AF345307

The Poll Book For The Election Of Two
Members To Represent In Parliament The
Southern Division Of The County Of Lincoln.
With A Report Of The Addresses, &c., April,
1857

THE
POLL BOOK

FOR THE

ELECTION OF TWO MEMBERS

TO REPRESENT IN PARLIAMENT

THE

SOUTHERN DIVISION OF THE COUNTY OF LINCOLN.

WITH

A REPORT OF THE ADDRESSES,

SPEECHES AT THE NOMINATION, &c., &c.,

APRIL, 1857.

SLEAFORD:

PRINTED AND SOLD BY WILLIAM FAWCETT;

PIPER, STEPHENSON, AND SPENCE, LONDON;

AND MAY BE HAD OF ALL BOOKSELLERS.

Price Five Shillings, in cloth, lettered.

SOUTH LINCOLNSHIRE CONTEST,

(1857)

THE first Parliamentary Contest for South Lincolnshire after the Reform Bill, took place at the General Election in 1841, when, on the retirement of Mr. Heathcote, (now Lord Aveland) the Candidates were

SIR JOHN TROLLOPE, CONSERVATIVE 4563
CHRISTOPHER TURNOR, Esq., CONSERVATIVE 4581
HENRY HANDLEY, Esq., LIBERAL 2948

At the succeeding General Election, in 1847, Mr. Turnor retired, and was succeeded by Lord Burghley, who, with Sir John Trollope, was then returned without opposition.

The Right Hon. Sir John Trollope was re-elected in March 1852, on his appointment to the Presidency of the Poor Law Board, under the Administration of Lord Derby.

The same Members were again returned, unopposed, at the General Election in July, 1852.

In March, 1857, the Government of Lord Palmerston having been defeated on the China question, the Parliament was dissolved, and at the General Election which ensued, Lord Burghley having announced his intention to retire, (for North Northamptonshire), the Conservative party addressed a requisition to Anthony Willson, Esq., of Rauceby, to offer himself as a Candidate in conjunction with the old Member, Sir John Trollope. The Liberals on this occasion decided to contest the County, and selected as their champion, George Hussey Packe, Esq., of Caythorpe, a gentleman supported by high family connections, and having the advantage in all the large Towns, of the Railway influence incident to his position as Deputy Chairman of the Great Northern Company. The three Candidates commenced their Canvass together, on Monday, the 16th of March, which was prosecuted with great vigour on both sides, and at the Close of the Poll, on the 4th of April, the Conservative principles were proved to be again triumphant, as recorded in the following pages, the numbers being

THE RT. HON. SIR JOHN TROLLOPE, 4020
A. WILLSON, Esq...................... 3636
G. H. PACKE, Esq. 3188

ADDRESSES, &c.,

ISSUED PREVIOUS TO THE DAY OF NOMINATION.

TO THE ELECTORS OF SOUTH LINCOLNSHIRE.

GENTLEMEN,

It having been announced that an immediate Dissolution will take place, I cannot delay in offering myself for a renewal of that confidence you have placed in me as your Representative in Parliament for so many years past.

I hope I may refer to my past votes in proof of having ever acted in accordance with those principles upon which you gave me your support in the first instance, and trust that an honorable consistency, with a close attention to the general business of the State, as well as the interests of my Constituents generally, will ensure me that goodwill and support, which I shall very shortly seek at your hands.

I have the honor to be Gentlemen,
Your very faithful Servant,

Sleaford, 16th March, 1857. JOHN TROLLOPE.

TO THE FREEHOLDERS AND ELECTORS OF SOUTH LINCOLNSHIRE.

GENTLEMEN,

Invited by a requisition numerously and most influentially signed, I offer myself as a Candidate for the honor of representing South Lincolnshire.

The principles which I profess are Conservative in character. Deeply attached to our Constitution in Church and State, I will ever advocate such measures as may be conducive to their true interests, whilst ready to reform any abuses which time or innovation may have introduced.

A supporter of the Church in all its purity, as opposed to every form of Romanism, I am at the same time justly tolerant of all who may conscientiously differ from us in their mode of worship.

I am adverse to constant changes in the Elective Franchise. I am opposed to the Ballot, because I think the Elector should exercise his trust openly, as is expected in return of the Member who represents him.

I will support any well devised National Scheme for the Education of the Children of the Poor.

I am a strenuous advocate for Economy in the Public Service, to the fullest extent consistent with the Honor and Safety of the Country.

In China I am of opinion that Sir John Bowring exceeded his powers, and should have been re-called.—No man has a right to involve his Country in War on his individual responsibility: But, those rash proceedings once taken, more serious danger to the commercial interests of the Country must have resulted from a retrograde movement, and I could not have supported Mr. Cobden's motion.

Brought up amongst you, I am a practical Agriculturist, and warm supporter of the united interest of Landlord and Tenant. Many of the burthens and taxes at present imposed on the land, and on the occupiers of the soil, in my judgment more fairly appertain to the community at large.

Gentlemen; should this brief exposition of my sentiments meet with your approval, and should you do me the honor to regard me as a fit and proper person to represent you in Parliament, I can only say that every effort on my part would be used to prove myself not unworthy of your confidence.

Purposing immediately to pay my personal respects to the Electors,
I have the honour to be, Gentlemen,
Your faithful and obedient Servant,

Rauceby, 13th March, 1857.　　　　　　　　　　　　　　A. WILLSON.

TO THE FREEHOLDERS & ELECTORS OF THE SOUTHERN DIVISION OF LINCOLNSHIRE.

GENTLEMEN,

Having been solicited by a numerous and influential portion of the Freeholders of the Southern Division of Lincolnshire; I beg to offer myself as a Candidate for the honour of representing you in Parliament. I am a firm and independent supporter of Lord Palmerston, and think from the manner the late War has been conducted, he is entitled to the confidence of the Country, and I trust that the present premature appeal will respond to his eminent Services as he deserves.

You will find me ever a steady promoter and supporter of Civil and Religious Liberty, and an advocate to the Settlement of the Church Rate Question.

I shall give my best consideration to any and every measure of Reform which may be brought forward, and should you do me the honor of returning me, you will always find I shall exert myself strenuously for the Agricultural Interest, my welfare being identified with your own.

I shall advocate every retrenchment and economy in the Public expenditure possible, consistent with the establishment of our Naval and Military Service, necessary to preserve the maintenance of Peace.

I remain, Gentlemen,
Yours faithfully,

Caythorpe, 16th March, 1857.　　　　　　　　GEORGE HUSSEY PACKE.

TO THE INDEPENDENT FREEHOLDERS AND ELECTORS OF SOUTH LINCOLNSHIRE.

GENTLEMEN,

Having now visited most of the principal Towns in your Division, I am enabled to form an opinion as to the feeling of the constituency on one great question, which as it appears to me is involved in this contest, viz: whether LORD PALMERSTON is not, under the circumstances of the times, the best man to fill the office of Prime Minister of this Country.—That there is the strongest possible feeling in favor of this view admits of no doubt—and coming forward as I do the firm, though at the same time, independent supporter of LORD PALMERSTON, I look forward with the greatest confidence to the issue of the Election, and can only repeat that if you do me the honor to return me one of your Representatives you will ever find me faithful to my trust—the strenuous advocate of that rational progress which is identified with the principles of the great Liberal Party of this Country, and at all times ready to do battle for the honor and independence of your Division, assailed as it is, on this occasion, *by an open and avowed coalition*, which I trust to your determination to defeat.

I have the honor to remain,
Gentlemen,
Yours faithfully,

Caythorpe, March 30th, 1857.   GEORGE HUSSEY PACKE.

SOUTH LINCOLNSHIRE ELECTION. 1ST APRIL. 1857.

GREAT NORTHERN   STEAM *versus* JOCKEYSHIP.   The best run of the season.

SOUTH LINCOLNSHIRE ELECTION 4TH APRIL, 1857.

METTLE *versus* VAPOUR.

THE NOMINATION.

The Nomination for the Southern Division of the County, took place this day. The Hustings as usual were erected in the Market-place, and among those present, were the High Sheriff, (George K. Jarvis, Esq., of Doddington Hall,) the Candidates, viz.—The Right Hon. Sir John Trollope, Bart., of Casewick, Anthony Willson, Esq., Rauceby, George Hussey Packe, Esq., Caythorpe ; also, Charles Chaplin, Esq., The Right Hon. R. C. Nesbit Hamilton, Viscount Goderich, M. P., F. L. Hopkins, Esq., Major Sibthorp, M.P., Charles Allix, Esq., The Hon. A. Bertie, The Rev. John King, The Hon. and Rev. Richard Cust, The Rev. Basil Beridge, George Whichcote, Esq., Charles Moore, Esq., William Parker, Esq., R. W. Myddleton, Esq., Spencer Skelton, Esq., Charles Derry, Esq., James Calthrope, Esq., Capt. Peacock, Col. Reynardson, The Rev. Edward Fane, &c., &c.

The HIGH SHERIFF having opened the proceedings in the usual manner, and appealed to the Electors to hear both sides with attention and impartiality,—called upon any Gentleman who had a Candidate to propose, to come forward :—

F. L. HOPKINS, Esq., of Boston, said he stood before them with pride and confidence to nominate the Rt. Hon. Sir John Trollope as a fit and proper person to represent the electors of that division. (Loud applause.) In proposing the hon. baronet he was not introducing a new candidate or a fresh aspirant for parliamentary honours, but a gentleman who had faithfully, and for the long period of sixteen years, discharged the important duties entrusted to him. (Hear, hear.) During that period he (Sir John) had firmly upheld the dignity of the Crown, he had been an unflinching supporter of the Conservative interest—an interest best calculated to maintain with honour those great and noble institutions which had conferred so many blessings upon the country—(hear)—he had always been a firm supporter of the Agricultural interest—(cheers)—and the time had not yet arrived when that interest was to be treated as a second-rate interest. It behoved the electors to send to the House of Commons representatives who would fight, as Sir John had fought, manfully on their behalf, and who would vote against a Statistics Bill, or any other measure of an inquisitorial nature. (Hear.) He appealed to them to elect the gentleman he had named, on account of his honourable conduct, his attention to the interests of the county, and the readiness with which he had always lent his aid to business measures. Even Sir John's political opponents had spoken approvingly of his talents, his urbanity, the courtesy with which, on all occasions, he had treated those great questions that had been submitted to him, and he (Mr. Hopkins)

kins) therefore asked the electors to place the right hon. gentleman at the head of the poll (cheers, and cries of " We will"), and by so doing pay a just tribute to his integrity and merit, and confer an honour not only upon him, but upon the county at large. (Cheers.) He was confident that, on Saturday next, Sir John would be returned; that they were not yet prepared to desert him, but would still stand by one who had faithfully served them for sixteen years, who had acted with fidelity to his Queen and his country, and who, in the ensuing session, would pay every attention to those great measures which, in all probability, would be brought before Parliament. (Loud cheers.)

C. DERRY, Esq., of Fleet, said he seconded the nomination of the right hon. baronet with great pleasure, but he wished the honour had rested upon some one of greater influence and standing than himself; nevertheless he would not shrink from the performance of the duty he had undertaken. (Hear.) Sir John Trollope had been before them as their representative for sixteen years; he had served his constituents faithfully —no member more so; he would, there was no doubt, still pursue the same straight-forward course, and enable them, as they had always done, to look upon their member with unfeigned satisfaction. (Cheers.)

Major SIBTHORP said he appeared before the electors that day in much the same capacity as he had done the previous day at Lincoln,—to nominate a fit and proper person to represent the electors of that (the Southern) division of the County. He could not, as had been done in the case of the hon. baronet just proposed, claim for his candidate the merit of having had a seat in Parliament; but he was of high standing amongst the gentry of the county, and of irreproachable character—a kind neighbour—an indulgent landlord, and nothing could be said of him that could possibly create a blush for the gentleman he was about to propose. He did not stand there as the exponent of the political principles of the gentleman he had alluded to; he had given an outline of those principles in his address, and he was, no doubt, prepared to answer any questions they might think fit to put to him. (Hear.) He would make a passing remark with respect to the question which had led to a dissolution of Parliament; he considered that the House of Commons came to a righteous conclusion upon that question; the resolution adopted was to the effect that the proceedings that had taken place at Canton were not justifiable, and his vote was intended as a vote of censure upon those proceedings, because he thought Sir John Bowring had acted in direct violation of his instructions. What was the difficulty with respect to Canton—was it the question of the Arrow? Certainly not. He would not detain them with any further observations upon that question, as a great deal of argument might be the result. The dissolution, however, had led to the cry of " Palmerston for ever," and he really did not know what that cry meant. He had the highest respect for the noble lord individually, but he deprecated his meddling policy; he believed the cry that had been got up meant in effect that they should be subject to increased taxation for the purpose of upholding irresponsible power. (Cheers.) After referring to that portion of Lord Palmerston's address to the electors of Tiverton which alluded approvingly to the reduction of the Income-tax—a reduction which he (Major Sibthorp) contended was effected by the voice of the people, he concluded by proposing as a candidate for their suffrages Anthony Willson, Esq., of Rauceby, whose name was received with loud applause.

SPENCER SKELTON, Esq., of Long Sutton, seconded the nomination, and said the electors could not have a more useful and zealous man to represent them in parliament. (Hear.) They wanted men of talent: but what did the constituencies in the large towns say? They say " We want commercial men." Why, the House of Commons was swamped with commercial men. Mr. Willson would be an able second to Sir John Trollope and would, he felt assured, pay every attention to questions of local as well as of national interest : they must get their members to turn their attention to measures of reform, and reform was requisite with respect to the question of weights and measures. He hoped they would show, by their polling on Saturday, that they were determined to have Mr. Willson in parliament. (Cheers.)

Major ALLIX said he had the honor to propose as a candidate George Hussey Packe, Esq. (Hear, hear.) He felt grateful to that gentleman for coming forward to emancipate that division of the county : the Liberals of South Lincolnshire had a fair claim to one representative, and in Mr. Packe they would have a supporter of Lord Palmerston, a nobleman who came forward during the necessities of the war to rescue this great nation from the danger which threatened it. (Hear.) That war must have happened in the course of time had it not occurred as it did, for such was the ambition of the late Emperor of Russia that he would only have waited until he had been better prepared and a great deal more bloodshed would probably have been the result. The war with China was now the principal question of the day, and upon that subject he (Major Allix) considered that Lord Palmerston had been exceedingly ill-used. A large party, headed by Mr. Cobden—a man bitterly opposed to the agricultural interest—took occasion to introduce a motion which was in effect a vote of censure upon the noble lord and his Government; feeling that the interests of the country were at stake, Lord Palmerston properly dissolved Parliament, and one of the results of that dissolution was that Mr. Cobden himself had been turned out. He was happy to observe, however, that the war with China was nearly at an end, for the Emperor had instructed his minister to make peace, which he hoped would be effected by the aid of Lord Elgin, and that trade with that country would again be prosperous. (Hear.) Mr. Packe was a friend to the constitution, to civil and religious liberty, to the reduction of taxation, and to such an amount of retrenchment as was consistent with the honour and safety of the country, he (Mr. P.) was also a consistent member of the Church of England, granting however to every man the right to worship the Almighty according to the dictates of his conscience, but an antagonist to either Popery or Puseyism. Such was the man he had the honour to propose to them, and he hoped they would return him as one of their representatives. (Cheers.)

WILLIAM PARKER, Esq., of Hanthorpe House, said the honour devolved upon him of seconding the nomination of Mr. Packe. (Cheers.) The battle they were called upon to fight was the battle of the Constitution and of the Government of the day : it was their duty and to their interest to support the government of Lord Palmerston. (Hear.) It was not for him to make any severe strictures with respect to the candidates who appeared before them that day ; he had an equal regard, personally, for all of them ; but he regretted he had occasion to dissent from the opinions expressed by Sir John Trollope. He (Mr. P.) had heard something said about China. The war with that country had brought them before the electors prematurely, otherwise, probably, the Parliament would have continued to the end of the period at which it would have been dissolved as a matter of course. However, a factious, and he considered a most contemptible, motion—(no, no)—had been moved in the House of Commons—(uproar)—he hoped he should be heard ; he was speaking the truth and making statements in accordance with the general feeling of the country. (No, no.) He was about to allude to the motion introduced by Mr. Cobden, and he (Mr. Parker) certainly felt disgusted that his party should unite with such a man for the purpose of ousting the Government. Had not the Government brought the war with Russia to a successful and honourable termination ? Lord Palmerston stepped in at the eleventh hour and corrected all those lamentable blunders by which the lives of many valuable soldiers had been sacrificed—the victims to mismanagement. (A voice—"What about the ballot?")—Mr. Parker: I shall see to that presently ; I mean to be thorough-going to-day. The vote adverse to the Government was a factious one ; but it was satisfactory to him to know that, in all probability, the war with China would soon be at an end. They had had their ears saluted with sounds of war, bloodshed, and cruelty. It was not an attribute of Englishmen to indulge in acts of cruelty. With respect to the Chinese question, the real object was to turn out the government, and to effect this there was a quintruple alliance of Peelites, Cobdenites, Puseyites, bad Whigs and worse Tories. Had they any hope from such a constitution? If they gave power to such men they would shortly bring their country to ruin. Was there anything to hope from men with half-a-dozen opinions ? He felt he had trespassed too much upon their attention and would retire. (Cries of " Go on.") Well, then, as they had kindly urged him to go on, he would just advert to Mr. Locke King's motion for an extension of the franchise. They had been told by Sir Frederic Thesiger that that motion was democratical and revolutionary. If so, why was Lord Palmerston to be condemned for having stopped it ? He had no hesitation in saying that the proposal to give 10l. house-holders a vote for counties was a proper motion. (Hear.) He (Mr. Parker) was a Tory, and so was Lord Palmerston, and one too, of the deepest dye. He hoped he should not be accused of turning round ; he had not deserted his party ; they had deserted him. Although a Tory, he now felt disgraced by that name. He could not advocate vote by ballot ; he thought such a measure would lead the country into difficulties, and it would be an un-English system. Before he retired, he was anxious to say one or two words with respect to the position in which he then stood : he came there with perfect consistency, and was confident as to the merits of Mr. Packe and Mr. Willson as fit and proper men to represent them ; he should give the preference to Mr. Packe who, he felt sure, would vote with the Government, and if they returned Mr. Willson he hoped he would support Lord Palmerston. He was afraid Sir John Trollope was tinctured by party—(no, no)—and the probability was that, so far as his seat in the house was concerned, he would occupy an insignificant position. The electors must have a man who would represent them : from any other they had no hope. Mr. Parker concluded by advocating the return of Packe and Willson. (Applause.)

Sir JOHN TROLLOPE then proceeded to address the assembly. He was received with loud cheers, mingled with hooting from the Packe party. The right hon. baronet said he appeared before the electors of South Lincolnshire for the fifth time as a candidate for the honourable position of their representative. (Cheers and uproar.) If they would keep silent for a few minutes and hear what he had to say, he had no doubt he should be able to satisfy all present that he was a proper person to be returned as their member. (Cheers.) He came before them, not as a stranger, but as one who had been tried, and he hoped he had not been found wanting. He and two hon. friends of his own appeared before the electors as candidates for their suffrages. And he must join with his worthy friend the High Sheriff in congratulating them upon having as candidates, men who, by birth, by education, by standing in the county, were deeply identified with all their interests ; and although they might differ, and no doubt did differ, upon some points, yet he thought they would find, when they came to hear his two hon. friends as well as himself, that there was no very material difference between them (hear, hear); for although the last speaker, Mr. Parker, had drawn a somewhat distinct line between himself (Sir John) and his hon. friend Mr. Willson, he thought he could show the electors, and show Mr. Parker also, that he had acted the part of a truly independent country gentleman as one of their representatives. Now he did not stand before them upon professions for the future; he would rather go upon what was on record of the past. And he would recall to their recollection the circumstances under which he was induced, in the first instance, to offer himself as a candidate for this county. It was in the year 1841, when the country was tired of the then existing Government, and wished to recall Sir Robert Peel—a name which would be familiar with too many of them. They were desirous of placing Sir Robert in power, and he (Sir John) came forward as one determined to support him, thinking he could never differ from the hon. baronet. But it was not very long before he found his confidence misplaced. He found great reason to doubt the sincerity of Sir Robert Peel's professions; or, at all events, Sir Robert changed his opinions as Mr. Parker had done. (Laughter and cheers.) Well, he blamed no man for changing his opinions, but that was no reason why he (Sir John,) should go along with Sir R. Peel. Therefore, he took an early opportunity of voting out of power the very man he went into Parliament to serve, and whom he had often been proud to serve. He quoted this fact as an illustration of his having acted the part of an independent member. (Hear, hear.) Since that time he could call to mind numerous occasions on which he had voted against what was called his own party—the Conservative party—when he thought them wrong, and also numerous instances in which he had supported a Whig Government when he thought them right. Having done these things, he appealed to the electors whether he had not acted the part of an independent representative. Now he did not want to go far back; but allusion had been made to the great war which had been concluded with Russia. What was his conduct in reference to that war? Did he offer a factious opposition to the government? Not so. In every instance where he thought them in the right, he gave them his humble support; and he did so in accordance with the views of his constituents. (Hear.) But great credit had been accorded to the head of the present government, Lord Palmerston, for concluding that war. He (Sir John) wished to give the noble lord every credit for what he had done; but let them inquire into facts. Was not Lord Palmerston a member of that very Cabinet that brought about the disastrous state of things in the Crimea? He was a member of the very government called by Lord John Russell to witness the horrible and heart-rending sufferings of our brave and gallant army before Sebastopol. (Hear, hear.) And when Mr. Roebuck moved for a committee of inquiry, who was one of the first to vote for it but their own representative. He (Sir John) voted for that inquiry. The result of that motion was the unseating of the government, of which Lord Palmerston was a member, and that enabled the noble lord to take the guidance of affairs. Therefore he (Sir John) might take some credit to himself for helping Lord Palmerston to be prime minister. (Hear, hear.) But they would perhaps recollect that it was the people of England who concluded the Russian war. It was the people of England who taxed themselves freely to conduct that war as it ought to be conducted—who raised the militia—who brought the army to the pitch of perfection which it ultimately attained—who sent out those sinews of war contained in our splendid navy. Yes, it was the people of England who insisted that the honor of this country should not be sullied. (Cheers.) When peace was concluded, they were not very well satisfied: they did not think they had got enough glory. But their allies, the French, thought they had had enough of it. They were tired of paying for the war, and the people of England were tired of the income tax. Though he did not think we had done enough—and for this reason, because we were not prepared for the emergency; and when we made peace, we were just about fit to go to war. (Hear, hear.) He, however, found no fault with that: he hoped he was a man of peace and desirous of putting a stop to blood-shed. (Hear, hear.) But, as he was saying, though we did not think we had done enough, the people of England concurred with Lord Palmerston's government in making what was thought a satisfactory and honourable peace. Now since that time he (Sir John) had been endeavouring to do what he could to lighten the burdens of the people. He had assisted in taking off taxation, and the government, from the pressure put on them, did not venture to go to a division on the subject. They were obliged to take 9d. in the pound off the income-tax. They were asked for 2d. more, but that could not be obtained. Twopence was a small figure, but it represented 2,000,000l. of taxation. Every penny in the pound paid to the income-tax represented a million of money. The sooner we got rid of paying those millions the better. (Hear, hear.) If he were asked what Parliament had been doing for the last three years, he scarcely knew that they had done anything with the exception of reducing the Income-tax and passing a Police Bill. They were going to have the police introduced into the quiet, honest county of Lincoln, where there was so little crime that their services were not required. He voted against that measure. Don't let it be said, therefore, that he had not given votes in favor of their interests and for the reduction of taxation. (Hear, hear.) Those were matters of history. Now let him come to the present war with China. They had been told that the late Parliament was very suddenly dismissed. And why was it thus dismissed? Because there suddenly came from a distant country, 13,000 miles from them, intelligence that we were engaged in warfare with a miserable race of people, who scarcely knew how to defend themselves. Our emissary in China had made war without the authority of the home Government. He did not refer to the Government at home. He did not say, "Am I right in bombarding Canton, in slaughtering its inhabitants, in burning their dwellings ?" He did it first and then asked for the sanction of the home Government. That was rather what he (the speaker) called *ex poste facto* law. He thought it would have been a wiser course to have sent home and said that a difficulty had arisen. (Cheers and slight uproar.) He knew well what the answer would have been. It would have been an instruction of the Government never to go to war with the Chinese without orders from home. And the orders were, not to enforce the terms of an existing treaty which it was more than probable would lead to bloodshed. Sir John Bowring disregarded orders, but Government thought fit to sanction his conduct, and he was now waiting for reinforcements. Would it not have been better to instruct him to make peace rather than that we should send out soldiers to that pestilent climate at a very great cost? Three millions of money was already being raised for the expenses of this armament. He (Sir John) only hoped that the news recently received might be true—that the Emperor of the Chinese was inclined to make peace; and he trusted our Government would meet him more than half way, because the war was stopping trade, and, probably, leading to great slaughter. He, for one, never gave a more conscientious vote—one more free from party feeling, or less obnoxious to the imputation cast upon it by Mr. Parker, of being a factious opposition to the Government—than the vote he gave upon the occasion of the Chinese debate. And he would say this—he did not repent of that vote, and if he had the opportunity he would give the same vote again. (Cheers.) He might have been wrong; but when he told them that he gave it on his conscience as an honest vote, he did not think they could blame him.

(Hear, hear.) Now there were a great many questions that must come under the consideration of the next Parliament; and he had no doubt that any one of the three candidates before them would be able to devote as much care and attention to those subjects as they could wish. He might allude first to the important question of education. He desired to concur with Government in affording every assistance in the establishment and support of schools founded upon a true scriptural basis, which alone could lead to happiness. He also wished to tell the electors that he had voted in accordance with their petition upon various subjects—amongst others in regard to the desecration of the Sabbath. He had presented many petitions from that part of the country, against the opening of the Crystal Palace, British Museum, and other places on a Sunday, and he had supported the prayer of those petitions. He had also opposed the introduction of bands into the Parks of London on Sundays. What was the consequence of that proceeding? It emptied the churches and chapels, and filled the public-houses. (Hear, hear.) He wished to see the Sabbath kept as a Christian people ought to keep it—holy—and that it should not be desecrated. He had a very strong opinion upon the subject, and he should always support that opinion. In reference to church rates, he and his fellow candidates were perfectly agreed. They all three of them, he believed, most entirely repudiated that horrible principle that would make a difference between man and man, both professing a Christian faith—that it should be kept up as a contention between Church and State; and he for one should be most happy to lend an earnest aid in settling a question, which must be settled, with due regard to the interests of that Church of which he hoped to continue a humble member. Another question of great importance to them was that of agricultural statistics. They recollected the nature of the bill introduced into Parliament upon that subject—namely, to have their stock counted up, and not only to require a return of the quantity of each species of corn grown, but also the yield per acre. It they did not produce a correct return they were to be fined, and if they did not pay the fine to be imprisoned. He did not think that a just measure, and he opposed it. (Hear, hear.) Don't accuse him of being an opponent of Lord Palmerston's Government because he resisted a measure like that. He had to look to his constituents —not to the Government. He wanted nothing from the Government. But he would say this—that if Lord Palmerston or any body else brought forward good measures he would support them. (Cheers.) But he did not pledge himself to Lord Palmerston. He (Sir John) was too old a bird for that. (Laughter and cheers.) He had been caught once. And it would be well for his friend Mr. Packe to take care not to pledge himself too deeply. (Cheers.) If he fixed himself at the back of Lord Palmerston, and was carefully looked after by the whipper-in, he would have a very uneasy time of it with his constituents when he came before them again. (Renewed laughter and cheers.) He (Sir John) believed he had pretty nearly accounted for the past. Let him say one word only in regard to the future. He did not hesitate to say that he had had so successful a canvass of the county that he entertained no doubt whatever of his election. And if that were so, don't let them suppose, if it should be the pleasure of the electors to return either of the other candidates—whether his friend on the right (Mr. Willson,) or his friend on the left (Mr. Packe)—don't let it be supposed that he should not cordially act with either the one or the other to promote the interests of the constituency. They were his own personal friends, and he had great faith in their honor. (Hear.) Wherever he had gone he found the same well-known faces, the same honest hands, the same stout hearts prepared to support him as they had done before, and he had no right to entertain the slightest doubt as to the result of this election. (Cheers.) Cordially thanking the assembly for the kindness with which they had heard him, he would only say, in conclusion, that he hoped he had been found a faithful servant, and he was satisfied they would not desert him. (The right hon. baronet closed his address amid loud applause, which was reiterated again and again.)

ANTHONY WILLSON, Esq., was the next speaker. He said he conceived that one of the first duties of any one standing in the proud position of a candidate for the representation of this great county in Parliament, was personally to pay his respects to the electors at the first opportunity that presented itself. And he regretted that so short a period had elapsed since the dissolution of Parliament, or rather since the announcement of the probable dissolution, that he had not had that opportunity he could have wished to pay to them personally his respects, and to explain to them in person the sentiments and political opinions on which, on that occasion, he asked for their suffrages. (Hear, hear.) He had, however, taken the only steps that time or opportunity left him: he had attended during the last fortnight at various fairs in the principal towns in South Lincolnshire to explain to the electors as clearly as he possibly could, the opinions which he professed, and which he hoped he should advocate, if they returned him as their representative to Parliament. Their late member (Sir John Trollope) who had addressed them, was able to explain to them and to state the votes he had given; whereas it only fell to the lot of a candidate to offer promises; and he should, therefore, proceed to explain to them, as briefly as possible, the political opinions which he professed. He need not say that he was an admirer of the constitution of this great country; for show him the Englishman that was not. Ours was a Government which was carried on with a due regard to the fair administration of the law; it was a Government which was the pride of Englishmen and the envy of surrounding countries. But they were aware that there never yet was a Government designed and framed by the human mind that was entirely free from imperfection; and they must be aware that imperfections would intrude themselves into the English constitution as they would into any other. And, therefore, he should be prepared to reform whatever had become obsolete or objectionable, so that our Government might continue to work in the same smooth manner as heretofore. (Cheers.) In a great country like this they must be aware that there must exist great differences of opinion on all subjects, and more particularly on that subject which must interest men both temporarily and eternally: he alluded to religion; and he for one was anxious that every man dissenting conscientiously from himself should have the freest and most liberal opportunity of religious worship he could possibly possess. (Hear, hear.) He was himself a Church-man, educated in the principles of the Established Church, and an enemy and opponent of all extreme opinions, whether Tractarianism as tending to Popery, or any other that had a tendency to introduce discord into that Church, which ought to be a Church of peace and unity. It was, he might say, the poor man's Church *par excellence*: its doors always stood open, and the members of the Church were ever anxious to receive all comers with amity and friendship. (Cheers.) He was an enemy to the ballot, because he considered it an un-English and unnecessary mode of exercising the franchise, which we professed to hold as the dearest possession of an Englishman. (Hear, hear.) He would not have any man go sneaking to the ballot-box with a lie upon his lips when he professed to vote differently to what he was prepared to do. They had heard questions asked and opinions given with regard to the extension of the franchise. There was one particular motion which had been brought forward, and which had gone by the name of Locke King's motion, the object of which was, as has been stated, to give to 10*l.* householders in counties the same privileges which 10*l.* householders possessed in boroughs and cities, and at first sight nothing could seem fairer. But there was this distinction between the 10*l*. franchise in towns and the 10*l*. franchise in counties. At the present moment, he thought all would admit, counties did not possess too large a share of power in the representative system. They comprised a very large amount of wealth and intelligence, and the proportion of power they possessed was considerably less than was awarded to the large towns. Now the effect of giving the franchise to 10*l*. householders in counties would be this—that it would throw the power of the representation entirely into the hands of the large towns. It would do so because many of those towns which were not yet sufficiently populous to demand to be admitted into the list of boroughs would still have a sufficient number of 10*l*. householders entirely to swamp the whole of the land-owners and occupiers in their immediate district. (Uproar.) Looking around him, he said that the agriculturists of that great county had a right to be fairly represented—(a voice: "Come to the labourer.")—and it would not be the case if this power were given to the large towns. With regard to education he was an advocate for it in its most extended sense. He was anxious that every parish, every hamlet, every village should possess one or more schools, that all might have an opportunity of acquiring the proper and necessary elements of education. He would thus have all start fair in the race of life. It had been said that in this great country there was no man, however humble, who might not hope to attain the exalted position of High Chancellor of England. Now he did not say that such a goal would be reached by many; but possessed of education a man was better qualified for any situation, whether as a labourer, a shopkeeper, or any other. (Cheers.) Therefore he would educate the people; and he would make it a national education. He would give national grants in aid of private charity rather than levy local rates as had been proposed, because he considered that the education of the people was a national, and not a merely local benefit. (Hear, hear.) He need not tell them that he was an earnest advocate for economy in the administration of the Government, because it was by the strictest economy alone that we could hope for that remission of taxation which every man had a right to demand. They had heard that we had already got a remission of a portion of the anti-English Income-tax, which was the more distasteful to the people of England from its inquisitorial character; and it would be by the strictest economy alone that we should be able to get rid of it altogether at the promised period in 1860. But he was anxious for the removal of other burdens besides that. He would have a reduction in the duties on tea and sugar, which would perhaps be as great a boon to the poor man as to the rich man. (Hear, hear, and cheers.) He had intended to allude to the subject of the abolition of church-rates, but Sir John Trollope had told them that in the course of the canvass they had been questioned in almost every town upon that particular subject, and he (the right hon. baronet) had himself explained the views which he (Mr. Willson) professed to hold, and which were also held by his worthy friend on the opposite side of the hustings, Mr. Packe. Therefore, he (Mr. W.) need not occupy further time on that subject. He should be an opponent of any measure on the question of agricultural statistics similar to that which was introduced in the late Parliament. Many of them had not the opportunity or ability to furnish those accurate accounts which that act demanded from agriculturists; and it would be a hardship against which the feeling of Englishmen would revolt were they compelled to make those returns under pain of fine and imprisonment. Therefore he was opposed to the bill in question on that account. (Cheers.) At the same time they were aware that it might be desirable for a great country like this to ascertain as nearly as possible the amount of corn in the country, and the probable amount of imports that would be necessary for the consumption. One of the first inquiries of a minister of finance or of a commercial man was as to the prospects of the ensuing harvest, because they were thereby enabled to foresee what would be the probable balance of trade in favour of or against this country. (Hear, hear.) And, therefore, if any measure could be devised that would, without possessing an inquisitorial character, inform the financial minister or the commercial man as to the probable amount of food in the country, that would be an entirely different question, and he should be ready to give such a measure careful consideration. (Hear, hear.) He did not know that there was any other subject on which he need particularly touch, except it was this—that he thought it desirable we should have a uniform system of weights and measures; for at the present time there existed very great variety in the manner in which corn was sold. In many cases they sold their wheat by the quarter, which consisted of eight strike or eight bushels; in other cases by the thirty-six stone; and the reason why it would be desirable to have, as nearly as possible, a uniform standard was its bearing upon the tithe question; for they were aware that the amount of composition they had to pay for tithe varied every year according to the average price of corn, and that average price was not truly and clearly ascertained, unless they were aware of the actual measure by which it was sold. (Hear, hear.) In conclusion, he thanked them for the attention with which they had listened to him, and hoped that if the sentiments he had expressed were in accordance with their own, they would place him, by their votes, on Saturday next, in the proud position of their representative in Parliament;— (cheers)—and should they do him that honor, he could assure them that his best endeavours and exertions should be given for their local, for their private, and for their general interests. (Loud cheers.)

G. H. PACKE, Esq., followed, and was received with cheers. He said he should not occupy their time long by going over the same story they had heard from the right hon. baronet, and from Mr. Willson, the other candidate; for on many points they perfectly agreed. But he would allude to those points where they materially differed. (Hear, hear.) In the first place he (Mr. Packe) came forward to seek their suffrages as an independent supporter of my Lord Palmerston and his government. (Cheers.) He, however, should not be the slave of Lord Palmerston if returned to Parliament; for if the noble lord did not go straight, he would not receive a vote from him (Mr. Packe.) They would well remember Lord Palmerston being called to the head of the government when things were in such a bad state in the Crimea—when our poor people were suffering and dying from cold and hunger, and our army was reduced to such a condition that we did not know whether we should not lose every man. The noble lord was then called to the helm; and what did he do? He came forward in the most vigorous manner to carry on the war, and he brought it to a termination which he (Mr. Packe) thought was most honourable to this country: and were they now to turn round upon his lordship on the first opportunity, and discard a minister who had served them so well? Ought they not rather to give him their fullest confidence? (Cheers.) He differed with his friend Sir John Trollope on the subject of China. He (Mr. Packe) thought Sir John Bowring was perfectly right, and that he had maintained the honor and character of this country. He suffered all the insults which Commissioner Yeh had put upon him, and it was not until he had tried every other course in vain that Sir John Bowring resorted to arms. This was borne out by the fact of the Emperor directing his commissioner to make peace on the terms proposed by Sir John Bowring. (Hear, hear.) Another thing which Lord Palmerston had done was this: as soon as the war had concluded, he made every possible reduction in the public expenditure, which enabled him to take 9_d._ in the pound off the income-tax. And if they did (Mr. Packe) the honor to elect him one of their representatives, they would find him at all times endeavouring, by every means in his power, to promote economy and retrenchment, so that the country might be further relieved from taxation. He should decidedly vote for every progressive measure of improvement, and he should support the extension of education, and all other beneficial measures which his friends on the right (Sir John Trollope and Mr. Willson) had told them they would support. They should never find him wanting in attention and perseverance in the discharge of his Parliamentary duties, and he trusted he should serve them as honestly, faithfully, and sincerely as any person who might be sent to Parliament. (Hear, hear.) He had received the greatest kindness, and he was happy to say had met with the greatest success on his canvass, and he confidently anticipated that the poll would result in his favor.

A beer-inspired "operative" here stood forward and asserted his right to speak. After exciting a little merriment, he called for "three cheers for Packe."

The HIGH SHERIFF then took a show of hands, which he declared to be in favour of Packe and Willson.

Mr. HOPKINS : On behalf of Sir John Trollope, I demand a poll.

The HIGH SHERIFF: A poll is demanded, and it will be held on Saturday next, commencing at eight and remaining open until five o'clock on that day. The declaration will be made at one o'clock on Monday, at this place.

Lord GODERICH, M.P., being upon the hustings, was called on to address the assembly. He expressed the great satisfaction with which he witnessed the show of hands in favour of his friend Mr. Packe, and trusted it might be ominous of the result which would be declared on Monday next. (Cheers.) To his friend Sir John Trollope he had but one objection, and it was that he had almost always voted in the opposite lobby to him in the House of Commons.

Sir JOHN TROLLOPE—Not upon China. (Cheers and uproar.)

Lord GODERICH said it was perfectly true that he voted with Sir John upon the question of China ; and he (Lord Goderich) gave an honest vote on that occasion. He had generally supported Lord Palmerston's Government in the House of Commons; Sir John Trollope had generally opposed it He (Lord Goderich) voted for the Government when they were endangered by the conduct of the Conservative party upon the question of the Turkish loan. He should like to ask Sir John Trollope how he voted on that occasion.

Sir JOHN TROLLOPE—Will you have the answer ? I did not vote against the Government on that occasion. Cheers.)

Lord GODERICH went on to say that Mr. Willson had told them nothing with regard to the course he would pursue in the House of Commons towards the Government of Lord Palmerston. Now upon that subject Mr. Packe had spoken openly and explicitly, and that point had been chiefly raised at this election. If, however, they were to go, as he trusted the electors would go into questions of general policy, not narrowing this election into a mere question of confidence in the Government, then there could be no doubt as to which of the three candidates before them was the best. He (Lord Goderich) stood in the happy position of a member of the new Parliament. The best wish he could give his friend Mr. Packe was, that he might find himself in that position at five o'clock on Saturday next. (Loud cheers.)

The proceedings were then brought to a close with a vote of thanks to the High Sheriff, moved by Sir JOHN TROLLOPE, and seconded by Mr. PACKE.

THE DECLARATION.

SLEAFORD, MONDAY, APRIL 6TH.

The official Declaration of the Poll was made this day by the High Sheriff. The Honourable Members were loudly cheered on appearing on the Hustings, and Mr. Packe, the defeated Candidate was also received with much cordiality.

The High Sheriff after a few preliminary remarks, declared the final close of the Poll to be as follows :—

TROLLOPE, ... 4016
WILLSON, ... 3632
PACKE, ... 3184

He therefore declared the Right Hon. Sir John Trollope, Bart., and Anthony Willson, Esq., to be duly elected as Members of Parliament for the South Division of Lincolnshire, (tremendous cheering, which lasted some time).

The Honourable Members proceeded to return thanks in a very cordial and hearty manner, and Mr. Packe also acknowledged "the distinguished position in which he had been placed by the Electors."

The business terminated with a vote of thanks to the High Sheriff for the impartial manner in which he had conducted the proceedings, the greatest good humour having prevailed throughout the contest.

———o—o———

FINAL CLOSE OF THE POLL,

APRIL 4TH, 1857.

	Trollope.	Willson.	Packe.	Total Polled.
SLEAFORD	447	729	375	868
BOURN	576	384	432	818
NAVENBY	279	352	187	472
GRANTHAM	508	382	465	824
HALF-WAY HOUSES	208	240	90	310
SPALDING	562	394	378	805
HOLBEACH	342	250	449	703
DONINGTON	321	297	259	515
BOSTON	777	608	553	1135
TOTAL	4020	3636	3188	6450

No. 1.—POLLING DISTRICT ASSIGNED TO SLEAFORD.

POLLED AT SLEAFORD.

Ancaster, West Willoughby, and Sudbrook.

Name of Elector.	Residence, if out of the Parish.	Qual.	T.	W.	P.
Allix, Charles, esq.	Willoughby Hall	Fr	0	0	1
Barber, Thomas	Sudbrook	Fr	1	1	0
Cooper, John	Ancaster	Fr	0	1	1
Elliott, Francis	Ditto	Fr	0	0	1
Garner, Thomas	Willoughby-heath	Rt	0	0	1
Garner, James	Willoughby	Rt			
Harvey, William Dodds	Sudbrook-hill	Rt	0	0	1
Hacket, John	Caythorpe	Fr			
Johnson, William	Ancaster	Rt	1	1	0
Leachman, William	Ditto	Fr	0	1	1
Muxlow, James	Sudbrook	Fr	0	1	1
Rudkin, Henry	Willoughby	Rt	0	1	1
Rowe, Daniel	Sudbrook	Fr	0	1	1
Slight, William	Willoughby	Rt			
Ward, William	Sudbrook	Rt	0	0	1
Walton, William	Ditto	Fr	0	1	1
Warren, Rev. Zachariah Shrapnall	Ancaster	Fr $\hbar$	0	1	1
Wilkinson, John	Ditto	Fr	0	1	1

Anwick.

Name of Elector.	Residence, if out of the Parish.	Qual.	T.	W.	P.
Ashington, Henry, Rev.	....	Fr	1	1	0
Birch, Jacob Thomas, esq.	Welbeck-street Middlesex	Fr			
Birch, William Henry, esq.	Ditto	Fr	0	0	1
Birch, Peregrine, esq.	Ditto	Fr	0	0	1
Edwards, Thomas	....	Fr	0	1	1
Faulkner, Thomas	....	Rt	1	1	0
Faulkner, Samuel	Walcot	Rt			
Faulkner, Charles	....	Rt	0	1	1

B

Anwick—continued.

Name of Elector.	Residence, if out of the Parish.	Qual.	T.	W.	P.
Garton, John	....	Rt	0	1	1
Graves, William	North Kyme	Fr	0	0	1
Milton, the Right Hon. Lord	Milton House, Northamptonshire	Fr			
Selby, Matthew	....	Rt	0	1	1
Winter, George	....	Rt	1	1	0
Wilkinson, Nelson, *Sol*	Peterborough	Fr			

Asgarby with Boughton.

Name of Elector.	Residence, if out of the Parish.	Qual.	T.	W.	P.
Green, John	Knipton	Rt	1	1	0
Sneath, Thomas	....	Rt	1	1	0
Tomlinson, Bruce	....	Rt	1	1	0

Aswarby.

Name of Elector.	Residence, if out of the Parish.	Qual.	T.	W.	P.
Baker, John	....	Rt	1	1	0
Caswell, John	....	Rt	1	1	0
Whichcote, Rev. Christopher	....	Fr			
Whichcote, Sir Thomas bart.	....	Fr	1	1	0

Aunsby.

Name of Elector.	Residence, if out of the Parish.	Qual.	T.	W.	P.
Dennis, William	....	Fr	1	1	0
Fairchild, William	....	Rt	1	1	0
Hufton, George	....	Fr	1	1	0
Locking, John	....	Rt	1	0	0
Rastall, Richard	....	Rt	1	1	0
Sardeson, William	....	Rt	1	1	0

Billinghay.

Name of Elector.	Residence, if out of the Parish.	Qual.	T.	W.	P.
Akrill, Richard	Colsterworth	Fr	1	1	0
Atkin, William	Walcot	Fr	0	1	1
Atkin, John	....	Fr	0	0	1
Abbott, Dennis	Timberland	Fr	1	1	0
Bailey, Ephraim	....	Fr	0	0	1
Bones, Edward	North Kyme	Fr	0	1	1
Bones, James	....	Rt	1	1	0
Benton, William Franklin	....	Fr	0	1	1
Bailey, Benjamin	....	Fr	0	0	1
Bailey, Ely	....	Fr	0	1	1
Bellamy, William	....	Rt	1	1	0
Bee, William	....	Fr	0	1	0
Berry, Enoch	....	Fr	0	1	1

Billinghay—continued.

Name of Elector.	Residence, if out of the Parish.	Qual.	T.	W.	P.
Croft, Thomas	....	Fr	1	1	0
Croft, William	Metheringham	Rt	1	1	0
Capps, Henry	....	Rt	0	1	1
Copping, Charles	....	Fr	0	1	1
Draper, James	....	Fr	1	1	0
Dickinson, Edward	....	Fr	0	1	1
Dickinson, Peter	....	Fr	0	1	1
Dickinson, John	....	Fr	0	0	1
Dixon, Joseph	Braunston	Fr			
Dickinson, Joseph	....	Fr	0	1	0
Eminson, Thomas	....	Fr	0	1	1
Friend, Charles William	Bardney	Fr	1	1	0
Flatters, Abraham	....	Fr	0	0	1
Fairweather, James	....	Fr	0	1	1
Grocock, Joseph	South Kyme	Fr			
Grocock, Isaac	....	Fr	0	1	1
Goose, John	Billinghay-dales	Fr	1	1	0
Goodwin, Samuel	....	Fr	0	1	1
Gadsby, William	....	Fr	1	1	0
Gilbert, Francis	....	Fr			
Green, William	....	Rt	1	1	0
Graves, Henry	Walcot	Fr	1	1	0
Harness, John Robert	....	Fr	0	0	1
Harrison, William	Dogdike	Fr	1	1	0
Holmes, John	South Kyme	Fr			
Hollinshead, Samuel	....	Fr	1	1	0
Holmes, Anthony	....	Fr	0	0	1
Holmes, John	Billinghay-fen	Fr	0	1	1
Jackson, Jabez	....	Fr	0	0	1
Jackson, Joseph	Billinghay-dales	Fr	0	0	1
Jenkins, Rev. Edward	....	Fr	0	1	1
Johnson, William	....	Fr	0	1	0
Kettleborough, George	....	Fr	0	1	1
Key, Thomas	....	Fr	0	1	1
Kent, James	....	Rt	1	1	0
Key, Jabez	....	Fr	0	1	1
Key, Timothy	Billinghay-fen	Fr	1	1	0
Key, Thomas Pearson	Billinghay-field	Rt	0	1	1
Key, Edward	Billinghay-field	Rt	0	1	1
Lamyman, Samuel	Coningsby	Fr	1	1	0
Lawson, Joseph	....	Fr	0	1	1
Lowe, John	....	Fr	0	1	1

Billinghay—continued.

Name of Elector.	Residence, if out of the Parish.	Qual.	T.	W.	P.
Loveday, John	....	Fr	1	1	0
Mastin, Henry	....	Fr	0	1	1
Maplethorp, Jackson	....	Fr	0	0	1
Maplethorp, Thomas	....	Fr	0	1	1
Paley, John	North Kyme	Fr	0	1	1
Poucher, Richard	....	Fr	0	0	1
Pigott, Key	....	Fr	0	1	1
Petchell, Luke	....	Fr	0	1	0
Rimes, John	....	Rt	0	1	1
Roberts, Edward	Billinghay-fen	Fr	1	1	0
Roberts, Joseph Garratt	Ancaster	Fr	0	0	1
Slack, Thomas	Walcot-dales	Fr			
Stringer, William	....	Tr	0	1	1
Siddons, William	....	Fr	0	1	1
Swinton, Jacob	....	Fr	1	1	0
Skinner, Thomas	....	Fr	0	1	1
Sharp, James	....	Fr	0	1	1
Sumpter, Edward	Walcot-dales	Fr			
Sampson, Henry	Billinghay-dales	Rt	1	1	0
Stevenson, John	....	Fr	0	1	1
Stubley, William	....	Fr	0	0	1
Smith, William	....	Fr	0	0	1
Stringer, William	....	Fr			
Torey, Henry	....	Fr	1	1	0
Taylor, Richard	....	Fr	1	1	0
Twells, Edward	Billinghay-dales	Fr	1	1	0
Thorpe, William	Kirkby Laythorpe	Fr	0	1	1
Wood, Joseph	Billinghay-dales	Fr	0	1	1
Williamson, James	Billinghay-fen	Fr	0	1	1
Wyles, Wright	....	Fr	0	1	1
Wray, Peter	....	Fr	0	0	1
Wheat, Henry, esq.	Norwood, Yorkshire	Fr			
Wilson, John	Martindales	Fr			
Wray, John	Billinghay-fen	Fr	1	1	0
Wilson, Matthew	Billinghay-dales	Rt	0	0	1
Wilson, William	....	Fr	1	1	0
Wilson, Joseph	....	Fr	0	1	1
Wilson, Parker	....	Fr	0	1	0
Wilson, John	....	Fr	0	1	0
Wood, Daniel Toynbee	Billinghay-dales	Fr	0	1	1

Bloxholm.

Name of Elector	Residence	Qual.	T.	W.	P.
Frudd, Francis	....	Rt	1	1	0

Bloxholm—continued.

Name of Elector.	Residence, if out of the Parish.	Qual.	T.	W.	P.
Hamilton, the Right Hon. Robert Christopher Nesbit	Bloxholm-hall, and Chesham-place, London	Fr	1	1	0
Linney, James	....	Rt	1	1	0
Mackinnon, Rev. John	....	Fr	0	1	0
Wilcock, John	....	Rt	1	1	0

Branswell, Dunsby and Temple Bruer.

Name of Elector.	Residence, if out of the Parish.	Qual.	T.	W.	P.
Blackbourn, David	Temple Bruer	Rt	1	1	0
Burnby, Matthew Coulson	Ditto	Rt	1	1	0
Dundas, Philip, esq.	Bloxholm	Fr			
Frankish, John	Temple Bruer	Rt			
Harvey, Thomas	Branswell	Rt			
Lowe, Ralph	Ditto	Rt	1	1	0
Maw, Thomas	Temple Bruer	Rt	1	1	0
Rylatt, William	Branswell	Rt	0	1	1

Burton Pedwardine.

Name of Elector.	Residence, if out of the Parish.	Qual.	T.	W.	P.
Brown, Rev Henry Handley	....	Fr	0	0	1
Edwards, Hon. William	Edmonthorpe Hall	Fr	*Peer*		
Gibson, Anthony	....	Rt	1	1	0
Hercock, George	....	Rt	1	1	0
Jones, Theophilus	....	Rt	0	1	1
Rippon, Thomas	....	Rt	1	1	0
Rippon, John	....	Rt	1	1	0

Cranwell.

Name of Elector.	Residence, if out of the Parish.	Qual.	T.	W.	P.
Clayton, Thomas Lucas	....	Rt	0	1	1
Lamb, William	....	Rt			
Sardeson, Charles	....	Rt	1	1	0
Sardeson, Francis	....	Rt	1	1	0
Scott, Rev. Robert Alan	....	Fr			

Culverthorpe.

Name of Elector.	Residence, if out of the Parish.	Qual.	T.	W.	P.
Blankley, Thomas	....	Rt	1	1	0
King, George	....	Rt	1	1	0

Dembleby.

Name of Elector.	Residence, if out of the Parish.	Qual.	T.	W.	P.
Bull, William	....	Rt	1	1	0
Widdowson, William	....	Rt	1	1	0

Digby.

Name of Elector.	Residence, if out of the Parish.	Qual.	T.	W.	P.
Cooke, George	....	Rt	0	1	1

Digby—continued.

Name of Elector.	Residence, if out of the Parish.	Qual.	T.	W.	P.
Cooke, Charles Frederick	....	Rt	0	1	1
Harmston, William	....	Rt	0	1	1
Idle, Robert	....	Rt	0	1	1
Jackson, John	....	Rt	0	1	1
Mitton, William	....	Rt	0	1	0
Mackinder, John	....	Rt	0	1	1
Sumner, Scholey	....	Rt	0	1	1

Dorrington.

Name of Elector.	Residence, if out of the Parish.	Qual.	T.	W.	P.
Bennett, Burrows	....	Fr	0	0	1
Carr, Isaac	....	Fr	1	1	0
Challand, Joseph	....	Rt	0	1	1
Dent, Joseph, esq.	Ribston-hall	Fr			
Dent, Dent John, esq.	Ribston-hall	Fr			
Dent, Dent William, *Esq*	Ribston-hall	Fr			
Dent, Dent Joseph Jonathan, *Clerk*	Richmond, Surrey	Fr			
Foster, William	Kelham, Notts.	Fr			
Frudd, Francis	....	Rt	0	1	1
Healey, Thomas	....	Rt	1	1	0
Harvey, Samuel	....	Fr	0	0	1
Lunn, William	....	Rt	0	1	1
Mackinnon, Rev. John	Bloxholm	Fr			
Snowden, William	....	Fr	0	1	1
Stow, James	....	Fr	1	1	0
Stow, Robert	....	Fr	1	1	0
Stevenett, William	....	Fr	0	0	1
Stevenett, William, jun.	....	Fr	0	1	1
Stevenett, William	Humber-street, Hull	Fr			
Thacker, William	....	Fr	0	1	0
Thornton, Jeremiah	....	Fr	1	1	0
Tomlinson, William	....	Fr	0	0	1
Tindall, John	....	Fr	1	1	0
Whittaker, James	....	Fr			
Warren, Rev. Zachariah	Ancaster	Fr			

Dogdike.

Name of Elector.	Residence, if out of the Parish.	Qual.	T.	W.	P.
Barnes, Joseph	....	Rt	1	1	0
Casswell, Thomas	Osbournby	Fr			
Clarke, Thomas	....	Fr	0	1	0
Emeris, Rev. John	Louth	Fr			
Lamyman, Amos	....	Rt	1	1	0

Dogdike—continued.

Name of Elector.	Residence, if out of the Parish.	Qual.	T.	W.	P.
Longthorn, James	....	Fr	1	1	0
Mayfield, Thomas	....	Fr	1	1	0
Mayfield, James	....	Rt	1	1	0
Mills, George	....	Fr	1	1	0
Watson, Richard	....	Rt	1	1	0

Evedon.

Burnett, Tindall Joseph	....	Rt	1	1	0
Pollard, Rev. Edward	....	Fr	1	1	0
Smith, George	....	Rt	1	1	0

Ewerby and Ewerby Thorpe.

Black, William	....	Fr	0	1	1
Burcham, William	....	Fr	0	1	1
Hardy, John	....	Rt			
Hubbard, James	....	Rt	0	1	1
Rowley, Andrews	New Sleaford	Fr	1	1	0
Smith, Thomas	....	Rt	0	1	1
Stennett, William	....	Fr	0	1	0
Thorpe, Thomas	....	Rt	1	1	0
Tindale, John	....	Fr	0	0	1
Tindale, John, jun.	....	Fr			
Wilson, John	....	Fr	0	1	1

Falkingham.

Barker, Thomas	....	Rt	0	0	1
Banks, William	....	Fr			
Blomfield, Charles, esq.	....	Fr	1	1	0
Casswell, John	....	Rt	1	0	1
Chambers, John	....	Rt	0	0	1
Heathcote, Arthur, esq.	Durdans, Epsom	Fr			
Howitt, Richard	....	Fr	0	0	1
Mitchell, Thomas	....	Rt	0	0	1
Martin, William	....	Rt	1	0	1
Morris, Edward	....	Rt	0	0	1
Owen, John	....	Rt	0	0	1
Rawnsley, Rev. Thomas Hardwicke	Halton Holgate	Fr	1	0	1
Stennett, Charles	....	Rt	0	0	1
Torrington, Edward	....	Fr	0	1	1
Ward, James	....	Fr	0	1	1
Wyer, Daniel	....	Rt	0	0	1

Great Hale.

Name of Elector.	Residence, if out of the Parish.	Qual.	T.	W.	P.
Bingham, Rev, Richard	Gosport	Fr			
Brown, John	Heckington	Rt	1	1	0
Blaze, John	New Sleaford	Fr	0	0	1
Bowles, Benjamin Ellis	Spalding	Fr			
Cobb, Robert	Bicker	Fr	0	0	1
Dawber, Robert	Lincoln	Fr	0	0	1
Everard, Richard	....	Fr	0	1	0
Fillingham, George, esq.	Syerston	Fr	*dead*		
Farrant, George Binstead	13, Green-street, Grosvenor-sq. Middlesex	Fr			
Fountain, Frederick	....	Fr	0	1	1
Freeman, Robert	....	Fr	0	0	1
Housley, John	....	Fr	0	1	1
Harris, Thomas	Great Hale-fen	Rt	0	0	1
Johnson, Edward	Great Hale-fen	Rt	0	0	1
Key, William	Brandon-plot	Fr	0	0	1
King, John	....	Fr	0	0	1
King, William	....	Fr	0	0	1
Knight, William	Great Hale-fen	Rt	0	1	0
Makins, John	....	Fr	0	0	1
Mason, John Marvin	....	Fr	0	0	1
Mason, Thomas	....	Fr	0	0	1
Read, Waddington	....	Rt	0	1	1
Rear, William	....	Rt	1	1	0
Sellars, Newton	Great Hale-fen	Rt			
Woodcock, John	Swineshead	Fr			-
Woods, Bettinson	....	Fr	0	0	1
Ward, Luke	....	Fr	0	0	1

Little Hale.

Name of Elector.	Residence, if out of the Parish.	Qual.	T.	W.	P.
Allett, Richard	Little Hale-fen	Rt	0	1	1
Cheales, Rev. Henry	Northend, near Fordingbridge	Fr	1	1	0
Clarke, George	....	Rt	0	0	1
Dickens, William	Little Hale-fen	Fr	1	1	0
Everard, Henry	Lincoln	Fr	0	0	1
Faulkner, Thomas	....	Rt	1	1	0
Faulkner, Francis Pogson	....	Rt	1	1	0
Farrant, Sir George, bart.	53, Upper Brook-street, London	Fr			
Fountain, Frederick	Great Hale	Fr			

Little Hale—continued.

Name of Elector.	Residence, if out of the Parish.	Qual.	T.	W.	P.
Godley, Thomas	Little Hale-fen	Fr	1	1	0
Godfrey, Joseph Silvester esq.	10, Gloucester-terrace, Regent's-park, London	Fr			
Green, Henry	....	Rt	0	1	1
Green, Thomas	....	Fr	0	0	1
Green, Benjamin	....	Rt	0	0	1
Hackett, John	....	Rt	1	1	0
Key, Richard	....	Fr	0	1	1
Luff, Richard	Horbling	Fr			
Milns, Thomas	Little Hale-fen	Rt	1	1	0
Newton, George	....	Fr	0	1	0
Ouzman, John	Little Hale-fen	Rt			
Orme, H., Capt.	Maiden-lane, Stamford	Fr	1	1	0
Sills, George	Casthorpe	Fr			
Thompson, George	....	Rt	0	1	1
Tindall, John	....	Rt	0	1	1

Heckington and Garrick.

Name of Elector.	Residence, if out of the Parish.	Qual.	T.	W.	P.
Almond, Henry	....	Fr	0	1	1
Almond, William	....	Fr	0	1	1
Arden, John	Garrick	Rt	1	1	0
Byron, William	....	Fr	1	1	0
Belton, Christopher	....	Fr	0	1	1
Bowles, Richard	Heckington-fen	Rt	1	1	0
Bancroft, Joseph	....	Fr	0	1	1
Bocock, William	....	Fr			
Barnatt, William	....	Fr	0	1	1
Bowles, Theophilus	Great Hale	Rt	0	1	1
Brocton, John	Farndon	Fr	1	1	0
Blain, George	Great Grimsby	Fr	1	1	0
Christopher, John	Winkhill-manor	Fr	1	1	0
Clarke, Joseph	Waddington	Fr	1	1	0
Clarke, George	Heckington-fen	Rt	0	1	0
Clarke, Henry, esq.	West Skirbeck	Fr	*dead*		
Cooper, John, jun.	Heckington-fen	Rt	1	1	0
Coupland, Daniel	Heckington-fen	Fr	0	1	1
Coupland, Edmund	....	Fr	0	1	1
Chapman, John	....	Fr	0	1	1
Cowlishaw, Henry	Shardlow, Derbyshire	Fr			

Heckington and Garrick—continued.

Name of Elector.	Residence, if out of the Parish.	Qual.	T.	W.	P.
De la Cour, Rev Charles	....	Fr	1	1	0
Daubrah, George	....	Fr	0	1	1
Elkington, Richard	....	Fr	0	1	1
Elmore, James	....	Fr	0	1	0
French, William, *Sol*	St. Mary's-street, Stamford	Fr			
Franks, Moses	....	Fr	0	0	1
Foster, James	....	Fr	0	1	1
Freestone, Henry	Sutterton	Rt	1	1	0
Foster, John Henry, *Sol*	New Sleaford	Fr	0	0	1
Godson, George	Heckington-fen	Fr	1	1	0
Godson, Richard	....	Fr	1	1	0
Godson, Joseph	....	Fr	1	1	0
Graves, Robert	....	Fr	0	1	1
Gibson, Anthony	Burton Pedwardine	Rt			
Godson, Edward	....	Fr	1	1	0
Hall, James	....	Fr	0	1	1
Hall, Henry	....	Fr	0	1	1
Hardstaff, William	....	Fr	1	1	0
Harrison, Samuel	Skirbeck	Fr	0	0	1
Holdershaw, William	....	Fr	0	1	1
Hoyes, Joseph	Heckington-fen	Fr			
Hill, Robert	....	Fr	0	1	0
Ingleton, Samuel	....	Fr	1	1	0
Lawson, William	....	Fr	0	1	1
Longlands, Thomas	Nottingham	Fr			
Lucas, Frederick, esq.	Louth	Fr			
Levesley, Benjamin	Heckington-fen	Rt	0	1	1
Levesley, John	Heckington-fen	Fr	0	1	1
Miller, John, jun.	Heckington-fen	Fr	0	1	1
Millns, Richard Godson	Lindhurst, Notts.	Fr	1	1	0
Miller, John	Heckington-fen	Rt	0	1	1
Miller, John	Heckington-fen	Fr	0	1	1
Miller, Richard	Heckington-fen	Fr	0	1	1
Mowberry, Charles	....	Rt	0	0	1
Millhouse, Oliver Howe	....	Rt	1	1	0
Minckley, Enoch	Heckington-fen	Fr	0	1	1
Morris, William	....	Fr	0	1	1
Moore, William	Heckington-fen	Fr	1	1	0
Newton, John	....	Fr	0	1	1
North, John	....	Fr	0	1	1
Newzam, Thomas William	Stamford	Fr			

Heckington and Garrick—continued.

Name of Elector.	Residence, if out of the Parish.	Qual.	T.	W.	P.
Nash, Sleightholme	....	Fr	0	1	1
Pearson, Charles, esq.	Tempsford Hall, St. Neots	Fr			
Pierce, Reverend William Matthews	West Ashby	Fr	0	0	1
Peart, Willey	Heckington-fen	Fr	1	1	0
Pierce, Francis Rockliffe, *West Ashby House	Fr			
Petchell, William	....	Rt	1	1	0
Partridge, Matthew	....	Fr	0	1	1
Pearce, Robert	Heckington-fen	Fr	0	1	0
Picker, John	Heckington-fen	Fr			
Pearce, Thomas	Bourn	Fr			
Potterton, John	....	Rt	0	1	1
Roberts, Naaman	Heckington-fen	Rt	1	1	0
Redshaw, Thomas, sen.	....	Fr	1	1	0
Redshaw, Thomas, jun.	....	Fr	0	0	1
Rilatt, George	....	Fr	0	1	1
Redshaw, Thomas, farmer	....	Fr	0	0	1
Redshaw, Thomas, jun.	Great Hale	Fr	0	1	1
Rippon, Thomas	Garrick	Rt	1	1	0
Scott, Sir Claude Edward, bart.	27, Bruton-street, Berkeley-square, London	Fr			
Simpson, Charles	....	Fr	0	1	1
Smith, Henry	....	Fr	1	1	0
Smith, John	....	Fr	1	1	0
Smith, Thomas	New Sleaford	Fr	1	1	0
Stanton, William	Manthorpe-cum-Little Gonerby	Fr	1	1	0
Smith, Robert James	Heckington-fen	Rt	0	1	1
Swan, Robert, esq *Sol*	Lincoln	Fr	1	1	0
Saunby, William	....	Fr	0	1	0
Taylor, Robert	....	Fr	0	1	1
Toynbee, Charles	Nocton	Rt			
Turner, John	....	Fr	0	1	1
Tomlin, Alfred	....	Fr	1	1	0
Turner, Edward	Heckington-fen	Fr	0	1	1
Weston, Richard	....	Fr	0	1	1
Wilkinson, John	....	Fr	0	1	1
Willson, Samuel	....	Fr	0	1	1
Wright, Robert	....	Fr	1	1	0

Helpringham and Thorpe Latimer.

Name of Elector.	Residence, if out of the Parish.	Qual.	T.	W.	P.
Almond, Giddings	....	Fr	0	1	0
Barnes, Joseph	Skillington	Fr	0	0	1
Bradley, John	....	Fr			
Bools, Charles	....	Fr	0	1	1
Bugg, George	Helpringham-fen	Fr	0	1	0
Bugg, Benjamin	....	Fr	0	0	1
Borman, John	....	Fr	1	1	0
Cook, Robert	....	Fr	0	1	1
Chambers, George	....	Fr	0	1	1
Codlin, Joseph	....	Fr			
Copeland, Thomas	Helpringham-fen	Rt	1	1	0
Creasey, James	Walcot	Fr	0	1	1
Cocks, John	Helpringham-fen	Rt	1	1	0
Elsom, George	Helpringham-fen	Fr	1	1	0
Foster, William, esq. *Sol*	New Sleaford	Fr			
Foster, John	....	Rt	1	1	0
Garratt, William	....	Fr	1	1	0
Garton, Samuel	Helpringham-fen	Fr			
Garton, John	....	Fr	1	1	0
Jones, Lewis	....	Rt	1	1	0
Johnson, Edward	....	Rt	0	0	1
Knight, William	....	Rt	1	1	0
Leak, John	....	Fr	0	0	1
Latham, Rev. Frederick	....	Fr	1	1	0
Pridgeon, Robert	....	Fr	1	1	0
Pell, Joseph	....	Fr	0	1	1
Pell, Samuel	....	Fr	0	1	1
Pearson, Charles, esq.	Tempsford Hall	Fr	1	1	0
Read, Joseph	....	Fr	0	0	1
Robinson, John	Heckington	Fr			
Robinson, Thomas	....	Fr	1	1	0
Robinson, Edward	....	Fr	0	0	1
Rippon, John	....	Fr			
Saunby, Anthony	....	Fr	1	1	0
Shaw, Thomas	Belper, Derbyshire	Fr			
Smith, Thomas	Swineshead	Fr	1	1	0
Smith, Edward	....	Fr	1	1	0
Smith, John	....	Fr	1	1	0
Taft, John	Helpringham-fen	Fr	1	1	0
Taft, William	....	Fr	1	1	0

Helpringham and Thorpe Latimer—continued.

Name of Elector.	Residence, if out of the Parish.	Qual.	T.	W.	P.
Thorlby, John	....	Fr	1	1	0
Thorlby, Joseph	....	Fr	1	1	0
Thorlby, William	....	Fr	1	1	0
Thorlby, Joseph Henry	....	Rt	1	1	0
Tomlinson, John	....	Fr	1	1	0
Tomlinson, Felix	Thorpe Latimer	Rt	1	1	0
Wilson, Rev. John	Wigtoft	Fr			
Whyman, John	....	Fr	0	1	1
Widdowson, Thomas	....	Fr	1	1	0
Widdowson, Thomas	Swaton	Fr			
Waddingham, Richard	....	Fr	1	1	0

Holdingham.

Name of Elector.	Residence, if out of the Parish.	Qual.	T.	W.	P.
Barnes, William	....	Rt	0	1	1
Clay, Thomas	....	Fr	0	0	1
Rippon, Frederick	....	Rt	0	1	0
Roberts, Thomas	....	Rt	0	1	1
Trevitt, William Squire	....	Rt	0	0	1

Horbling and Bridge-End.

Name of Elector.	Residence, if out of the Parish.	Qual.	T.	W.	P.
Baker, John	Bridge-End	Rt	1	1	0
Barnes, Robert	....	Rt	1	1	0
Baker, Thomas	Bridge-End	Rt	1	1	0
Blackbourn, Henry	Ditto	Rt	1	1	0
Brown, Rev. Edward	Lyndon, Rutland	Fr			
Brown, Colonel Henry	28, Soho-sq., London	Fr			
Bristo, John	Horbling-fen	Rt	0	1	0
Bristo, Marshall	....	Rt	1	1	0
Coates, Eli	Underwood, Nottinghamshire	Rt			
Coates, Samuel	Alfreton, Derbyshire	Fr			
Cragg, William, esq.	Threekingham	Fr			
Dods, John Thomas	Gosberton	Fr			
Dean, Seth Ellis	....	Rt	1	1	0
Harris, Rev. Henry	....	Fr	1	1	0
Luff, Richard	....	Rt	0	1	0
Pickwell, Thomas	....	Rt	1	1	0
Rimmington, Thomas	....	Rt	1	0	1
Smith, Henry	....	Rt	1	1	0
Smith, Benjamin, esq. Sol	....	Rt			
Tirrell, Philip	....	Rt	1	1	0
Taylor, Anthony Creasey	....	Rt	1	1	0

Horbling and Bridge-End—continued.

Name of Elector.	Residence, if out of the Parish.	Qual.	T.	W.	P.
Wass, Thomas	....	Rt	0	0	1
Wilson, Thomas	Azeby	Fr	1	1	0
Wiles, George, esq. *Sol*	....	Rt			

Howell.

Bett, William	....	Rt			
Dudding, John Walter	....	Fr	0	1	1
Machin, John Vessey, esq.	Gatesford	Fr	1	1	0
Sardeson, Henry	....	Rt	1	1	0
Werge, Henry Reynolds, esq.	Her Majesty's 55th Regiment	Fr			

Kelby.

Barrand, Edward	....	Rt	1	1	0
Cheales, Rev. John	Skendleby	Fr			
Everitt, William	....	Rt	1	1	0
King, John	....	Rt	1	1	0
Marratt, Thomas	....	Fr	1	1	0
Matkin, William	....	Rt	1	1	0
Pinder, Joseph	....	Rt	1	1	0
Parkinson, Charles	Wilsford	Fr			

Kirkby Laythorpe.

Barlow, John	....	Fr	0	1	1
Cartwright, Thomas	....	Rt	1	1	0
Childs, William	Little Hale	Fr			
Pickworth, John Gould	....	Rt	0	1	0
Sardeson, George	....	Rt	1	1	0

North Kyme.

Almond, William Porter	....	Fr	0	1	1
Broadgate, Theophilus	....	Fr	0	1	0
Berry, Thomas	Billinghay	Fr	0	1	1
Bailey, Jabez	....	Rt	1	1	0
Bellamy, Edward	....	Fr	0	1	1
Blackbourn, William	....	Fr	0	1	1
Blackbourn, Thomas	....	Rt	1	1	0
Beecher, John D., Rev.	Norwood-park,	Fr	1	1	0
Bellamy, Edward	....	Fr	1	1	0
Brooks, Jacob	....	Fr	0	1	1
Brooks, John	....	Fr	0	1	1
Bones, Richard	....	Rt	1	1	0
Dimond, Samuel	Billinghay	Fr			

North Kyme—continued.

Name of Elector.	Residence, if out of the Parish.	Qual.	T.	W.	P.
Garratt, William	Dogdike	Rt	0	1	0
Goodbarne, William Fisher	Kirkby Laythorpe	Fr	1	1	0
Goodman, Joseph, jun.	....	Fr	0	1	1
Goodman, Joseph	....	Rt	0	1	1
Harrod, Thomas	....	Fr			
Harness, John Robert	Billinghay	Fr			
Helpringham, William	....	Fr	0	1	1
Ireland, Charles	Wildmore-fen	Fr			
Jackson, Nathaniel	Ashby-cum-fenby	Fr	1	1	0
Jackson, Edward	Vachery	Rt	1	1	0
Jollands, Willie	....	Fr	1	1	0
Jillands, William	Anwick	Fr	0	1	1
Kirk, William	....	Fr	0	0	1
Key, Thomas	Billinghay	Fr			
Lunn, William	....	Fr			
Lynn, Robert	....	Fr	0	1	1
Lynn, John	....	Fr	0	1	1
Lanes, John	....	Fr	0	0	1
Lightfoot, Joseph	....	Fr	0	0	1
Mugliston, Samuel Stotherd	Billinghay	Fr	0	1	1
Martin, John	....	Rt	0	1	1
Peacock, Rev. Edward	Maddington, Wilts	Fr	1	1	0
Rook, Richard	Billinghay	Rt	0	1	1
Rear, William	Great Hale	Fr			
Ravell, Matthew	....	Fr	0	1	1
Stubley, John, jun.	....	Fr	0	1	1
Stubley, Joshua	Billinghay	Fr	0	0	1
Sutton, William	Billinghay	Fr	0	1	1
Sills, John	....	Fr	0	1	1
Stubley, John	....	Fr	0	0	1
Southern, Thomas	....	Fr	1	1	0
Smith, Rev. John, *D.D.*	Horncastle	Fr	*dead*		
Truswell, Sharp	....	Fr	0	0	1
Torey, Joseph	....	Fr	0	1	1
White, Henry	....	Fr	1	1	0
White, Thomas	....	Fr	0	0	1
White, Thomas, jun.	....	Rt			
White, Robert	....	Fr	1	1	0
Wilson, William	Ewerby	Fr	0	1	1
Walker, George	Spilsby	Fr	0	0	1

North Kyme—continued.

Name of Elector.	Residence, if out of the Parish.	Qual.	T.	W.	P.
Woulds, Robert	....	Fr	1	1	0
York, James Whiting, esq.	Walmsgate, Louth	Fr	*dead*		

South Kyme.

Name of Elector.	Residence, if out of the Parish.	Qual.	T.	W.	P.
Addison, Thomas	....	Rt	1	1	0
Addison, Benjamin	....	Rt	1	1	0
Baldwick, Samuel	....	Rt	1	1	0
Codd, John	....	Rt	1	1	0
Cust, the Hon. Charles Henry	Belgrave-square, London	Fr	1	1	0
Cust, the Hon. and Rev. Richard	Rectory, Belton	Fr			
Chambers, John	....	Rt	1	1	0
Chambers, Banks	....	Rt	1	1	0
Chambers, Thomas	....	Rt	1	1	0
Dodd, William	....	Rt	1	1	0
Dixon, George	....	Rt	1	1	0
Forman, William	....	Rt	1	1	0
Forman, Edward	....	Rt	1	1	0
Graves, George	....	Rt	1	1	0
Grewcock, Joseph	....	Rt	1	1	0
Hides, George	....	Rt	1	1	0
Hoyes, John	....	Rt	1	1	0
Neucatre, Rev. Henry Sidney	....	Fr	1	1	0
Oliver, William	Burtoft-in-Wigtoft	Rt			
Potter, John	....	Rt	1	1	0
Sharpe, James	....	Rt	1	1	0
Scholey, Robert	....	Rt	1	1	0
Thompson, Abraham	....	Rt	1	1	0
Ulyatt, Edward	....	Rt	1	1	0
Ulyatt, Edward	....	Rt	1	1	0
Vessey, William	....	Rt	1	1	0
Ward, James	....	Rt	1	1	0

Leasingham.

Name of Elector.	Residence, if out of the Parish.	Qual.	T.	W.	P.
Billiatt, Joseph	Syston	Fr	1	1	0
Billiatt, John	Honington	Fr			
Billiatt, William	Honington	Fr	1	0	1
Blackbourn, Samuel	....	Fr	0	1	1
Conington, Rev. John	Southwell	Fr			
Curtois, Rev. Peregrine	Hemingford Grey	Fr	1	1	0

Leasingham—continued.

Name of Elector.	Residence, if out of the Parish.	Qual.	T.	W.	P.
Covel, Thomas	....	Fr	1	1	0
Count, William	....	Fr			
Chevin, Henry	....	Rt	1	1	0
Francis, John	....	Rt	0	1	1
Hammond, Thomas	....	Rt	0	0	1
Hopkinson, William	Stamford	Fr			
Myddleton, Richard Wharton, esq.	....	Fr			
Mowbray, John	....	Fr			
Riggall, Joseph	....	Rt	1	1	0
Robinson, Matthew	Stubton	Fr			
Seawell, Charles Yorke, esq.	Buckden	Fr			
Sands, Charles	....	Rt	0	0	1
Seawell, Rev. Henry Walter	Little Berkhamp-stead	Fr			
Sumner, Henry	....	Rt	0	1	1
Stow, Mark	....	Rt	1	1	0
Sumner, Cooper	....	Rt	1	1	0
Smith, William	Ruskington	Fr			
Trollope, Rev. Edward		Fr	1	1	0
Wells, Samuel	....	Fr	1	1	0

Martin.

Name of Elector.	Residence, if out of the Parish.	Qual.	T.	W.	P.
Allett, John	Timberland-fen	Fr			
Burr, George	....	Fr	1	1	0
Cawdron, William	....	Fr	1	1	0
Cawdron, William	....	Fr	1	1	0
Cawdron, William Blackbourn	Billinghay	Fr	1	1	0
Clay, William	Martin-dales	Fr			
Clay, Thomas	Martin-dales	Fr			
Cartwright, John	Nocton	Fr			
Cawdron, Henry	....	Fr	1	1	0
Cook, John	....	Fr	1	1	0
Denman, the Hon. Thomas	38, Portland-square, London	Fr			
Farbon, Joseph	....	Fr	1	1	0
Farbon, William	....	Fr			
Farbon, William	Horncastle	Fr	1	1	0
Farbon, Robert	....	Fr	1	1	0
Fowler, Benjamin	Kirkstead	Fr	1	1	0

Martin—continued.

Name of Elector.	Residence, if out of the Parish.	Qual.	T.	W.	P.
Gash, Joseph	Martin-fen	Rt	1	1	0
Griffith, Robert	Horncastle	Fr			
Goose, James	Martin-fen	Rt	1	1	0
Goose, Solomon	....	Rt	1	1	0
Grayson, William	....	Rt	0	1	1
Haynes, James	Ingoldmells	Fr	1	1	0
Hollingshead, James	Martin-Moor	Rt	1	1	0
Holmes, Abraham	Martin-moor	Rt	1	1	0
Howard, Sampson	Martin-fen	Rt	1	1	0
Howard, Thomas	Martin-fen	Rt	1	1	0
Howard, John	Martin-fen	Rt	1	1	0
Hollingshead, Thomas	....	Fr	1	1	0
Hollingshead, Robert	Timberland	Fr	1	1	0
Idle, Thomas	Martin-moor	Rt	1	1	0
Kent, Richard	Martin-dales	Fr			
Kyme, William	Martin-dales	Fr	1	1	0
Knott, Joseph	Martin-dales	Fr			
Kent, Thomas	Martin-dales	Fr	1	1	0
Knott, Matthew	Martin-dales	Fr			
Mayfield, William	Martin-dales	Rt	1	1	0
Marshall, Joseph	Martin-dales	Fr	1	1	0
Marshall, William	Martin-fen	Rt	1	1	0
Picksley, Richard	Martin-moor	Rt	0	1	0
Read, James	....	Fr	1	1	0
Smith, John	Martin-fen	Fr	1	1	0
Sutterby, Thomas	Martin-fen	Rt			
Saxby, Joseph	Martin-dales	Fr	1	1	0
Spencer, William	....	Rt	1	1	0
Webster, Cornelius	....	Rt	1	1	0
Webster, William	....	Rt	1	1	0
Wright, Richard	Martin-dales	Rt	1	1	0
Welby, Henry	....	Fr	1	1	0
Ware, Samuel	....	Fr	1	1	0
Wilson, John	Martin-fen	Rt	1	1	0

Newton.

Name of Elector.	Residence, if out of the Parish.	Qual.	T.	W.	P.
Doughty, Samuel	....	Rt	1	1	0
Ellis, William	....	Rt	1	1	0
Ellis, John	....	Rt			
Holmes, William	....	Rt	1	1	0
Lynn, John Cragg	....	Rt	1	1	0
Sharp, Robert	....	Fr			
Welby, Rev. Arthur Earle	....	Fr	1	1	0

Osbournby.

Name of Elector.	Residence, if out of the Parish.	Qual.	T.	W.	P.
Barrand, Charles Foster	Aunsby	Fr			
Briggs, Richard	....	Rt	1	1	0
Bycroft, William	....	Rt	1	1	0
Clay, Richard	....	Rt	1	1	0
Casswell, Thomas	....	Rt			
Colton, Christopher	Horbling	Fr	1	1	0
Collingwood, William	....	Fr	1	1	0
Capps, John	....	Fr	1	1	0
Holmes, Samuel, jun.	....	Rt	1	1	0
Handley, Thomas	....	Fr	1	1	0
Handley, Robert	....	Fr	1	1	0
Hall, Robert	....	Rt	1	1	0
Holmes, Samuel	....	Fr	1	1	0
Johnston, Robert Henry	Grantham	Rt			
Mowbray, Joseph	....	Rt	1	1	0
Parnell, Thomas	....	Fr	0	1	1
Pawley, Robert	....	Rt	1	1	0
Pearson, Rev. John	....	Fr	1	1	0
Pheasant, John	Threekingham	Fr			
Spencer, Thomas	....	Fr	1	1	0
Thompson, Thomas George	....	Rt	1	1	0
Whichcote, George, esq.	Aswarby	Fr			
Whichcote, George, jun., esq.	....	Rt	1	1	0
Wright, John	....	Fr	0	1	1
Wright, William	....	Fr	1	1	0

Quarrington.

Name of Elector.	Residence, if out of the Parish.	Qual.	T.	W.	P.
Bellamy, James	New Sleaford	Rt			
Cubley, Tamberlain	....	Rt	1	1	0
Hervey, the Honourable Frederick William, commonly called Earl Jermyn	Ickworth-park	Fr	1	1	0
Hine, the Rev. Henry Thomas Cooper	....	Fr	1	1	0
Mason, Frederick	....	Fr	0	0	1
Peach, John	....	Fr	1	1	0
Tomlinson, Augustus	....	Rt	1	1	0

South Rauceby.

Name of Elector.	Residence, if out of the Parish.	Qual.	T.	W.	P.
Barber, Samuel	....	Fr	1	1	0

South Rauceby—continued.

Name of Elector.	Residence, if out of the Parish.	Qual.	T.	W.	P.
Gibson, Leonard	....	Rt	1	1	0
Petchell, Thomas	....	Rt			
Rowley, John	....	Rt	1	1	0
Rowley, George	....	Rt	1	1	0
Rowley, Edward	....	Fr	1	1	0
Scarborough, John	....	Rt	1	1	0
Willson, Anthony, esq.	....	Fr	1	1	0

North Rauceby.

Name of Elector.	Residence, if out of the Parish.	Qual.	T.	W.	P.
Harvey, George	....	Rt	1	1	0
Newton, William George Tinley	....	Rt	0	1	0
Pilkington, William	....	Rt	1	1	0
Roberts, Robert	....	Rt			
Thurlby, Jesse Miller	....	Rt	1	1	0
Thoroton, Rev. Charles	....	Fr	0	1	0
Wolf, William	....	Rt	1	1	0

Roxholm.

Name of Elector.	Residence, if out of the Parish.	Qual.	T.	W.	P.
Baldock, William	....	Rt	0	0	1
Birch, Wyrley, esq.	Wretham, Norfolk	Fr			
Clay, Richard	....	Rt	0	1	1
Green, Edward	....	Rt	0	0	1
Twidale, Joseph	....	Rt	0	0	1

Rowston.

Name of Elector.	Residence, if out of the Parish.	Qual.	T.	W.	P.
Andrew, William, esq.	Lincoln	Fr			
Blackbourn, John	Rowston	Rt	1	1	0
Blackbourn, John, jun.	Ditto	Rt	1	1	0
Gadd, Joseph	Digby	Fr	0	1	1
Love, John	Rowston	Rt	0	0	1
Pratt, Rev. Charles	Packington, Leicestershire	Fr	1	1	0
Phillips, William	Sheffield House	Rt	0	0	1

Ruskington and Haverholm Priory.

Name of Elector.	Residence, if out of the Parish.	Qual.	T.	W.	P.
Almond, Frederick	Ruskington-fen	Fr	0	1	1
Atkin, Benjamin	Ruskington-moor	Rt	1	1	0
Atkin, Thomas	....	Fr	0	0	1
Birch, Wyrley, esq.	Wretham	Fr			
Brewin, Thomas	....	Rt	0	0	1
Baxter, William	....	Fr	0	1	1
Brewin, John	....	Fr			

Ruskington and Haverholm Priory—continued.

Name of Elector.	Residence, if out of the Parish.	Qual.	T.	W.	P.
Blackbourn, George	....	Fr	0	0	1
Brown, Edward	....	Rt	1	1	0
Cartman, John	....	Rt	0	1	1
Christian, Robert	....	Fr	0	1	1
Collishaw, George	....	Fr			
Creasey, John	....	Rt	0	1	1
Dudding, John, esq.	Lincoln	Fr			
Dawson, Richard	....	Fr	0	0	1
Francis, Robert	....	Rt	0	0	1
Foston, Joseph	....	Rt	0	0	1
Frudd, John	Ruskington-road	Rt	1	1	0
Hudson, William	....	Fr	0	1	1
Heckford, Rev. James	....	Fr	1	0	1
Holmes, John	Billinghay	Fr			
Headland, John	....	Fr	0	0	1
Headland, William	....	Fr	0	1	1
Kelley, Thomas	....	Fr	0	1	1
Moor, John	....	Fr	0	1	0
Myers, Rev. Charles	Flintham	Fr			
Neale, William	Newton	Fr			
Newton, William	....	Fr	0	1	1
Ogden, Thomas	....	Fr	1	1	0
Oxenford, William	Cranwell	Fr	1	1	0
Pattinson, Samuel	....	Fr			
Parkes, William	....	Fr			
Prince, Thomas	....	Fr	0	1	1
Ragsdale, William	Bottesford, Leicestershire	Fr	0	0	1
Richards, Gibson	....	Fr	0	1	1
Riggall, Edmund	....	Rt	1	1	0
Rowley, Thomas	....	Rt	0	1	1
Reast, Joseph	....	Fr	1	1	0
Robinson, Robert	....	Rt	0	1	1
Snow, James	....	Rt	1	1	0
Stow, Richard	....	Rt	0	1	0
Sutton, Francis	....	Fr	0	1	1
Thurlby, Robert	Boston	Fr	1	1	0
Towler, Edward	Swinhop	Fr			
Thorpe, John	....	Fr	0	1	1
Wabey, Thomas	....	Fr	1	1	0
Wainer, William	....	Fr	0	1	1

Ruskington and Haverholm Priory—continued.

Name of Elector.	Residence, if out of the Parish.	Qual.	T.	W.	P.
Wainer, Thomas	....	Fr	0	1	1
Williams, Samuel	Sleaford	Fr			
Williams, Benjamin	Sleaford	Fr			
White, Thomas	South Kyme	Fr			
Wilkinson, George	Doddington	Fr			
White, Charles	....	Rt	0	1	1

Scredington.

Name of Elector.	Residence, if out of the Parish.	Qual.	T.	W.	P.
Banks, John	....	Fr	0	1	1
Burkitt, John	Halstead,Leicestershire	Fr			
Boss, Edward	....	Fr	0	1	1
Bailey, John	....	Rt	0	1	0
Bailey, Edward	....	Rt	0	1	0
Barnes, William	....	Fr	1	1	0
Chambers, George	Hocknold, Norfolk	Fr			
Dexter, Thomas	....	Rt	1	1	0
Dodds, Charles	....	Fr	0	1	0
Faulkner, John	Billingborough	Fr	1	1	0
Foyster, John	Threekingham	Fr	1	1	0
Hare, John	....	Fr	1	1	0
Holmes, William	....	Fr	1	1	0
Lowe, Edward Thomas	Aswarby	Fr	1	1	0
Marston, John Taylor	Market Deeping	Fr			
Neave, John	....	Rt	1	1	0
Palian, Henry	....	Fr			
Pawson, Thomas	Navenby	Fr			
Thompson, Dring	....	Rt	0	1	1
Wilson, William	....	Fr	0	1	0
Wilson, William	Falkingham	Fr			
Waltham, Rev. Joshua	Helpringham	Fr	0	1	0

Scott Willoughby.

Name of Elector.	Residence, if out of the Parish.	Qual.	T.	W.	P.
Baker, William	....	Rt	1	1	0
Burrows, Robert	....	Rt	1	1	0
Cust, the Hon. and Rev. Henry Cockayne	Cockayne Atley	Fr			

New Sleaford.

Name of Elector.	Residence, if out of the Parish.	Qual.	T.	W.	P.
Almond, John	....	Rt	0	1	1
Andrew, Thomas	Kinoulton	Fr			
Allen, Edward	....	Fr	1	1	0

New Sleaford—continued.

Name of Elector.	Residence, if out of the Parish.	Qual.	T.	W.	P.
Bailey, William	....	Rt			
Bailey, George	....	Rt	1	1	0
Baxter, John	....	Fr	0	1	1
Barrowcliffe, Joseph	....	Fr	0	1	1
Bailey, James	....	Fr	0	1	1
Brewitt, James Christopher	Old Sleaford	Fr	1	1	0
Butler, George	....	Rt	0	1	1
Bissill, John Henry	....	Fr	1	1	0
Bacon, John	....	Fr	0	1	1
Blaze, John	....	Fr			
Burrell, Samuel	Boston	Fr	1	1	0
Bacon, Solomon	....	Fr	0	1	0
Beeson, Stephen	....	Fr	1	1	0
Benstead, John	....	Fr	0	1	1
Black, James	....	Fr	0	0	1
Bennison, Marmaduke	....	Fr	0	1	1
Bates, Edward	Holloway	Fr	1	1	0
Cartwright, Edward	....	Rt	1	1	0
Clipsham, Thomas	....	Fr	0	1	1
Cubley, Tamberlain	Quarrington	Fr			
Camomile, Joseph	....	Fr	0	1	1
Cox, George	....	Fr	1	1	0
Codd, Benjamin	....	Fr	0	1	0
Clipsham, John	....	Fr	0	1	1
Darby, William	Old Sleaford	Rt	0	0	1
Darlow, Alfred	....	Fr	0	1	0
Dawson, Richard	....	Fr	0	1	1
Fawcett, William	....	Fr	0	1	1
Fawcett, William, jun.	....	Fr	1	1	0
Foster, William, esq. *Sol*	....	Fr	0	0	1
Foster, Edward	....	Fr	1	1	0
Fox, John	....	Fr	0	0	1
Gill, Baxter	....	Fr	0	1	0
Gibson, Joseph	....	Fr	0	0	1
Goodson, William	Market Raisen	Fr			
Gray, John	....	Rt	0	1	0
Green, Benjamin	....	Fr			
Goodwin, Abraham	Wilsford	Fr	0	1	1
Holdich, William Hungerford, esq. *Sol*	....	Fr	1	1	0
Harrison, Richard	....	Rt	1	1	0

New Sleaford—continued.

Name of Elector.	Residence, if out of the Parish.	Qual.	T.	W.	P.
Hipkin, Frederick	....	Fr	0	1	1
Hunt, William	....	Fr	0	1	1
Hill, Thomas	Ropsley	Fr	0	0	1
Handley, John	South Muskham	Fr			
Heald, William	....	Fr	1	1	0
Huelin, Rev. Elias	5, Somerset-place, Brompton	Fr			
Job, Charles	....	Fr	0	1	1
Johnson, Robert	Falkingham	Fr	0	0	1
Julian, John	....	Fr	0	1	1
Kirk, Charles	Old Sleaford	Fr	1	1	0
Lee, Edmund	....	Fr	1	1	0
Law, Elston	....	Rt	0	0	1
Martin, George	....	Fr	0	0	1
Manton, Rev. Henry	....	Fr	0	0	1
Martin, John	....	Fr	0	1	1
Marfleet, Joseph	Crowland	Fr			
Mastin, Waters Walker	....	Rt	0	1	1
Moore, Maurice Peter, esq.	....	Fr	1	1	0
Marston, John Taylor	Market Deeping	Fr			
Nickolls, John	....	Fr	1	1	0
Newton, Christopher Drake	Buckworth, Hunts	Fr	0	1	1
Obbinson, Thomas	....	Rt	1	1	0
Peake, Henry	....	Fr	1	1	0
Parry, Thomas	....	Fr	0	0	1
Parker, John	....	Fr	0	1	1
Payne, John, jun	....	Fr	0	1	1
Price, Edward	....	Fr	0	1	1
Pinder, Thomas	....	Fr	1	1	0
Roberts, Alfred	....	Rt	1	1	0
Roberts, John	....	Fr	1	1	0
Salmon, Richard	....	Fr	1	1	0
Simpson, William	....	Fr	0	1	0
Simpson, William, jun.	....	Fr	1	1	0
Sharpe, Robert	....	Rt	0	1	1
Steel, Charles	....	Fr	0	1	0
Steel, John	....	Rt	1	1	0
Snow, Benjamin	....	Fr	1	1	0
Simpson, Thomas	....	Fr	0	1	0
Smedley, Joseph	....	Fr			
Stennett, William	....	Fr	0	1	1
Tether, William	Newark	Fr			

New Sleaford—continued.

Name of Elector.	Residence, if out of the Parish.	Qual.	T.	W.	P.
Warwick, John	....	Fr	1	1	0
Williams, Rowland	....	Fr	0	1	1
Williams, Samuel	....	Fr	0	1	0
Williams, Benjamin	....	Fr	0	1	1
Weston, Thomas Fawcett	....	Fr	0	1	1
Webster, Thomas	....	Fr	1	1	0
Wilson, Joseph	Gainsborough	Fr	0	1	1
Weston, George	....	Fr	0	1	0
Yerburgh, Rev. Richard	....	Fr	1	1	0

Old Sleaford.

Name of Elector.	Residence, if out of the Parish.	Qual.	T.	W.	P.
Boyer, Charles	....	Fr	1	1	0
Chambers, Charles	....	Fr	0	0	1
Clements, Charles	....	Fr	1	1	0
Copeland, Robert	Dorrington	Fr	0	1	1
Newbatt, Edward	....	Rt	0	0	1
Smith, Joseph Slight	Quarrington	Fr	0	1	1
White, Anthony	....	Rt	0	1	1
Witherington, George	....	Fr	1	1	0

Spanby.

Name of Elector.	Residence, if out of the Parish.	Qual.	T.	W.	P.
Barnes, Thomas	....	Rt			
Bellamy, George	....	Rt	1	1	0
Chambers, George	Helpringham	Fr			
Dodsworth, John	....	Rt	1	1	0
Horsman, William	....	Rt	1	1	0
Lockwood, Robert, jun.	....	Rt	1	1	0
Speed, Robert	....	Fr	1	1	0

Swaton.

Name of Elector.	Residence, if out of the Parish.	Qual.	T.	W.	P.
Andrews, Joseph	....	Rt	1	1	0
Barber, William	....	Rt	0	1	1
Copeland, Johnson	....	Rt	1	1	0
Cooper, John	....	Rt	1	1	0
Cooper, William	....	Rt	1	1	0
Cropley, Crosby	....	Rt	1	1	0
Dennis, Joseph	....	Rt	1	1	0
Dean, Samuel	....	Rt	1	1	0
Hercock, George	....	Rt	1	1	0
Knapp, Rev. Henry	....	Fr	1	1	0
Mansfield, William	....	Rt	1	1	0
Mann, Thomas Stirling	....	Rt	1	1	0

Swaton—continued.

Name of Elector.	Residence, if out of the Parish.	Qual.	T.	W.	P.
Modd, John	....	Rt	1	1	0
Morris, William	....	Rt	1	1	0
Pepper, Robert	....	Rt	1	1	0
Scott, Rev. Thomas	Bromley Cottage, Kent	Fr			
Stubley, William	Horbling	Rt			
Stennett, John	....	Rt	0	1	1
Widdowson, Thomas	....	Rt	1	1	0

Swarby.

Name of Elector.	Residence, if out of the Parish.	Qual.	T.	W.	P.
Barrand, Charles	Crofton	Rt	1	1	0
Birch, Charles	....	Rt	1	1	0
Elston, Thomas	....	Rt	1	1	0
Foster, John	....	Fr	1	1	0
Gratton, John	....	Fr	1	1	0
Munton, John	Exton	Fr	1	1	0

Threekingham and Stow.

Name of Elector.	Residence, if out of the Parish.	Qual.	T.	W.	P.
Andrew, John	Stow	Rt	0	0	1
Bellamy, George	Spanby	Rt			
Cragg, William, esq.	Threekingham	Fr	1	1	0
Cragg, Edward	Ditto	Rt	1	1	0
Creasey, Robert	Stow	Rt	0	0	1
Dean, Clement Ellis	Threekingham	Rt	0	0	1
Ellicott, Rev. Charles Spencer	Whitwell, Rutland	Fr	1	0	1
Gilbert, John	Threekingham	Rt	0	0	1
Gilbert, Richard	Ditto	Rt	0	0	1
Henson, Thomas	Stow	Rt	1	1	0
Owen, George	Threekingham	Rt	0	0	1
Pheasant, John	Ditto	Rt	0	0	1
Rudge, Samuel Nouaille esq.	No. 6, Harley-street, Cavendish-sq., London	Fr			
Stones, Oliver	Threekingham	Fr	1	1	0
Wood, Joseph	Ditto	Rt	1	1	0

Thorpe Tilney.

Name of Elector.	Residence, if out of the Parish.	Qual.	T.	W.	P.
Collishaw, Edward	ThorpeTilney-dales	Rt	1	1	0
Dowse, James	Ditto	Rt	1	1	0
Elmitt, Thomas	Ditto	Rt	1	1	0
Gash, David	....	Rt	1	1	0
Holmes, Phineas	....	Rt	1	1	0
Whitby, Thomas	....	Rt	1	1	0

Timberland.

Name of Elector.	Residence, if out of the Parish.	Qual.	T.	W.	P.
Abbott, William	....	Rt	0	1	1
Allett, John	Timberland-fen	Rt	0	1	1
Creasey, John	Timberland-fen	Rt	1	1	0
Cartwright, James	....	Rt	1	1	0
Clifton, Joseph	....	Rt	1	1	0
Clifton, Thomas	....	Fr	1	1	0
Clay, John	Bardney Dairies	Fr	0	1	1
Cartwright, John	....	Rt	1	1	0
Creasy, Thomas	Thorpe Tilney	Fr	1	1	0
Elkington, Thomas	Timberland-fen	Fr			
Farnsworth, Edmund	Washingborough	Fr	1	1	0
Guttridge, John	....	Fr	0	1	1
Hollingsworth, Robert	Heckington	Fr	1	1	0
Huggins, Henry	Timberland-dales	Fr	1	1	0
Hallam, John	....	Fr	1	1	0
Milnes, Robert Pemberton, esq.	Fryston Hall, Yorkshire	Fr			
Meanwell, Wright	Coningsby	Fr			
Milnes, Richard, esq.	Fryston Hall, Yorkshire	Fr			
Pinder, Robert	Timberland-field	Rt	1	1	0
Pinder, Abraham	....	Rt	1	1	0
Short, William	Tattershall	Fr	0	1	1
Sneath, William	Timberland-fen	Rt	1	1	0
Taylor, John	Timberland-dales	Rt	1	1	0
Tatam, Thomas	Timberland-dales	Rt	1	1	0
Toynbee, Samuel	....	Fr	1	1	0
Wells, William	Timberland-fen	Rt	1	1	0
Wright, Robert	....	Fr			
Willcock, William	Timberland-dales	Rt	1	1	0
Wheat, Rev. Carlos Coney	....	Fr			
West, Atkin	....	Rt	1	1	0
Wheat, John, esq.	Treeton, near Rotherham	Fr	1	1	0
Wheat, Samuel	....	Rt	1	1	0

Walcott, near Falkingham.

Name of Elector.	Residence, if out of the Parish.	Qual.	T.	W.	P.
Coles, Rev. Thomas Henry, D.D,	Honington vicarage	Fr			
Ducket, John	....	Fr	0	0	1
Faulkner, Samuel	....	Rt	0	1	1
Meadows, Edward	....	Rt	0	0	1

Walcott, near Falkingham—continued.

Name of Elector.	Residence, if out of the Parish.	Qual.	T.	W.	P.
Oliver, John Warren	....	Rt			
Oliver, John Paul	....	Rt	0	0	1
Sumner, George	....	Fr	1	0	0
Smith, Edward	....	Rt	1	1	0
Tomblin, Rev. Charles	Langtoft	Fr			
Woolley, Robert	....	Rt			

Walcott, near Billinghay.

Name of Elector.	Residence, if out of the Parish.	Qual.	T.	W.	P.
Burrell, Charles Pettinger	Walcott-dales	Rt	0	1	1
Bralsford, Crosha	....	Fr	0	1	0
Burrell, Charles	Walcott-dales	Fr	0	1	1
Burrows, John	Walcott-fen	Fr	0	1	0
Brand, John	....	Fr	1	1	0
Brand, Richard	....	Fr	0	1	0
Boothby, James	Walcot-dales	Fr	1	1	0
Brand, Joseph	....	Fr	1	1	0
Bralsford, Crosha	....	Fr	0	1	1
Bralsford, Robert	....	Fr	0	1	0
Catton, William	....	Fr	1	1	0
Creasy, David, jun.	....	Rt	0	1	1
Creasey, Abraham	....	Rt	0	0	1
Creasey, Thomas	....	Fr			
Creasey, Robert	....	Fr	1	1	0
Cook, Joseph	Walcott-dales	Fr	1	1	0
Cook, William	Tattershall	Fr	1	1	0
Duckle, Robert	Gainsborough	Fr			
Duckle, Edward Samuel	Ditto	Fr			
Franklin, William, sen.	Walcott-fen	Fr	1	1	0
Graves, John	....	Rt	1	1	0
Holmes, John	....	Rt	0	1	1
Harris, John	Walcott-dales	Fr			
Harrison, John	....	Rt	1	1	0
Harrison, Joseph	....	Rt	1	1	0
Jackson, John	Digby-fen	Fr			
Marris, William	Walcott-fen	Rt	0	1	0
Osgerby, James	....	Fr	1	1	0
Peacock, Wilkinson, esq.	Greatford	Fr			
Peacock, Rev. Wilkinson Affleck	Ulceby, near Alford	Fr	1	1	0
Peacock, W. H., esq.	Thorpe Tilney	Fr	1	1	0
Peacock, Rev. John	Wellingore	Fr			
Pickworth, Thomas	Walcott-dales	Rt	0	1	1

Walcott, near Billinghay—continued.

Name of Elector.	Residence, if out of the Parish.	Qual.	T.	W.	P.
Parker, William	....	Rt	1	1	0
Rollitt, John, sen.	Kyme-fen	Fr	0	1	0
Rollitt, John	....	Rt	1	1	0
Slack, Thomas	Walcott-dales	Rt	0	1	1
Sleaford, William	Walcott-fen	Fr	0	1	1
Sumpter, Edward	....	Fr	1	1	0
Skelton, Moses James	Wellingore	Fr	0	0	1
Skelton, Robert	....	Fr	0	1	1
Tylor, John	Blankney-dales	Fr	1	1	0
Taylor, Thomas	....	Fr	1	1	0
Tong, Joseph	Walcott-dales	Rt	1	1	0
Wells, John	....	Fr	1	1	0
Woulds, Edward	....	Rt	1	1	0
Willson, Anthony, esq	South Rauceby	Fr			

Silk Willoughby.

Name of Elector.	Residence, if out of the Parish.	Qual.	T.	W.	P.
Burkitt, John	Swayfield	Rt			
Chambers, John Beeston	....	Rt	0	1	1
Codd, William	....	Fr			
Cooper Robert	Whaplode-drove	Fr			
Hack, Matthew	....	Rt	0	0	1
Hack, Richard Smith	Brook, Rutland	Rt			
Money, Thomas	....	Rt	0	1	1
Newton, Samuel	....	Rt	0	1	1
Tinley, John	....	Rt	0	1	1
White, Edward Chambers	....	Rt	0	0	1

Wilsford and Hanbeck.

Name of Elector.	Residence, if out of the Parish.	Qual.	T.	W.	P.
Cooper, Samuel	....	Rt	0	0	1
Everard, John	....	Rt	1	1	0
Eaton, Freeman	Ancaster; Wilsford-side	Fr			
Garner, James	....	Rt	0	0	1
Healey, Anthony	Little Gonerby	Fr			
Hodson, Maxey	....	Fr	0	0	1
Knight, William	Helpringham	Rt			
Mitchell, John	....	Fr	0	0	1
Nixon, Henry	Wilsford-warren	Rt	1	1	0
Palmer, Robert Jackson	West Willoughby	Fr	0	0	1
Parkinson, Thomas	....	Fr	1	1	0
Parkinson, Charles	Wilsford-hall	Fr	0	1	0
Patchett, Thomas	Brandon	Fr	1	1	0

Wilsford and Hanbeck—continued.

Name of Elector.	Residence, if out of the Parish.	Qual.	T.	W.	P.
Peach, John	....	Fr	1	1	0
Preston, John	....	Fr	0	1	1
Rowlatt, John	....	Rt	0	1	1
Roberts, Richard	....	Rt	0	0	1
Sleight, John	....	Rt			
Smart, William	....	Fr	1	1	0
Sumner, John	....	Rt	0	1	1
Thompson, Henry, esq. *Grantham		Fr			
Younge, Rev. John Par- kinson	....	Fr	1	1	0

No. 2.—POLLING DISTRICT ASSIGNED TO BOURN.

Aslackby and Millthorpe.

Name of Elector.	Residence.	Qual.	T.	W.	P.
Alderson, Rev. Edmund	Aslackby	Fr	0	0	1
Blankney, Musson Ben- jamin	Ditto	Rt	1	0	1
Brown, Rev. Edward	Lyndon, Rutland,	Fr	1	1	0
Brown, John	Aslackby	Fr			
Casswell, Thomas	Ditto	Rt	1	1	0
Dale, Anthony	Ditto	Rt	0	1	1
Eastland, John	Walpole, St. Andrew's Norfolk	Fr			
Gray, Edward	Graby	Rt	0	0	1
Hunt, John	Aslackby-decoy	Rt	1	1	0
Hatton, William	Hambleton	Fr			
Healey, Charles	Uppingham,	Fr	0	0	1
Johnson, Thomas	Millthorpe	Rt	1	1	0
Moore, Rev. William, D.D.	Spalding	Fr			
Palmer, William	Pointon	Fr	0	1	1
Richards, William	Aslackby-field	Fr	0	1	1
Smith, Benjamin, esq. *Horbling		Fr			
Steel, Rev. John	Totteridge	Fr			
Sharpe, Thomas	Pointon	Rt			
Sanderson, William	Aslackby	Rt	0	0	1
Wilkinson, Joseph	Ditto	Rt	1	0	1
Wilkinson, William	Ditto	Rt	1	1	0
Wells, Joseph	Ditto	Fr	1	1	0
Willson, William	Rippingale	Fr	0	0	1

Barholm.

Name of Elector.	Residence, if out of the Parish.	Qual.	T.	W.	P.
Arden, Avery	Hertford	Fr	1	1	0
Banks, George William	....	Rt	1	1	0
Cliff, Robert	....	Rt	1	1	0
Cave, Thomas	Longtoft-fen	Rt	1	1	0
Charity, John	....	Rt	1	1	0
Greenwood, Thomas	....	Rt	1	1	0
Hurn, Daniel	....	Rt	1	1	0
Nidd, George	Barnack	Rt			
Parkinson, Richard	....	Fr	1	1	0
Parkinson, Richard, jun.	....	Co	1	1	0
Turner, Rev. William	....	Fr	1	1	0
Warn, Abraham	....	Rt	1	1	0

Baston.

Name of Elector.	Residence, if out of the Parish.	Qual.	T.	W.	P.
Andrew, Edmund	Carlby	Co			
Bland, Thomas	....	Fr			
Bland, Richard Gray	Baston-lodge	Rt	1	1	0
Camm, John	Wilsthorpe	Co	1	1	0
Carpenter, Robert	....	Fr	1	1	0
Cave, William	....	Rt	1	1	0
Cole, John	....	Co			
Cole, William	....	Fr	1	1	0
Comfort, William Henshaw	15, Hillmarton Villas, Camden-road, Holloway, London	Fr	1	1	0
Dring, Francis	Baston-fen	Co	1	0	1
Frisby, William	....	Co	1	0	1
Gray, Thomas	....	Co	1	1	0
Gibson, William	....	Fr	1	1	0
Halford, William	Greatford	Co	0	1	1
Halford, John	Greatford	Co	0	1	1
Hill, Joseph	....	Fr	1	1	0
Hudson, George	....	Rt	1	0	1
Hill, John Peter	....	Fr	1	0	1
Johnson, Frederick William	....	Fr	1	1	0
Lenton, John	....	Co	1	1	0
Marriott, Richard	....	Rt	1	1	0
Palmer, John	Great Ponton	Co	1	0	1
Parkinson, William	Braceborough	Co	1	0	1
Peasgood, Aquila	....	Co	1	0	1
Phipp, Edward	Grantham	Co	1	1	0
Philpot, Richard Seaton	Oakham	Fr	0	0	1

Baston—continued.

Name of Elector.	Residence, if out of the Parish.	Qual.	T.	W.	P.
Pilkinton, George	....	Rt	1	0	0
Roberts, William	....	Co	1	0	0
Rosbe, John James	....	Rt	1	0	1
Smith, Middleton	....	Rt			
Skeath, William	....	Rt	1	1	0
Stephens, Robert	....	Fr	1	1	0
Skrimshire, Edward Augustus	Castor, Northamptonshire	Fr			
Warn, William	....	Co	1	0	1
Watson, John	....	Fr	1	0	1

Birthorpe.

Name of Elector.	Residence, if out of the Parish.	Qual.	T.	W.	P.
Armstrong, Robert	....	Fr	1	1	0
Grice, Peniston	....	Fr	1	1	0

Billingborough.

Name of Elector.	Residence, if out of the Parish.	Qual.	T.	W.	P.
Abel, Joseph	....	Rt	1	1	0
Andrew, William	....	Fr	0	1	1
Bothamley, Thomas	....	Fr			
Bray, Isaac	....	Fr	0	1	1
Banks, John	Scredington	Rt			
Barrand, William	....	Fr	1	0	1
Blasson, Thomas	....	Fr	0	0	1
Codling, James	....	Fr	1	0	1
Crosby, John	....	Fr	0	0	1
Dean, Seth Ellis	Horbling	Fr			
Everingham, Thomas	....	Fr	1	1	0
Goodacre, James	....	Rt	1	1	0
Goodacre, Robert	....	Fr	0	0	1
Gould, James, jun.	Birthorpe	Rt			
Henson, William	Allington	Fr	1	1	0
Kynaston, John *Vicar*	....	Fr	0	1	1
Leak, John Baxter	....	Fr			
Linney, Joseph	....	Rt	1	1	0
Nelson, Robert	....	Fr	1	1	0
Pikett, Thomas	....	Fr	1	0	1
Pickworth, James	....	Fr			
Pikett, William	....	Fr	1	0	0
Penn, John	....	Fr	1	0	1
Rugely, John	....	Fr	1	0	1
Stubley, William	....	Fr	1	1	0
Sewards, George	....	Rt	0	1	1

Billingborough—continued.

Name of Elector.	Residence, if out of the Parish.	Qual.	T.	W.	P.
Stevenson, Thomas	. . . .	Rt	1	0	1
Smith, Joseph	. . . .	Fr	1	0	1
Sharp, John	. . . .	Fr	0	0	1
Taylor, John	Westgate, Grantham	Fr			
Westmoreland, William	. . . .	Fr	1	0	1
Wright, William	Stamford	Tr	0	0	1

Bourn, with Dyke, Cawthorpe, and Tongue-End.

Name of Elector.	Residence, if out of the Parish.	Qual.	T.	W.	P.
Andrews, Stephen Wilson	Bourn	Co	1	1	0
Aitkin, Andrew	Deeping-fen	Rt	0	0	1
Aitkin, Thomas	Ditto	Rt	0	0	1
Allen, William	Stainby	Fr			
Ash, William	Dyke	Fr	1	0	1
Arden, John	Ditto	Rt			
Andrew, Joseph	Bourn-fen	Rt	1	0	1
Arnold, William	Bourn	Co	1	0	1
Banks, William	Falkingham	Fr	1	1	0
Beetham, Edward	Lincoln	Fr			
Beedzler, Dixon	Bourn	Co	0	0	1
Bettinson, Richard	Cawthorpe	Rt	0	0	1
Bettinson, George	Bourn	Fr	1	0	0
Bott, Henry	Ditto	Fr	0	1	1
Bott, John	Ditto	Fr	0	0	1
Brudenell, Joseph	Bourn South-fen	Fr	0	0	1
Benstead, Simon	Bourn	Fr	1	1	0
Bell, William David	Ditto	Co	1	0	1
Bray, William	Ditto	Co	0	0	1
Bellingham, Francis	Ditto	Fr	1	1	0
Bellingham, Francis James	Ditto	Rt	1	1	0
Brand, Charles	Ditto	Fr	1	0	1
Banton, Edward	Ditto	Rt	1	0	1
Bray, John	Ditto	Fr	0	0	1
Bray, John, jun.	Ditto	Fr	0	0	1
Cealey, William	Ditto	Fr	1	1	0
Darby, Robert	Morton	Fr	0	1	1
Dawson, John	Bourn	Rt	1	1	0
Daniell, William	Downham, Norfolk	Co	0	0	1
Dewey, John	Bourn	Rt	0	1	1
Dewey, William	Ditto	Co	1	0	1
Dodsworth, Rev. Joseph	Ditto	Fr	1	1	0
Dove, Henry Draper	Cawthorpe	Rt	1	1	0

Bourn, &c.—continued.

Name of Elector.	Residence, if out of the Parish.	Qual.	T.	W.	P.
Dove, Rev. Thomas Dove	Stamford and Cambridge	Co			
Elfleet, William	Bourn	Co	0	1	1
Eldret, Edward	Ditto	Rt	1	1	0
Farrer, James	Ditto	Fr	0	0	1
Ferraby, Benjamin	Ditto	Rt			
Ferraby, William	Ditto	Rt	1	1	0
Farrer, John	Ditto	Fr	1	1	0
Fish, Joseph	Downham Market	Fr	1	1	0
Fisher, Dale	near Bourn	Ex Pa			
Ford, Thomas	Bourn	Fr	1	0	1
Foster, John	Dyke	Rt	0	1	1
French, William *Sd*	Stamford	Co			
Gentle, Joseph	Bourn	Rt			
Gibson, John	Oakham	Co			
Goodyear, James	Cawthorpe	Rt	0	1	1
Gray, William	Dyke	Fr			
Gresswell, Barton	Bourn	Fr	0	0	1
Grummitt, Joseph	Bourn North-fen	Co	1	1	0
Gilby, John	Bourn	Fr	1	1	0
Grummitt, John	Elsthorpe	Rt			
Heathcote, Sir Gilbert John, Bart.	Normanton-park	Fr	*Peer*		
Harrison, John	Bourn	Co	1	1	0
Hack, Matthew	Pickworth	Fr	1	1	0
Hardwicke, John Walker	Dyke	Rt	0	1	1
Halford, Charles	March-fen	Co			
Hopkinson, William, esq.	Stamford *Sd*	Fr	1	1	0
Hunt, Henry	Bourn	Co	0	0	1
Ingle, John	Colsterworth	Fr	0	0	1
Lenton, George	Burton Coggles	Fr			
Lincoln, Timothy	Stamford	Fr	1	1	0
Lloyd, Edwin	Edenham	Fr	0	0	1
Longland, John	Bourn	Co	0	0	1
Mawby, Robert	Ditto	Fr	0	1	1
Mawby, Thomas Turnell	Ditto	Rt	1	1	0
Mills, Rev. Thomas	Peterborough	Co	*dead*		
Mullett, William	Bourn	Co	0	0	1
Maile, Matthew Edis	Falkingham	Fr	1	1	0
Mills, Robert Mason	Bourn	Rt	0	1	1
Martin, Robert	Ditto	Co	0	0	1
Mansfield, John	Ditto	Fr	0	0	1

Bourn, &c.—continued.

Name of Elector.	Residence, if out of the Parish.	Qual.	T.	W.	P.
Munton, Robert N.	Bourn	Fr	1	1	0
Munton, George Octavius	Ditto	Co			
Nicholls, George John	Ditto	Co	1	1	0
Osborn, Robert	Glaston, Rutland	Fr	0	0	1
Osborn, Thomas	Bourn	Rt	1	1	0
Osborn, Henry	Ditto	Co	1	1	0
Peacock, Wilkinson, esq.	Greatford Hall	Fr	1	1	0
Pochin, William Ann, esq.	Barkby Hall, near Leicester	Fr			
Palmer, William	Bourn	Rt	1	1	0
Presgrave, Thomas	Ditto	Co	0	0	1
Presgrave, Charles	Wing	Fr	1	1	0
Phillips, Charles	Bourn	Rt	1	1	0
Porter, George	Great Casterton	Fr	1	1	0
Presgrave, John	Bourn	Co	0	0	1
Phillips, Joseph	Bourn-fen	Rt	1	0	1
Pilkington, Thomas	Bourn	Fr			
Pridmore, William	Morcott	Fr			
Porter, Daniel	Aslackby	Fr	1	1	0
Redmile, Campain	Dyke	Rt	0	1	1
Redmile, William	Ditto	Co			
Richardson, William	Stamford	Fr			
Roberts, Charles	Bourn	Co	0	0	1
Roberts, Robert	Holbeach	Fr	0	0	1
Roberts, John Bellars	Bourn	Rt	0	0	1
Shilcock, James	Ditto	Fr	1	1	0
Smith, Francis	Ditto	Co	1	0	1
Sherwin, John	Ditto	Co	0	0	1
Storey, Joseph	Ditto	Co	0	1	1
Shippey, Thomas	Ditto	Rt	1	1	0
Spreckley, Charles	Ditto	Co	0	0	1
Smith, William Emlyn	Redmile	Fr			
Swift, William, jun.	Morton	Fr	0	0	1
Swift, George	Bourn	Fr	1	1	0
Shillaker, John	Bourn-fen	Rt	1	0	1
Todd, John Thomas	Bourn	Fr	1	1	0
Thorp, John	Ditto	Co	0	0	1
Tye, Thomas	Ditto	Fr	0	0	1
Tyler, Edward	Exton	Fr	0	0	1
Ward, William Wallis	Bourn	Co	0	0	1
Wherry, Edward	Ditto	Fr	0	0	1
Worsdall, Francis	Ditto	Co	0	1	1

Bourn, &c.—continued.

Name of Elector.	Residence, if out of the Parish.	Qual.	T.	W.	P.
Wherry, William	Bourn	Co	0	0	1
Woolley, John	Ditto	Co	0	0	1
Wyles, George	Ditto	Co	0	0	1
Wyles, Francis	Ditto	Co	1	0	0
Wyles, William	Ditto	Fr	1	0	0
Welldon, Thomas	Ditto	Fr	1	0	1

Braceborough and Shillingthorpe.

Name of Elector.	Residence, if out of the Parish.	Qual.	T.	W.	P.
Berridge, John	Braceborough	Rt	1	1	0
Jacklin, John	Ditto	Rt	1	1	0
Mountain, Thomas	Ditto	Rt	1	1	0
Parkinson, William	Ditto	Rt	1	0	1
Quincey, James	Ditto	Fr	1	0	1
Rogers, Rev. George	Ditto	Fr	1	0	1
Smith, William	Ditto	Rt	1	1	0
Willis, Francis, esq., M.D.	Shillingthorpe	Fr	1	1	0

Castle Bytham.

Name of Elector.	Residence, if out of the Parish.	Qual.	T.	W.	P.
Berridge, John	Careby	Fr			
Bowder, Robert	....	Fr	0	0	1
Beecraft, Richard	Woodford-bridge, Essex	Fr			
Branston, George Green	....	Fr	1	0	1
Beaupre, Joseph	16, Shepherd's Court Mayfair, London	Fr			
Burchnall, Francis	....	Fr	0	0	1
Coverley, John	....	Fr	0	0	1
Dawson, John	....	Rt	1	0	0
Duncombe, John	St. Martin's, Stamford	Fr	1	1	0
Harrison, Thomas	....	Fr	0	0	1
Harris, Francis	....	Fr	1	0	0
Heathcote, The Hon. Gilbert Henry	Normanton-park, Rutland	Fr	1	0	1
Harris, John	Little Bytham	Fr	1	1	0
Harris, John	....	Rt	1	1	0
Lank, Thomas	South Witham	Fr	1	0	0
Ormond, Henry	Laughton	Fr			
Piccaver, John	....	Rt	0	0	1
Pilkington, Matthew	Clipsham, Rutland	Fr	1	0	1
Phillips, Joseph	St. Martin's, Stamford	Fr			
Piccaver, John Northen	....	Rt	0	0	1
Richardson, Joseph Ferguson	....	Le	1	0	1

Castle Bytham—continued.

Name of Elector.	Residence, if out of the Parish.	Qual.	T.	W.	P.
Stanham, Hugh	....	Rt	0	0	1
Stanton, John	....	Fr	0	0	1
Sharpe, Richard	....	Fr	1	0	1
Steel, Thomas	....	Rt			
Sharpe, Thomas	....	Fr	1	0	0
Sharpe, Thomas	Little Bytham	Fr	0	0	1
Selley, Thomas	....	Rt	0	0	1
Thorpe, Henry	....	Fr			
Wade, William	....	Rt	0	0	1
Wing, William	....	Fr	1	0	0
Wing, John	....	Fr	1	0	0
Webster, Thomas	....	Rt	1	0	1

Little Bytham.

Name of Elector.	Residence, if out of the Parish.	Qual.	T.	W.	P.
Agar, Thomas	....	Fr	1	0	1
Harris, John	....	Rt			
Harris, Francis	Castle Bytham	Rt	1	1	0
Herring, Matthew	Holywell	Fr	1	1	0
Nixon, John	....	Fr	1	0	0
Ormond, John	....	Rt	1	0	0
Patchett, William	....	Fr	1	0	1
Pilkington, William	....	Rt	1	0	0
Phillips, Joseph	St. Martin's, Stamford	Fr			
Sivers, Thomas	Deeping-gate, North-amptonshire	Fr	0	0	1
Wheelwright, Reverend Charles Apethorpe	Tansor	Fr			

Careby.

Name of Elector.	Residence, if out of the Parish.	Qual.	T.	W.	P.
Berridge, Benjamin	....	Rt	1	0	1
Berridge, John	....	Rt	1	1	0
Clarke, William Christian	....	Rt	1	0	0
Chapman, George	....	Rt	1	1	0
Reynardson, Rev John Birch	....	Fr	1	1	0

Carlby.

Name of Elector.	Residence, if out of the Parish.	Qual.	T.	W.	P.
Andrew, Edmund	....	Rt	1	1	0
Barratt, William	....	Rt	1	1	0
Briggs, John	....	Rt	1	1	0
Cross, Henry	....	Rt	1	1	0
Hurt, Rev. Robert	....	Fr	1	1	0

     PARTS OF KESTEVEN.

Carlby—continued.

Name of Elector.	Residence, if out of the Parish.	Qual.	T.	W.	P.
Reynardson, Charles Birch, esq.	Holywell	Fr			
Reynardson, Henry Birch, esq.	Holywell	Fr	1	1	0
Reynardson, Rev. John Birch	Careby	Fr			
Reynardson, Rev. George Eastland Birch	Rectory, Faversham, Kent	Fr	1	1	0
Reynardson, Edward Birch, esq.	Holywell	Fr	1	1	0
Stevenson, Jonathan	....	Rt	1	1	0
Templeman, James	....	Rt	1	1	0
Templeman, John	....	Rt	1	1	0
Woods, Thomas	....	Rt	1	1	0
Woods, Thomas, jun.	....	Rt	1	1	0

Counthorpe.

Name of Elector.	Residence, if out of the Parish.	Qual.	T.	W.	P.
Nidd, Clement	....	Rt	1	1	0
Nidd, Clement William	....	Rt	1	1	0
Sharp, Thomas	....	Rt	1	1	0
Steel, Thomas, jun	....	Rt	1	1	0

Corby.

Name of Elector.	Residence, if out of the Parish.	Qual.	T.	W.	P.
Barefield, Henry	....	Fr	1	0	0
Bellamy, Richard	Ponton	Rt			
Bellamy, George Searson	....	Fr	1	0	1
Bradford, Frederic Eminson	Corby Birkholme	Rt	1	0	0
Brown, Thomas	....	Rt	1	1	0
Branston, Richard	Spittlegate	Fr			
Branston, John Searson	....	Rt	1	0	1
Brewster, William	....	Le			
Clark, William	31, Coleshill-street, Birmingham	Fr			
Collingwood, Joseph	....	Rt	1	0	1
Collingwood, Edward	....	Le			
Collingwood, William	....	Rt	1	1	0
Ellis, Thomas	....	Le	1	0	1
Farebrother, Rev. Charles	Corby Vicarage	Fr	1	0	1
Healy, George	Stoke Doyle	Fr			
Hare, Samuel	....	Rt	1	0	0
Heritage, William	....	Fr			

Corby—continued.

Name of Elector.	Residence, if out of the Parish.	Qual.	T.	W.	P.
Lank, John	....	Le	1	0	0
Musson, John	....	Fr	1	0	0
Nichols, John	....	Rt	1	1	0
Osborn, John	....	Fr	1	0	1
Rawlinson, Thomas Litchford	....	Fr	1	0	0
Rawlinson, James	....	Fr	1	0	1
Robinson, Thomas	Corby Heath	Rt	1	0	1
Sandall, William	Rippingale	Fr	0	0	1
Stokes, Matthew	....	Rt	1	0	1
Wilkinson, Richard Septimus, Esq.	121, Pall Mall, London	Fr	1	0	1

Creeton.

Name of Elector.	Residence, if out of the Parish.	Qual.	T.	W.	P.
Botherway, William	....	Rt	1	1	0
Blake, Thomas	Creeton Lodge	Rt	1	1	0
Layng, Rev. William	....	Fr	0	0	1
Millington, Bryan	....	Rt	1	0	1
Nidd, Clement William	....	Rt	1	1	0

West Deeping.

Name of Elector.	Residence, if out of the Parish.	Qual.	T.	W.	P.
Addy, Myhill	....	Fr			
Atter, John	Toft	Fr	1	0	1
Green, John	....	Fr	1	0	1
Greaves, James	Leicester	Rt	0	0	1
Gunning, Rev. George	Frenchay, near Bristol	Fr			
Hetley, Henry	Orton Longville	Fr	0	0	1
Haynes, James Haynes	13, South-square, Gray's Inn, London	Fr	1	1	0
Molecey, John Molecey Twigge	....	Rt			
Morley, Christopher	....	Rt	1	1	0
Morley, Joseph	....	Rt	1	1	0
Phillips, Joseph, jun.	St. Martin's, Stamford Baron	Co	1	1	0
Pickering, John	....	Fr	1	1	0
Smith, Seth	....	Fr	1	1	0
Sharpe, John Crutchfield	Deeping-gate	Rt			

Market Deeping.

Name of Elector.	Residence, if out of the Parish.	Qual.	T.	W.	P.
Allen, William	....	Co	0	0	1
Andrew, John	Deeping St. James	Co	1	0	0

Market Deeping—continued.

Name of Elector.	Residence, if out of the Parish.	Qual.	T.	W.	
Addy, John	....	Co	1	0	1
Barber, John	....	Co	1	1	0
Bland, William	Baston	Rt			
Butler, Charles	Baston	Rt	1	0	1
Barber, John Thomas	....	Co	0	0	1
Banks, George William	Barholm	Co			
Barber, Edward	Stamford	Fr			
Bellairs, John	....	Co	1	0	0 ·
Bordman, William	....	Co	0	0	1
Bellairs, Sir William	Mulbarton, Norfolk	Fr			
Barnes, Edward	....	Fr	1	1	0
Buzzard, James	....	Fr	1	1	0
Chesterfield, Thomas	....	Co	1	0	1
Creet, John	....	Fr			
Collins, John	....	Co	1	0	1
Charity, John	Barholm	Co			
Dods, John Thomas	Gosberton	Co			
Fox, John	....	Co	1	0	1
Franks, Daniel	....	Fr	1	1	0
Franks, George	....	Co	1	0	1
Gray, Henry	....	Co	1	0	1
Goodale, John	....	Fr	1	1	0
Harrison, Thomas	Clipsham	Fr	0	0	1
Hildyard, Rev. William	rectory in this parish	Fr	1	1	0
Holland, James	....	Fr	0	0	1
Hare, Daniel	....	Co	1	1	0
Holland, William	....	Fr	1	1	0
Ingman, George	....	Co	1	0	1
Kelly, James	....	Rt	1	0	0
Limmex, Joseph	....	Rt	1	0	1
Linnell, George	....	Co	1	1	0
Lenton, John	....	Co	1	0	1
Markham, William, sen.	....	Fr	1	0	1
Markwell, John	....	Co			
Marston, John Taylor	....	Fr	0	0	1
Mawby, Joseph Beecraft	....	Co	1	1	0
Mossop, Rev. Charles	Helpstone	Co	0	0	1
Molecey, John Molecey Twigge	West Deeping	Fr	1	1	0
Moore, Maurice Peter, esq.	Sleaford	Fr			
Mann, Frederick	Stowgate	Rt			

Market Deeping—continued.

Name of Elector.	Residence, if out of the Parish.	Qual.	T.	W.	P.
Miller, John Kitchen	... .	Co	0	0	1
Perkins, John	....	Co	1	1	0
Pollard, Joseph	St. Martin's Stamford	Fr	1	1	0
Phillips, Joseph, jun	Stamford	Fr			
Page, William	....	Fr	1	1	0
Plowright, James	....	Co	1	1	0
Peck, William	....	Co			
Rockliffe, William	Deeping St. James	Co	1	0	1
Stimson, John	....	Co	1	0	1
Shillaker, Thomas	....	Co			
Shillaker, Basil Thomas	....	Co	1	1	0
Sharpe, Rev. Thomas Henry	Codicote, Herts	Co	0	0	1
Sharpe, Samuel Johnson	....	Co	1	1	0
Sharpe, Samuel Bates	....	Co	1	1	0
Sharpe, John Crutchfield	Deeping-gate Meadow	Fr	1	1	0
Stapleton, Harvey	....	Fr	1	1	0
Swann, Thomas	....	Co	1	0	1
Shillaker, William	....	Co	1	1	0
Sneath, John Powdrell	....	Co	1	0	1
Stubbs, John	Northborough	Co	1	1	0
Tomlin, William	Deeping St. James	Co	1	0	0
Thorpe, John	....	Fr	1	1	0
Todd, Henry	Peterborough	Co	0	0	1
Todd, John,	....	Fr	1	0	1
Thistleton, Thomas	....	Co	1	0	1
True, Thomas	....	Co	0	0	1
Wherry, John	....	Co			
Wade, John	....	Co	1	0	1
Wyles, John Alfred	....	Co	1	0	0

Deeping St. James, and that part of Deeping-Fen, Extra-parochial, which is within the parts of Kesteven.

Name of Elector.	Residence, if out of the Parish.	Qual.	T.	W.	P.
Allen, William	....	Rt	1	0	0
Allam, George	....	Fr	1	0	0
Ashby, John	....	Co			
Arch, James	....	Co	1	1	0
Andrew, George	....	Co	1	0	1
Ball, Josiah	South Luffenham	Co	0	0	1
Barr, Richard	....	Fr	1	1	0
Baker, James	....	Fr	1	1	0

Deeping St. James.—continued.

Name of Elector.	Residence, if out of the Parish.	Qual.	T.	W.	P.
Barker, John Hyde	....	Rt	0	0	1
Baker, Benjamin	....	Fr	1	0	1
Baker, John	Deeping-gate	Fr	1	1	0
Baker, John	....	Fr	1	1	0
Barsby, Allin	....	Co			
Beavus, William	....	Fr	1	1	0
Bell, Thomas	Deeping-gate	Co	1	0	0
Bellairs, Rev. Henry	Bedworth, Warwick-shire	Fr			
Bilton, Robert	....	Fr	1	1	0
Brown, George	....	Fr	1	1	0
Bolland, Thomas	....	Co			
Burton, William	Park-st., King's-cliff	Fr			
Barron, James	Crowland-common	Fr			
Bennett, George	....	Fr	1	0	0
Buckle, Samuel Charles Watson, *Esq.*	Peterborough	Fr			
Buck, Thomas	....	Fr	1	1	0
Bullimore, Richard	Deeping-fen	Rt	1	1	0
Bains, John	....	Co	1	1	0
Baker, George	St. Mary's Stamford	Co	0	0	1
Butler, Bellars	Caldecott, Rutland	Co			
Carrington, Thomas	....	Co	1	1	0
Carrington, Jonathan	....	Co			
Cansdale, Thomas Merriman	....	Fr			
Chesterfield, Mann	....	Co	1	1	0
Chesterfield, George	....	Rt	1	1	0
Chesterfield, William	....	Co	1	1	0
Chesterfield, John	....	Fr	1	0	1
Chesterfield, Thomas	Northborough	Co	1	0	1
Chesterfield, Thomas	....	Co	1	1	0
Cook, William	....	Fr	1	1	0
Creet, William	....	Fr	1	1	0
Cooper, Rev. John Mawbey	Peckleton	Fr			
Desborough, William	....	Co	1	1	0
Eldret, John	Deeping-fen	Rt	1	0	1
Ellis, William	....	Rt	1	1	0
Fairchild, Francis	Deeping-fen	Fr	0	0	1
Frisby, George	Crowland	Fr			
Frisby, Matthew	Deeping-fen	Fr			
Frisby, John	....	Fr	1	0	1

Deeping St. James—continued.

Name of Elector.	Residence, if out of the Parish.	Qual.	T.	W.	P.
Frisby, James	....	Rt	1	1	0
Fowler, Francis	....	Rt	1	1	0
Farrow, Thomas	....	Co			
Garford, Thomas	....	Co	1	1	0
George, Rev. John	*Vicar.*	Fr	1	1	0
Godwin, Benjamin	....	Fr	1	1	0
Goodyer, Richard	Tinwell, Rutland	Co	1	1	0
Gregory, Thomas	Hatfield, Herts	Fr	1	1	0
Green, James	....	Co	1	1	0
Grossmith, William	Bainton .	Co	1	1	0
George, Thomas	Bythorne, Hunts	Fr	1	1	0
Hare, John	Hacconby	Co	0	0	1
Hare, James	....	Co	1	0	0
Hare, Charles	Deeping-fen	Rt	1	1	0
Huffer, John	Deeping-gate	Co	1	0	1
Hainsworth, William	Market Deeping	Co	0	0	1
Hopkins, Samuel .	....	Fr	1	1	0
Holland, William	Market Deeping	Rt			
Haynes, William	....	Rt	1	0	1
Huston, Samuel	....	Fr	1	0	1
Ireland, John	....	Fr	1	1	0
Johnson, John	....	Co	1	1	0
Jackson, William	....	Fr	1	0	1
Jenkinson, Robert	Northborough	Co	1	1	0
Jones, Thomas	Stamford	Co			
Johnson, Tealby	....	Co	1	1	0
Kenney, Mark	....	Fr	1	1	0
Lake, Joseph	....	Fr	1	1	0
Lincoln, William	....	Rt	1	1	0
Lake, James	Deeping-fen	Co	1	1	0
Lake, Jonathan	....	Rt	1	1	0
Lake, Baker	Deeping-gate	Co	1	0	1
Lake, Edward	....	Co	1	1	0
Lake, Jonathan	....	Co	1	0	0
Lake, William	....	Co	1	1	0
Lambert, George	....	Co	1	0	1
Leaton, Joseph	Deeping-bank	Rt			
Leaton, Samuel	Deeping-fen	Co			
Lincoln, Richard	....	Fr	1	0	1
Morton, John	....	Fr	1	1	0
Measures, Edward	....	Co	1	1	0
Morton, William	....	Fr	1	1	0

Deeping St. James, &c.—continued.

Name of Elector.	Residence, if out of the Parish.	Qual.	T.	W.	P.
Merilion, Mark	....	Fr	1	0	1
Nurse, Thomas	....	Co	1	1	0
Nutt, James	Market Deeping	Co	1	1	0
Parrott, Samuel	....	Co			
Pawlett, Edmund	....	Rt	1	1	0
Percival, William	....	Tr	1	0	0
Parr, John	St. Paul's-street, Stamford	Co	1	1	0
Percival, John	....	Co	1	0	1
Pollard, Joseph	St. Martin's Stamford	Fr			
Peak, William	....	Fr			
Plowright, Michael	Market Deeping	Co	1	1	0
Price, Thomas	Helpstone	Fr	1	1	0
Rastall, James	....	Co	1	1	0
Riddington, William	....	Rt	1	1	0
Roberts, Rev. Robert	Aldwinckle, Northamptonshire	Fr	1	1	0
Rippon, Henry	....	Fr	1	0	1
Russell, John	Market Deeping	Fr	1	0	1
Savage, William, jun.	....	Fr	1	0	1
Searson, Robert	....	Rt	1	1	0
Sanderson, Thomas	....	Fr	1	0	0
Shales, Thomas	....	Fr	1	0	1
Smith, Henry	....	Fr	1	1	0
Sharpe, Samuel Johnson	Market Deeping	Co			
Smith, Benjamin	....	Rt	1	1	0
Sindall, Thomas William	Weston Hills	Co			
Swift, Daniel	....	Rt	1	1	0
Smith, Robert	Wood Newton, Northamptonshire	Co			
Smith, George	....	Co	1	1	0
Swift, Thomas	....	Co	1	1	0
Sharpe, John Crutchfield	Deeping-gate	Co			
Smith, William Baker	....	Fr	1	0	1
Taylor, William	....	Co	1	0	0
Tomlin, Tobias, jun.	....	Co	1	1	0
Templeman, John	Deeping-gate	Fr			
Templeman, Thomas	Ditto	Fr	1	0	1
Torey, John	....	Fr	1	1	0
Tomlin, John	....	Co	1	1	0

Deeping St. James, &c.—continued.

Name of Elector.	Residence, if out of the Parish.	Qual.	T.	W.	P.
Walpole, William	Grove-street, South Town, near Great Yarmouth,Suffolk	Co			
Wenham, William	....	Fr	1	1	0
Wiles, James	....	Co	1	1	0
Withno, Samuel	....	Fr	1	1	0
Wright, Joseph	....	Rt			
Wright, William	....	Rt	1	1	0
Wensor, George	Deeping-fen	Rt	1	1	0
Wenham, Matthew	....	Co	1	1	0
Wright, John	....	Fr	1	1	0

Dowsby and Graby.

Name of Elector.	Residence, if out of the Parish.	Qual.	T.	W.	P.
Bunning, Robert	Graby	Rt	0	0	1
Claypole, John	Dowsby	Fr	1	1	0
Casswell, Henry	Ditto	Rt	0	0	1
Dean, Seth Ellis	Ditto	Rt	1	1	0
Foster, Rev. Kingsman	Ditto	Fr	1	1	0
Lucas, Richard	Edithweston	Fr	1	1	0
Lound, Thomas	Pinchbeck	Fr			
Scales, Edward	Dowsby	Rt			
Scales, Edward	Ditto	Fr	1	1	0
Scales, Joseph	Ditto	Rt	0	1	1

Dunsby.

Name of Elector.	Residence, if out of the Parish.	Qual.	T.	W.	P.
Keightley, Rev. George Wilson	....	Fr	1	1	0
Lawrance,William Munton	....	Rt			
Wadsley, John	....	Rt	1	0	1

Edenham, Grimsthorpe, Elsthorpe, and Scottlethorpe.

Name of Elector.	Residence, if out of the Parish.	Qual.	T.	W.	P.
Adcock, William Daniel	Edenham	Rt	1	1	0
Birch, Henry	Grimsthorpe	Rt	1	0	1
Burgess, John	Edenham	Rt	1	0	0
Brothwell, William Turnball	Ditto	Rt	1	0	1
Birch, Charles	Ditto	Rt	1	0	0
Carrington, Samuel	Ditto	Rt			
Carter, John	Leighton	Rt			
Coddington, William	Edenham	Rt	0	1	0
Clarke, Kirby	Elsthorpe	Rt	1	0	0
Gillson, Thomas	Grimsthorpe	Rt	1	0	0
Gillson, Joseph	Grimsthorpe	Rt	1	0	0
Grummitt, John	Elsthorpe	Rt	1	0	1

Edenham, Grimsthorpe, &c.—continued.

Name of Elector.	Residence, if out of the Parish.	Qual.	T.	W.	P.
Grummitt, William	Elsthorpe-grange	Rt	1	0	1
Hoyles, George	Edenham	Rt	1	0	1
Johnson, James	Grimsthorpe	Rt	1	0	1
Jones, William	Scottlethorpe	Rt	1	0	1
Matkin, William	Ditto	Rt	1	0	1
Ormond, William	Ditto	Rt	1	0	0
Robertson, Robert	Whitfield	Rt			
Scott, George Gordon	Edenham	Rt	1	0	1
Sharman, George	Ditto	Rt	1	0	1
Sharp, Job	Scottlethorpe	Rt	1	0	1
Shelton, Thomas	Edenham	Rt	1	0	1
Wilkin, James	Tinwald-downs	Rt			

Greatford.

Name of Elector.	Residence, if out of the Parish.	Qual.	T.	W.	P.
Burrows, John	. . . .	Fr	1	0	1
Bowman, Frederic	Duddington	Fr	1	1	0
Cavendish, the Hon. Charles Compton	Burlington-house, London	Fr			
Gilbert, George	. . . .	Fr	1	1	0
Parkinson, John	. . . .	Rt	1	0	1
Pratt, Frederick	. . . .	Rt			
Smith, Robert	. . . .	Rt	0	0	1
Thompson, Edward Lawrence	. . . .	Rt	1	0	1
Wilde, Rev. Albert Sidney	. . . .	Fr	1	1	0

Hacconby and Stainfield.

Name of Elector.	Residence, if out of the Parish.	Qual.	T.	W.	P.
Barnes, Joseph	Terry Booth	Rt			
Bonney, Rev. Thomas Kaye	Normanton	Fr			
Brown, William	Hacconby	Rt	0	0	1
Batty, Charles	Hacconby-fen	Rt	0	0	1
Chapman, Robert Wyer	Hacconby	Rt	0	0	1
Chapman, John	Ditto	Rt	0	0	1
Eldret, Edward, jun.	Hacconby-fen	Fr			
Eldret, Joseph	Hacconby	Rt	1	0	1
Grummitt, Edward	Stainfield	Rt	0	0	1
Grummitt, John	Hacconby	Rt	0	0	1
Grummitt, Joseph	Stainfield	Rt	0	1	1
Holmes, James	Ditto	Rt	1	1	0
Lawrance, Thomas	Dunsby	Fr			
Lawrance, Thomas, jun.	Hacconby	Rt			
Teesdale, Isaac	Ditto	Rt	1	0	1

Holywell and Aunby.

Name of Elector.	Residence, if out of the Parish.	Qual.	T.	W.	P.
Chambers, Charles	Aunby	Rt	1	1	0
Dainty, John	Holywell	Rt	1	1	0
Howett, Robert	Ditto	Rt	1	1	0
Mowbray, William	Aunby	Rt	1	1	0
Reynardson, Charles Thomas Samuel Birch, esq.	Holywell	Fr			
Robinson, William	Ditto	Rt	1	1	0
Sharpe, John	Ditto	Rt	1	1	0

Irnham, Bulby, and Hawthorpe.

Name of Elector.	Residence, if out of the Parish.	Qual.	T.	W.	P.
Chapman, Joseph	Southwood Lodge	Rt	1	1	0
Healey, Samuel	Irnham	Rt			
Harwood, Edward	Bulby	Rt	1	1	0
Hodgkin, Hardwicke	Hawthorpe	Rt	1	0	1
Smyth, Rev. William Watson	Bulby	Fr			
Searson, Robert	Irnham	Rt	1	1	0
Searson, John	Bulby	Rt	1	1	0
Wright, Thomas	Ditto	Rt	0	1	1
Wright, Stephen	Irnham	Rt	1	1	0
Wright, John Gilbert	Ditto	Rt	1	1	0
Woodhouse, William Hervey, esq.	Irnham Park	Fr			

Kirkby Underwood.

Name of Elector.	Residence, if out of the Parish.	Qual.	T.	W.	P.
Duckett, William	....	Rt	0	0	1
Emly, Rev. Frederick Septimus	....	Fr	1	1	0
Gill, Cuthbert	....	Rt	0	0	1
Hodgkin, Henry	....	Rt	0	0	1

Laughton.

Name of Elector.	Residence, if out of the Parish.	Qual.	T.	W.	P.
Ball, William	Rydall, Westmoreland, & the Grove, Tottenham, Middlesex	Fr			
Blundy, John	....	Rt			
Casswell, John Henry	....	Rt	1	1	0
Ormond, Henry	....	Rt	1	1	0

Langtoft.

Name of Elector.	Residence, if out of the Parish.	Qual.	T.	W.	P.
Belton, William	....	Co	1	0	1

Langtoft—continued.

Name of Elector.	Residence, if out of the Parish.	Qual.	T.	W.	P.
Bickerdike, William	....	Co	0	0	1
Cooke, Richard Thomas	Park-street, West Luton	Fr			
Cox, Daniel Cole	Maxey	Co	0	0	1
Cooke, John	Alconbury Hill	Fr			
Costall, John	Market Overton	Fr	1	1	0
Collins, William	....	Fr	1	0	1
Dickins, John	....	Rt	1	0	1
Foster, Charles	....	Co	0	0	1
Foster, Charles Noah	3, New Wharf, White-friars, London	Co	0	0	1
Franklin, George	....	Co	1	1	0
Gee, John, sen.	....	Fr			
Gibbs, Thomas	....	Co	1	1	0
Gee, John, jun.	....	Rt	1	0	1
Gee, John, sen.	....	Fr			
Gee, Edward	....	Co	1	0	1
Horden, William Rear	Stamford	Co	1	1	0
Haynes, James	West Deeping-fen	Fr	1	1	0
Holmes, William, sen.	....	Fr	1	0	1
Holmes, Joseph	....	Fr	0	0	1
Hudson, John	....	Co	1	0	1
Johnson, Thomas	....	Rt	1	0	1
Johnson, Edward	....	Co	1	0	1
Johnson, Edward, jun.	Maxey	Rt	1	0	1
Johnson, Edis	....	Rt	1	1	0
Jibb, Jesse	....	Co	1	0	1
Mee, John	....	Co	1	0	1
Mee, James	....	Co	1	0	1
Nidd, George	....	Rt	1	1	0
Nidd, George	Barnack	Co	1	1	0
Peasgood, George	....	Rt	0	0	1
Peasgood, Henry Aquila	....	Fr	0	1	1
Porter, Robert	....	Rt	0	0	1
Rowell, Richard	....	Rt	0	0	1
Rubbins, Edward	Baston	Fr	1	1	0
Rowell, Richard, jun.	....	Rt			
Shillaker, George	....	Co	1	0	1
Turnbull, Christopher	Wittering	Fr	1	1	0
Tomblin, Rev. Charles	....	Fr	1	1	0
Wright, William	Ryhall	Fr	1	1	0
Ward, William	....	Fr	1	0	1

Manthorpe.

Name of Elector.	Residence, if out of the Parish.	Qual.	T.	W.	P.
Ansell, Henry Michael	....	Fr	1	0	1
Ansell, John Newcomb	Stretton, Rutland	Fr	1	0	1
Howett, William	....	Fr	0	0	1
Nixon, Thomas	Bowthorpe-park	Rt	1	0	1
Smeaton, David	....	Fr	1	0	1
Taylor, William	....	Rt	1	1	0
Woolley, William	....	Fr	1	0	0

Morton and Hanthorpe.

Name of Elector.	Residence, if out of the Parish.	Qual.	T.	W.	P.
Andrew, James	Morton	Fr	0	1	1
Arden, John Lawrence	Dyke	Fr	1	1	0
Baker, Joseph Pare	Morton	Fr	1	1	0
Bartholomew, Henry	Reading, Berks	Fr			
Bugg, William	Morton	Fr	0	1	1
Bullock, John George	Ditto	Rt	1	1	0
Butler, William	Ditto	Fr	1	1	0
Batterham, Thomas Christian	Ditto	Rt	0	0	1
Caparn, John	Enderby, Leicester	Fr			
Clarke, Edward	Morton	Fr	1	0	1
Chambers, Thomas	Ditto	Co	0	1	1
Christian, William	Ditto	Rt	0	1	1
Christian, Thomas	Hanthorpe	Rt	0	1	1
Castle, Samuel	Grantham	Fr			
Dring, John	Hanthorpe	Fr	0	1	0
Dring, Thomas	Ditto	Fr	0	1	1
Eayrs, Samuel	Keele, Staffordshire	Fr			
Eayrs, William	Pickworth, Rutland	Fr	1	1	0
Ellingworth, John	Morton	Fr	0	0	1
Faulkner, Henry	Ditto	Rt	1	1	0
Freeman, Edward	Ditto	Rt	0	1	1
Freeman, John	Ditto	Rt	0	1	1
Freeman, William	Barkby, Leicestershire	Fr	0	1	0
Fairchild, Thomas	Morton	Co	1	0	1
Howitt, William	Hanthorpe	Fr	0	1	1
Holdsworth, Reverend Thomas Colbeck	Morton	Fr	1	1	0
Lister, John	Ditto	Fr	0	1	1
Lawrance, Thomas	Hacconby	Fr	1	0	1
Larkin, Rev. Edmund Roberts	Burton, by Lincoln	Fr	0	0	1
Mowson, Alfred	Morton	Fr			

Morton and Hanthorpe.—continued.

Name of Elector.	Residence, if out of the Parish.	Qual.	T.	W.	P.
Maykins, William	Dyke	Fr	1	0	1
Newton, Robert,	Morton	Co	0	0	1
Parker, William, esq.	Hanthorpe House	Fr	0	1	1
Parker, Captain William, jun.	Hanthorpe House	Fr			
Parker, Captain Charles John Bullivant	Hanthorpe House	Fr	0	1	1
Parker, Robert	Morton	Fr	1	0	1
Palmer, John	Ditto	Fr	0	1	1
Rodgers, Anthony	Ditto	Fr	1	0	1
Rodgers, Charles	Sleaford	Co	0	0	1
Rodgers, William	Morton	Rt	0	1	0
Rodgers, Charles	Ditto	Rt	0	1	1
Rodgers, John	Hanthorpe	Rt	0	1	1
Rodgers, George	Morton	Fr	0	0	1
Rollings, Thomas	Ditto	Fr	0	0	1
Sandall, John	Gosberton	Fr	0	1	1
Simpson, John	Upwell, Cambs	Fr	1	1	0
Smith, Edward	Morton	Fr	0	1	1
Sandall, Robert	Ditto	Fr	0	0	1
Summerfield, Thomas	Hanthorpe	Rt	0	1	1
Thurlby, John	Morton	Fr	1	0	1
Thompson, Edward	Tallington	Fr			
Tathwell, Captain George Baker	Head Quarters of her Majesty's 33rd Regiment	Fr			
Wingfield, Rev. Edward Oldfield	Market Overton	Fr			
Wingfield, George, esq.	Glatton	Fr	1	1	0
Wingfield, Thomas Henry, esq	Head Quarters of her Majesty's 32nd Regiment	Fr	1	1	0
Waters, John Wilson	Morton	Fr	0	0	1

Osgodby.

Cooper, William, sen.	. . . .	Rt	0	0	1
Cooper, William, jun.	. . . .	Rt			
Howitt, Thomas	. . . .	Rt	0	0	1

Pointon.

Ato, Thomas	Pointon-fen	Fr	1	1	0
Atkinson, Joseph	. . . .	Fr	0	1	1

Pointon—continued.

Name of Elector.	Residence, if out of the Parish.	Qual.	T.	W.	P.
Barnett, Richard Clay	....	Fr	0	0	1
Banks, Benjamin Brown-low	Horbling	Fr	1	1	0
Boyfield, Richard	Aslackby	Fr	1	1	0
Briggs, Francis	....	Fr			
Carter, Richard	Pointon-fen	Fr			
Carter, John	Dunsby	Fr	0	0	1
Casswell, Thomas	Dunsby-fen	Fr			
Dennis, William	....	Fr	1	1	0
Gray, Edward	Graby	Fr			
Hackett, William	....	Fr			
Handley, Benjamin, esq.	....	Fr	0	1	1
Hill, William	....	Rt	0	0	1
Hubbard, John	....	Fr	0	0	1
Marshall, William	Pointon-fen	Rt	1	1	0
Michelson, William	Pointon-fen	Fr	1	1	0
Mansfield, James	....	Rt	1	1	0
Passmore, John	....	Fr	1	1	0
Parr, Charles	....	Rt	1	0	1
Pattinson, William Gold-ing	Burgh-in-the-Marsh	Fr			
Raines, Henry	....	Fr	0	0	1
Sharpe, Thomas	....	Fr	0	1	1
Shillcock, John	....	Rt	1	1	0
Sindall, Robert	....	Fr	1	1	0

Rippingale.

Name of Elector.	Residence, if out of the Parish.	Qual.	T.	W.	P.
Atkinson, Thomas	....	Fr	0	0	1
Atkinson, Thomas	....	Rt	0	0	1
Atkinson, William	....	Rt	0	0	1
Bromley, Henry	....	Rt	0	0	1
Chapman, Henry	....	Rt	0	0	1
Cooper, Rev. William	....	Fr	1	0	1
Claypole, William	....	Rt	0	0	1.
Gale, William	....	Fr	1	0	1
Healey, Edward	....	Rt	0	0	1
Hill, William	....	Fr	1	0	1
Heathcote, William Henry, esq.	North Luffenham	Fr	1	0	1
Heathcote, Lionel Edward, esq.	Grove End-road, St. John's wood, London	Fr			

Rippingale.—continued.

Name of Elector.	Residence, if out of the Parish.	Qual.	T.	W.	P.
Hind, Robert	....	Rt	0	0	1
Jaques, Thomas	....	Rt	1	0	1
Pacey, Daniel	....	Rt	1	0	1
Pawlett, John Thomas	....	Fr	0	0	1
Quincey, Richard	....	Rt	0	0	1
Richards, John	....	Rt	0	0	1
Smith, Abel	....	Rt	0	0	1
Shield, Thomas	....	Fr	0	0	1
Sandall, Thomas	....	Fr	0	0	1
Wilson, Albert	....	Rt	1	0	1
Younger, Robert	....	Fr			

Sempringham.

Name of Elector.	Residence, if out of the Parish.	Qual.	T.	W.	P.
Gould, James	Birthorpe	Fr	1	1	0
Houghton, Trolley	....	Rt	0	0	1
Jackson, William	....	Rt	1	1	0
Mackinder, Draper	....	Rt	1	1	0
Pickworth, Francis	Surfleet	Rt			

Stow.

Name of Elector.	Residence, if out of the Parish.	Qual.	T.	W.	P.
Bullock, William	....	Rt	1	1	0

Swinstead.

Name of Elector.	Residence, if out of the Parish.	Qual.	T.	W.	P.
Atton, Mansfield	....	Fr	1	0	1
Branston, William	....	Rt	1	0	1
Burgess, William	....	Rt	1	0	1
Chapman, Rev. Edward Martin	Grimsthorpe Cottage	Fr	1	0	1
Jones, John	....	Rt	1	0	1
Lamb, William	....	Rt	1	0	1
March, William	....	Rt	1	0	1
Melsom, Richard	....	Rt	1	0	1
Perkins, Thomas	....	Rt	1	0	1
Rosling, Samuel	....	Rt	1	0	1
Sharman, Thomas	....	Rt	1	0	1
Ward, William	....	Rt	1	0	1
Ward, John	....	Rt	1	0	1
Willoughby, the Honble. Alberic Drummond	142, Piccadilly, London	Rt			

Swayfield.

Name of Elector.	Residence, if out of the Parish.	Qual.	T.	W.	P.
Almond Thomas	....	Fr	0	1	1
Bullimore, John	....	Fr	0	1	0

Swayfield—continued.

Name of Elector.	Residence, if out of the Parish.	Qual.	T.	W.	P.
Batty, Spencer	....	Rt	1	1	0
Birkett, John	....	Rt	0	1	0
Doubleday, William	....	Rt	0	1	1
Elson, William	Goadby Marwood, Leicestershire	Fr			
Maile, Matthew Edis	Falkingham	Fr			
Noel, the Honourable Charles George	*Viscount Campden* Exton	Fr			
Parker, John	Nottingham	Fr			
Porter, William	....	Rt	1	1	0
Sharp, Samuel	....	Fr	1	0	1
Tirrell, John	....	Rt	0	0	1
Thraves, John	....	Rt	0	0	1
Thraves, Matthew	....	Rt	0	1	1
Wyer, John	Bedford	Fr			

All Saints, Stamford.

Name of Elector.	Residence, if out of the Parish.	Qual.	T.	W.	P.
Atter, James, *Sol*	Barn-hill, Stamford	Fr	0	0	1
Bunney, George	Scotgate, Stamford	Rt	.1	1	0
Colls, George	Rutland-terrace, Stamford	Fr			
Dawson, Thomas	High-st., Stamford	Fr	1	0	1
Hinman, John	Market Overton	Fr			
Herbert, John James	Grantham	Fr *dead*			
Jones, Rev. Dennis Edward	St. Martin's Stamford Baron	Fr	1	1	0
Linton, Thomas	Fotheringhay	Fr			
Mills, Rev. Thomas	Wittering	Fr	1	1	0
Mitton, William	St. Martin's, Stamford Baron	Fr			
Myers, Rev. Charles John	Flintham, Notts	Fr	1	1	0
Norton, Noah	Tinwell-road	Fr	1	1	0
Newcomb, Robert Nicholas	High-st., Stamford	Fr *Esq*			
Percival, Thomas	Wansford	Fr	1	0	1
Palmer, Robert	St. George's-square, Stamford	Fr			
Porter, William George	Peterborough	Fr			
Philpot, Joseph Charles	15, Rutland-terrace	Fr	0	0	1
Richardson, James	Barn-hill, Stamford	Fr	1	0	0
Roberts, Thomas	St. Peter's-street, Stamford	Rt	1	1	0
Richardson, Charles	Ditto	Fr	1	0	0

All Saints, Stamford—continued.

Name of Elector.	Residence, if out of the Parish.	Qual.	T.	W.	P.
Sykes, John	North-street	Fr	1	0	1
Thompson, Richard *Sol*	Barn-hill, Stamford	Fr	1	1	0
Torkington, James *Sol*	10, Rutland-terrace, Stamford	Fr	1	1	0
Torkington, John *Sol*	St. Peter's-hill, Stamford	Fr *Bishop*	1	1	0
Wareing, Rev. William, D.D.	Northampton	Fr			
Walters, Rev. Nicholas	Broad-st., Stamford	Fr			
Warren, Thomas	Empingham	Fr	0	0	1
Willson, Robert William	George-street, Nottingham	Fr			
Wingfield, John Muxloe, esq.	Tickencote	Fr	1	1	0
Wright, Horace	All Saints'-street	Fr	0	1	1
Waterfield, William Wright	St. Peter's-street	Rt	1	0	1

Saint George, Stamford.

Name of Elector.	Residence, if out of the Parish.	Qual.	T.	W.	P.
Burton, John	Uffington	Fr	0	0	1
Beadsworth, John	High-street	Fr	0	0	1
Boyden, George	St. Martin's, Stamford	Fr	1	1	0
Boyden, William	Ditto	Fr	0	0	1
Barns, Henry	Ditto	Fr			
Brown, Richard	Wothorpe	Fr	1	1	0
Clapton, Jeremiah	St. Mary's-street	Fr	1	1	0
Clayton, Beaumont	Ketton, Rutland	Fr	1	0	1
Gretton, Rev. Frederick Edward	St. Paul's-street, Stamford	Fr	1	1	0
Handson, Charles Henry	Ironmonger-street	Fr	1	1	0
Hamilton, Joseph	St. George's-square	Fr			
Hind, William Maltby	St. Mary's-place	Fr	1	0	0
Jeffs, Goodliff	Barn-hill, Stamford	Fr	1	1	0
Knight, Richard	Ironmonger-street	Rt			
Knight, Richard	Ditto	Fr			
Laxton, Thomas	St. Paul's-street	Fr	1	1	0
Lowe, John	Ryhall	Fr	1	1	0
Ludlam, James	St. Paul's-street	Fr	1	1	0
Lumby, Joshua	High-st., Stamford	Fr	1	0	1
Milner, Thomas	Adelaide-street	Fr	1	0	1
Newcomb, Robert Nicholas	High-street	Fr			
Oswin, William	Tickencote	Fr	1	1	0

Saint Mary, Stamford.

Name of Elector.	Residence, if out of the Parish.	Qual.	T.	W.	P.
Broom, William	Ryhall, Rutland	Fr	0	0	1
Jackson, Thomas Hippis-ley, esq.	St. Mary's-street, Stamford	Fr	1	1	0
Newcomb, Robert Nicholas	High-street	Fr			

Saint Michael, Stamford.

Name of Elector.	Residence, if out of the Parish.	Qual.	T.	W.	P.
Althorp, James	High-st., Stamford	Fr	1	1	0
Billings, John	Crane's-ct., High-street	Fr	1	0	1
Betton, Rev. Joseph	Wooton-under-Edge	Fr			
Broom, William	Ryhall	Fr			
Cayley, Edward	Broad-st., Stamford	Fr			
Cooch, Thomas	Tinwell, Rutland	Fr	1	0	1
French, William	Broad-street	Fr			
Gadsby, John	Wittering	Fr			
Horden, William Andrew	High-street	Fr	1	1	0
Howes, John	All Saints'-place, Stamford	Fr			
Lumby, John	High-st., Stamford	Fr	0	0	1
Lumby, John	Ditto	Fr			
Lightfoot, Samuel	Saint Leonard-st.	Fr	1	0	1
Lowe, Charles	Broad-st., Stamford	Fr	1	0	1
Lowe, Charles	Broad-street	Fr			
Michelson, Robert	St. Martin's, Stamford	Fr	1	1	0
Newzam, William Thomas	St. George's-square, Stamford	Fr	1	1	0
Newcomb, Robert Nicholas	High-street	Fr	0	0	1
Porter, William George	Peterborough	Fr	1	0	1
Reed, William	Broad-st., Stamford	Fr			
Richardson, James, sen.	Barn-hill, Stamford	Fr			
Rogers, Silvester	Broad-st., Stamford	Fr	1	1	0
Spencer, William	Emlyn's cottages	Fr	1	1	0
Tebbutt, Henry	High-st., Stamford	Fr	1	0	1
Warrington, Leonard	Witney	Fr			
West, George Breton	Welland-street, Stamford	Fr	0	0	1

Saint John, Stamford.

Name of Elector.	Residence, if out of the Parish.	Qual.	T.	W.	P.
Ashby, Thomas Wood-house	St. John's-street	Fr	0	0	1
Boor, Henry	St. Martin's	Fr	1	1	0

Saint John, Stamford—continued.

Name of Elector.	Residence, if out of the Parish.	Qual.	T.	W.	P.
Brooks, Charles	St. Mary's	Fr	1	0	1
Brumhead, John	St. John's-street	Fr			
Coulson, William	All Saints'-street	Fr	1	0	1
Coulson, George	Scotgate	Fr	1	0	1
Coulson, George	Scotgate	Fr			
Carroll, John	North-street	Fr	1	0	1
Desborough, James George	St. Peter's-hill	Fr	1	1	0
Dawson, William	St. Mary's-street	Fr	0	0	1
Duncombe, John	St. Martin's, Stam-ford	Fr			
Huddlestone, John	Red Lion-street	Fr			
Johnston, John	52, Market-pl., Hull	Fr			
Moss, William Barker	St. Mary's-street	Fr	1	0	1
Muggleton, Samuel	Cole's Hill-street, Birmingham	Fr			
Newcomb, Robert Nicholas	High-street *Esq*	Fr			
Oswin, John	Red Lion-square	Fr	0	0	1
Richardson, William	Scotgate	Fr	0	0	1
Thompson, Richard *Sol*	Barn-hill	Fr			
Wade, John	St. Mary's-hill	Fr	1	0	0

Tallington.

Name of Elector.	Residence, if out of the Parish.	Qual.	T.	W.	P.
Bertie, Hon. Montague Peregrine	Uffington	Fr	0	0	1
Brown, Thomas	....	Rt	0	0	1
Idle, John	....	Rt	0	0	1
Phillips, Joseph	St. Martin's, Stamford	Fr	1	1	0
Phillips, John	Royston	Fr	1	0	1
Paine, John	....	Rt	1	0	1
Pine, Henry	....	Rt	0	0	1
Robinson, James	....	Fr	1	1	0
Searson, George	....	Rt	0	0	1
Staplee, John	....	Rt			
Thompson, Edward	....	Rt	1	0	1

Toft and Lound.

Name of Elector.	Residence, if out of the Parish.	Qual.	T.	W.	P.
Atter, John	Toft	Rt	1	0	1
Bell, Henry Cecil	Ditto	Fr	1	0	1
Elston, Henry	Lound	Rt	0	0	1
Foster, Edward Sladen	Toft	Rt	0	0	1
Howitt, John	Corby	Fr	1	0	1
Pick, Robert	Toft-lodge	Rt	0	0	1

Toft and Lound—continued.

Name of Elector.	Residence, if out of the Parish.	Qual.	T.	W.	P.
Smith, Stephen	Lound	Rt	0	0	1
Wass, Thomas	Toft	Rt	0	0	1
Wass, William	Toft-lodge	Rt	0	0	1

Thurlby and Obthorpe.

Name of Elector.	Residence, if out of the Parish.	Qual.	T.	W.	P.
Austin, John	Thurlby Northorpe	Rt	1	0	1
Barber, Michael	....	Fr	0	0	1
Bunning, Robert	Empingham	Fr	0	0	1
Bettinson, John	....	Rt	1	0	1
Bryan, Henry	Thurlby Northorpe	Co	0	0	1
Bland, William	Obthorpe	Rt	1	0	0
Cappitt, John	....	Fr	1	0	1
Carrington, Samuel	Edenham	Rt	1	0	0
Fields, John	....	Fr	0	0	1
Gentle, Joseph	Bourn	Fr	1	1	0
Hayes, Richard	....	Fr	0	0	1
Harrison, Everson, esq.	Tolethorpe-hall	Fr			
Hill, William	....	Rt	1	1	0
Harvey, Samuel	Thurlby Northorpe	Co	0	0	1
Hubbard, William	Thurlby-grange	Rt	0	1	1
Hubbard, Thomas Cook	Thurlby-grange	Rt	0	1	1
Inkly, George	....	Fr	1	1	0
Jackson, James	....	Fr	1	1	0
Knipe, Francis	Thurlby Northorpe	Rt	0	0	1
Knipe, Eldret	....	Co	1	0	1
Knipe, John	Thurlby Northorpe	Fr	0	0	1
Lenton, George	Burton Coggles	Co			
Peasgood, William	....	Fr	1	0	1
Peasgood, William	....	Fr			
Pope, Thomas	....	Rt	1	1	0
Pope, Thomas	....	Fr			
Rowden, William	....	Fr			
Ringham, Matthew B.	Northorpe	Co	1	0	1
Sandall, Robert	Stamford	Co	1	0	1
Sandall, William	....	Rt	1	1	0
Smith, Edis	....	Rt	0	0	1
Spencer, William	....	Fr	1	0	1
Stevenson, William	....	Fr	1	1	0
Sneath, John	....	Rt	0	0	1
Tucker, Peter	....	Rt	0	0	1
Tyler, William	....	Co	1	1	0
Wade, Robert	Thurlby Northorpe	Co	1	0	1

Thurlby and Obthorpe—continued.

Name of Elector.	Residence, if out of the Parish.	Qual.	T.	W.	P.
Wass, Thomas	Toft	Rt			
Worsley, Rev. Charles Pennyman	....	Fr	1	1	0
Wade, John, sen.	....	Fr	0	0	1
Wade, John, jun.	....	Fr	1	0	1
Wade, William	....	Fr	1	0	1
Ward, George	Thistleton, Rutland	Fr	1	1	0
Wright, Edward	Thurlby Northorpe	Rt	1	1	0

Uffington and Casewick.

Name of Elector.	Residence, if out of the Parish.	Qual.	T.	W.	P.
Brown, Elmer	Uffington	Rt	0	0	1
Barnard, Lonsdale East	Ditto	Rt	1	1	0
Cooper, Thomas	Ditto	Rt	0	0	1
Gee, George	Deeping-fen	Fr	1	0	1
Hare, Charles	Ditto	Rt			
Herd, William	Uffington	Rt	0	0	1
Layard, Rev. Brownlow Villiers	Ditto *absconded*	Fr			
Martin, Robert	Ditto	Rt	1	1	0
Pegus, Rev. Peter William	Uffington House	Rt	0	0	1
Pierrepont, Henry Bennett, esq.	Laywell House, Brixham, Devon	Fr			
Pateman, Taylor	Uffington	Rt	0	0	1
Stevenson, James, esq.	Clifton, Gloucester	Fr			
Sibcy, Samuel	Uffington	Rt	0	0	1
Stokes, John	Ditto	Rt	0	0	1
Trollope, the Right Hon. Sir John, bart.	Casewick-hall	Fr			
Trollope, Captain Arthur	Lincoln *Stamf*	Fr *distributor*			
Trollope, Captain Charles	Casewick-hall	Fr			
Webster, James	Uffington	Rt			

Wilsthorpe.

Name of Elector.	Residence, if out of the Parish.	Qual.	T.	W.	P.
Peacock, Christopher Gilbert	Greatford	Rt	1	1	0
Ullett, Abel	....	Fr			
Wilson, Joseph	....	Rt	1	1	0
Whincup, Henry	St. Martin's, Stamford	Rt	1	1	0

Witham-on-the-Hill.

Name of Elector.	Residence, if out of the Parish.	Qual.	T.	W.	P.
Brown, William	....	Rt	0	0	1
Duncombe, Philip Duncombe Pauncefort, esq.	Great Brickhill Manor, Bucks	Fr	1	1	0

Witham-on-the-Hill.—continued.

Name of Elector.	Residence, if out of the Parish.	Qual.	T.	W.	P.
Johnson, William Augustus, esq.	....	Fr	0	0	1
Johnson, Rev. William Henry	....	Fr	1	0	1
Lloyd, Edward	....	Rt	0	0	1
Moxon, Thomas	....	Rt	1	0	0
Pick, Richard	....	Rt	0	0	1
Woolley, Edward	....	Fr	0	0	1

No. 3.—POLLING DISTRICT ASSIGNED TO NAVENBY.

Ashby-de-la-Laund.

Name	Residence	Qual.	T.	W.	P.
Clarke, Joseph	....	Rt	1	1	0
Dixon, Matthew	....	Rt	1	1	0
Gambles, John	....	Rt	1	1	0
Graves, Robert	....	Rt	1	1	0
King, Rev. John William	....	Fr	1	1	0

Auborn.

Name	Residence	Qual.	T.	W.	P.
Bavin, William	....	Rt	1	1	0
Dalton, William	....	Rt	1	1	0
Dalton, George	....	Rt	1	1	0
Grimes, Joseph	....	Rt	0	0	1
Mansford, William	Marlbrough	Rt	1	1	0
Reynolds, Benjamin	....	Fr	0	0	1
Start, Joseph	....	Fr	0	0	1
Weightman, Hugh	Bassingham	Rt			
Willan, Rev. Francis Miles	....	Fr	1	1	0

Beckingham and Sutton.

Name	Residence	Qual.	T.	W.	P.
Blackshaw, Samuel	Sutton	Fr	1	1	0
Brooksby, Francis	Ditto	Fr	0	1	1
Crosby, Thomas	Beckingham	Fr	0	0	1
Crosby, John	Ditto	Fr	0	0	1
Cropley, William	Barkston	Rt			
Darcy, George	Beckingham	Fr	1	1	0
Darcy, William	Balderton-gate, Newark	Fr	0	0	1
Dickinson, Thomas	Beckingham	Fr	1	1	0
Dunn, George	Ditto	Fr	0	0	1
Else, Joseph	Ditto	Le			

Beckingham and Sutton—continued.

Name of Elector.	Residence, if out of the Parish.	Qual.	T.	W.	P.
Elkington, Robert	Great Hale	Fr	0	0	1
Forrest, William	Gainsborough	Fr	1	1	0
Handley, John, esq.	North Muskham	Fr			
Holland, Rev. William	Cold Norton, Essex	Fr			
Johnson, Joseph	Beckingham	Rt	1	1	0
Johnson, Robert	Ditto	Fr	0	0	1
Johnson, John	Ditto	Fr	1	1	0
Marsland, Rev. George	Ditto	Fr	1	1	0
Moore, John	Ditto	Fr	0	1	1
Rimington, Thomas	Ditto	Fr	0	1	1
Squires, John	Ditto	Rt	0	0	1
Torry, John	Ditto	Rt	0	1	0

Blankney and Linwood.

Name of Elector.	Residence, if out of the Parish.	Qual.	T.	W.	P.
Bott, Charles	Blankney-heath	Rt			
Bridges, Rev. Brook George	Blankney	Fr	1	1	0
Brown, Richard	Ditto	Fr	1	1	0
Bavin, Thomas	Blankney-fen	Rt	1	1	0
Chaplin, Charles, esq.	Blankney-hall	Fr	1	1	0
Cartwright, James	Blankney-fen	Rt	1	1	0
Cottingham, Henry	Linwood	Rt	1	1	0
Cartwright, Nathaniel	Haugham	Rt	1	1	0
Challans, William	Blankney-fen	Rt	1	1	0
Challans, Richard	Ditto	Rt	0	1	0
Gilbert, William	Blankney-grange	Rt	1	1	0
Goose, Daniel	Linwood-hall	Rt	0	1	0
Greenham, John	Blankney-barf	Rt	1	1	0
Greenham, James	Blankney-fen	Rt	1	1	0
Knott, Thomas	Blankney-barf	Rt	1	1	0
Pears, Thomas	Blankney	Rt	1	1	0
Sharp, Jonathan Plowright	Blankney-fen	Rt	1	1	0
Tyler, John	Linwood-fen	Rt			
Tatam, Thomas	Blankney-fen	Rt			
Willson, William	Blankney-barf	Rt	1	1	0

Boothby and Somerton Castle.

Name of Elector.	Residence, if out of the Parish.	Qual.	T.	W.	P.
Burnby, Matthew Coulson	Boothby	Rt	1	1	0
Daubney, John	Ditto	Rt	0	0	1
Everett, William	Ditto	Rt	0	0	1
Marfleet, Frederick	Navenby	Fr	1	1	0
Marfleet, John Isaac	Winthorpe	Fr	1	1	0
Marfleet, Henry	Boothby	Fr	1	1	0

Boothby and Somerton Castle—continued.

Name of Elector.	Residence, if out of the Parish.	Qual.	T.	W.	P.
Rylatt, Charles	Boothby	Rt	0	0	1
Spafford, Edward	Boothby-heath	Rt	1	0	1
Turnor, Benjamin	Boothby	Rt			

Brant Broughton.

Name of Elector.	Residence, if out of the Parish.	Qual.	T.	W.	P.
Andrews, John	Broughton Clays	Rt	1	1	0
Bradley, Richard	....	Fr	1	1	0
Bush, John	....	Fr	0	1	1
Briggs, Thomas	....	Fr			
Catton, George	....	Fr			
Coldron, William	....	Rt	1	1	0
Dunn, Thomas	....	Fr	0	1	1
Dunn, William	....	Fr	1	1	0
Dunn, Charles	....	Fr	1	1	0
Gibson, Richard	....	Rt	1	1	0
Harrison, George	....	Fr	1	1	0
Hucknall, Richard	....	Fr	0	1	1
Heald, Benjamin	....	Fr			
Houson, Rev. Henry	....	Fr	1	1	0
Johnson, Joseph	Broughton Clays	Rt	1	1	0
Lawson, John	....	Fr	1	1	0
Lister, Jackson Joseph Upton	West Ham, Essex	Fr			
Lister, William Henry	....	Rt			
Newton, William	....	Rt	1	1	0
Newstead, John	....	Fr	0	1	1
Rycroft, John	....	Fr	1	0	1
Rollison, William	....	Rt	0	1	0
Robinson, Richard	....	Fr	0	1	1
Scatliff, Joseph	....	Rt	1	1	0
Scott, William	....	Fr	0	1	1
Shaw, John	....	Fr	1	1	0
Weightman, Hugh	....	Rt	1	1	0

Caythorpe and Frieston.

Name of Elector.	Residence, if out of the Parish.	Qual.	T.	W.	P.
Atkin, John Horton	Caythorpe	Fr	0	0	1
Barnes, John	Ditto	Fr			
Barnes, Henry	Caythorpe-heath	Rt	0	0	1
Bates, William	Frieston	Rt	0	0	1
Bennett, George	Caythorpe	Fr	0	0	1
Bemrose, John	Ditto	Fr	0	0	1
Bemrose, Henry	Ditto	Rt	0	0	1

Caythorpe and Frieston—continued.

Name of Elector.	Residence, if out of the Parish.	Qual.	T.	W.	P.
Berry, Thomas	Caythorpe	Fr	1	0	1
Berry, Newton	Ditto	Fr	0	1	1
Blackbourn, Elias	Ditto	Rt	0	0	1
Chapman, William Thomas	Biggleswade	Fr	0	0	1
Crofts, Rev. Charles Daniel	Caythorpe	Fr			
Dennis, William	Crofton	Fr			
Eatch, William	Caythorpe	Rt	0	0	1
Francis, Robert	Ditto	Rt	0	0	1
Garton, John	Ditto	Fr	0	1	1
Glover, William	Ditto	Rt	0	0	1
Harvey, Thomas	Frieston	Rt	0	0	1
Hancock, Thomas	Frieston	Fr	0	1	1
Hunt, George	Caythorpe	Fr	0	1	1
Hackett, John	Ditto	Rt	0	1	1
Laughton, Philip	Ditto	Fr	0	1	1
Machers, William	Frieston	Fr	0	0	1
Machers, William, jun.	Caythorpe	Fr	0	0	1
Matkin, Thomas	Ditto	Fr	0	1	1
Minnitt, Edward	Ditto	Rt	0	0	1
Musson, William	Ditto	Fr			
Nettleship, Thomas	Lincoln	Fr	0	0	1
Packe, George Hussey, esq.	Caythorpe-house	Fr			
Paley, John	Caythorpe	Rt	0	0	1
Palmer, Thomas William	No. 1, Prime-street, Hull	Fr	0	0	1
Pogson, Samuel	Caythorpe	Rt	0	0	1
Redshaw, William	Ditto	Fr	0	0	1
Robinson, William, jun.	Brandon	Rt			
Simpson, John	Long Bennington	Fr			
Smith, Parker	Frieston	Fr	0	1	1
Shelbourn, Matthew	Ditto	Rt	0	0	1
Shelbourn, George	Ditto	Rt	0	0	1
Thurlby, John	Ditto	Fr	0	0	1
Vere, James, esq.	United University Club House, Suffolk-street, Pall Mall East, Middlesex	Fr			
Watson, Richard	Caythorpe	Rt	0	0	1
Walker, Richard	Ditto	Fr	0	0	1
White, Thomas	Ditto	Fr	0	0	1
Wilson, James	Ditto	Rt			

Caythorpe and Frieston—continued.

Name of Elector.	Residence, if out of the Parish.	Qual.	T.	W.	P.
Woodcock, Edward Walker	Oakham	Fr	0	0	1
Woodcock, Rev. George Henry	Sixhills, Wragby	Fr	0	1	1
Williams, Charles	Carlton-le-Moorland	Fr	0	1	1
White, William	Caythorpe	Fr	0	1	1
Woodcock, Edward Walker	Thurmaston vicarage, Leicestershire	Fr			

Coleby.

Name of Elector.	Residence, if out of the Parish.	Qual.	T.	W.	P.
Auckland, Samuel	....	Fr	0	0	1
Beet, Edward	Waddington	Fr	0	0	1
Bland, George	....	Rt	0	0	1
Challans, Robert	....	Rt	0	0	1
Crosby, Thomas	....	Rt	0	0	1
Crosby, Thomas, jun.	....	Fr	0	0	1
Commins, Robert	Coleby Heath	Fr	0	0	1
Elkington, William	Metheringham	Fr			
Garratt, John	Coleby Heath	Fr	1	1	0
Garratt, William	Coleby Heath	Fr	1	1	0
Harvey, John	....	Fr	0	0	1
Lister, Charles	Coleby Heath	Rt	0	0	1
Penrose, Rev. Thomas Trevanon	....	Fr			
Phillips, Robert	Navenby	Fr			
Pullen, William	....	Fr	0	0	1
Sykes, Robert	Spridlington	Fr	0	0	1
Skinner, Robert	....	Fr	0	0	1
Thompson, Edward	....	Fr	0	0	1
Taylor, John	Cromwell, Notts	Fr			
Tempest, Sir Charles Robert, bart.	Broughton Hall, Yorkshire	Fr			
Trafford, George	Coleby Heath	Rt	0	0	1
Ward, John	Welbourn	Fr			

Dunston.

Name of Elector.	Residence, if out of the Parish.	Qual.	T.	W.	P.
Brown, Thomas	....	Rt	0	0	1
Cartwright, John	Dunston-fen	Rt	0	0	1
Cartwright, Thomas	Dunston-heath	Rt	0	0	1
Cartwright, Edward Richardson	Dunston-fen	Rt	0	0	1
Crosby, William Horner	Reepham	Fr			
Dawson, William	Dunston-field	Fr	1	1	0

Dunston—continued.

Name of Elector.	Residence, if out of the Parish.	Qual.	T.	W.	P.
Fox, Francis	....	Rt	0	0	1
Goose, Daniel	Linwood	Fr			
Gresham, Thomas	Dunston-fen	Fr	0	1	1
Horner, Thomas Foster	....	Fr	0	1	1
Kirk, Joseph	....	Rt	0	1	1
Lloyd, Rev. Gamaliel Yarburgh	....	Fr			
Robinson, George	....	Rt	0	0	1
Scoley, Edward	Nocton	Rt	0	0	1
Scoley, Matthew	....	Rt	0	0	1
Vere, James, esq.	United University Club-house, Pall Mall East, Middlesex	Fr			

Fenton.

Name of Elector.	Residence, if out of the Parish.	Qual.	T.	W.	P.
Andrews, Thomas	Broughton	Rt	1	1	0
Frederick, Sir Richard, bart.	Burwood-park, Surrey	Fr			
Gilbert, Henry	Barnby	Fr	1	1	0
Handley, John, jun., esq.	Newark	Fr	0	1	1
Hague, Samuel	....	Rt	1	0	1
Ripley, Joseph	....	Fr	1	0	1
Rycroft, John	Broughton	Fr	1	1	0

Fulbeck.

Name of Elector.	Residence, if out of the Parish.	Qual.	T.	W.	P.
Bains, William	....	Rt	1	1	0
Burtt, Joseph	....	Rt	1	1	0
Capp, Jonathan	Fulbeck Low-field	Rt	1	1	0
Chambers, Charles	Fulbeck Low-field	Rt			
Collingwood, William	....	Rt	1	1	0
Crosby, Joseph	....	Rt	0	1	1
Dunn, Charles	Leadenham	Fr			
Dunn, John	Leadenham	Fr			
Ellis, Robert	....	Fr	1	1	0
Elliott, John	....	Rt	0	1	0
Else, John	....	Fr	1	1	0
Emerson, Edward	Fulbeck Low-field	Rt	1	1	0
Fane, Lieut.-Col. Henry	....	Fr	1	1	0
Fane, Rev. Edward	....	Fr	1	1	0
Fane, Lieut.-Col. Henry Edward	Avon, Hampshire	Fr			

Fulbeck—continued.

Name of Elector.	Residence, if out of the Parish.	Qual.	T.	W.	P.
Hayward, Thomas	Wellingore	Fr			
Hayward, John	St. Martin's, Lincoln	Fr			
Humphrey, Edward	....	Fr	1	1	0
James, George William	....	Fr	0	1	1
Lamb, John	....	Rt	1	1	0
Lee, Wold, esq. *S.L*	Lincoln	Fr	1	1	0
Lawson, Christopher	Leadenham	Fr			
Minnitt, William	Fulbeck-heath	Rt	0	1	0
Marshall, William	....	Fr	1	1	0
Morris, Henry	....	Fr	0	0	1
Miller, John	Saxby, Leicestershire	Fr			
Marshall, William	....	Fr	0	1	1
Newton, Thomas	....	Fr	1	1	0
Newton, John	....	Rt	1	1	0
Norris, Thomas	....	Fr	1	1	0
Ostler, William, esq.	Grantham	Fr	1	1	0
Parker, Edward Howard	....	Rt	1	1	0
Seely, Robert	187, High-street, Lincoln	Fr			
Smith, Charles	Mablethorpe	Fr			
Tomlin, Robert	....	Fr			
Watson, William	....	Fr	1	1	0
Watson, John	....	Fr	1	1	0
Watson, Thomas	....	Fr	0	1	0
Watson, Robert	....	Fr	1	1	0

Harmston.

Name of Elector.	Residence, if out of the Parish.	Qual.	T.	W.	P.
Barnes, Henry	....	Rt	0	1	0
Bastin, John	....	Rt	0	1	1
Burt, Edward	Welbourn	Fr	1	1	0
Catton, James	....	Fr	0	1	1
Clarke, Rev. Henry	Harmston vicarage	Fr			
Dixon, John	....	Rt	1	1	0
Day, Samuel	....	Rt	0	0	1
Danby, John William *S.L*	Lincoln	Fr	1	1	0
Hood, John	Nettleham Hill	Fr	1	1	0
Moore, Robert	Coddington	Fr	0	0	1
Metheringham, William	Windsor-terrace, Norwich	Fr	0	0	1
Mills, Thomas	....	Rt	0	0	1
Sharpe, Samuel	....	Rt	0	1	0

Harmston—continued.

Name of Elector.	Residence, if out of the Parish.	Qual.	T.	W.	P.
Turner, Samuel	....	Fr	0	1	1
Thorold, Benjamin Hart, *Esq.*....		Fr	1	0	1
Wilson, William	....	Fr	1	1	0

Heighington.

Name of Elector.	Residence, if out of the Parish.	Qual.	T.	W.	P.
Bailey, Charles	Newark	Fr	0	0	1
Bainbridge, George	High-street, Lincoln	Fr	1	1	0
Blyton, Edmund	Lincoln	Fr	1	1	0
Curtois, Rev. Atwill	Longhills	Fr	1	1	0
Clarke, Robert	....	Rt	1	1	0
Chamberlain, John	....	Fr	1	1	0
Calvert, Thomas	Branston	Fr	1	1	0
Cook, John	Branston	Fr			
Cooling, Robert	....	Fr	1	1	0
Coupland, William	....	Rt	1	1	0
Curtois, Rev. Peregrine	Hemingford Grey	Fr			
Cuthbert, George	....	Rt	1	1	0
Dance, William	....	Fr	0	0	1
Dance, John	Washingborough	Fr	0	0	1
Duckett, William	....	Rt	0	1	1
Day, William	Branston	Fr	1	1	0
Day, Rev. Frederick	....	Fr	1	1	0
Day, Robert	....	Fr	1	1	0
Durance, Joseph	19, Lindum-road, Lincoln	Fr	1	1	0
East, William	....	Fr	1	1	0
Foster, John	....	Fr			
Gilby, William Robinson	Newbigin, Beverley	Fr			
Gurnhill, Robert	Lincoln	Fr	1	1	0
Gresham, Robert	Branston	Fr	1	1	0
Harrison, William	Branston	Rt	1	1	0
Hurton, John	....	Fr	1	1	0
Hurton, Joseph	....	Fr			
Hodson, Thomas	....	Fr	1	1	0
Harrison, Stephen	Lincoln	Fr	1	1	0
Hammons, Christopher	....	Fr	1	1	0
Hodson, Thomas	Harby, Notts	Fr			
Howard, Henry	....	Fr	1	1	0
Jaques, Robert	....	Fr	0	0	1
Jackson, George	....	Rt			

Heighington—continued.

Name of Elector.	Residence, if out of the Parish.	Qual.	T.	W.	P.
Jackson, Charles	. . . .	Rt			
Kirk, Joseph	Dunston	Rt			
Kirk, John	. . . .	Rt	0	0	1
Knight, John	Blyton	Fr			
Lowe, Septimus	Lincoln	Fr	1	1	0
Lovely, Thomas	Branston	Fr	1	1	0
Moore, Joseph, esq. & Minster-close, Lincoln		Fr	1	1	0
Marshall, Edward	. . . .	Fr	1	1	0
Moore, Henry, esq.	Redbourne	Fr			
Pask, Michael	. . . .	Fr	1	1	0
Pask, John	Glentham	Fr			
Quincey, George	. . . .	Fr	1	1	0
Robinson, Robert	. . . .	Fr	1	1	0
Sibthorp, Rev. Humphrey Waldo	Washingborough	Fr			
Sibthorp, Gervaise Tottenham Waldo, esq.	Hackthorne	Fr	1	1	0
Shepherd, James	. . . .	Rt	1	1	0
Skepper, Original	Fiskerton	Fr	1	1	0
Squire, Francis	. . . .	Fr	0	1	1
Seeley, Charles, esq.	. . . .	Fr	0	0	1
Taylor, Joshua	. . . .	Fr	1	1	0
Taylor, Stephen	Branston	Fr	0	1	1
Ward, Charles	Newland, Lincoln	Fr	1	1	0
Wilson, William	Owmby	Fr			
Wooldridge, Joseph	Branston	Fr	0	1	1
Walker, John	. . . .	Fr	1	1	0
Wright, Thomas	. . . .	Rt	1	1	0

Kirkby-Green.

Name of Elector.	Residence, if out of the Parish.	Qual.	T.	W.	P.
Fullalove, Thomas	Scopwick	Fr	1	1	0
Gibson, William	. . . .	Rt	1	1	0
Pears, William	Scopwick mills	Fr	1	1	0
Woolfitt, William	. . . .	Rt	1	1	0
Young, Thomas	. . . .	Le	1	1	0

Leadenham and Bayard's-Leap.

Name of Elector.	Residence, if out of the Parish.	Qual.	T.	W.	P.
Abbott, William	. . . .	Fr	0	1	0
Brown, Benjamin Handley, esq.	. . . .	Rt			
Bestall, Richard	Bayard's-leap	Rt	1	1	0

Leadenham and Bayards Leap—continued.

Name of Elector.	Residence, if out of the Parish.	Qual.	T.	W.	P.
Bland, Thomas Colley	....	Rt	0	1	1
Burrows, William	....	Rt	1	1	0
Capp, Robert	Claypole	Fr	0	0	1
Capp, John	Holbeach	Fr	0	0	1
Chapman, John	....	Rt	1	1	0
Dunn, John	....	Fr	0	1	1
Fisher, James	....	Fr	0	1	1
Gibson, William	Lincoln	Fr	1	1	0
Harvey, Robert	....	Rt	1	1	0
Lawson, Christopher	....	Fr	1	1	0
Linney, Thomas	....	Rt	1	1	0
Morley, Joseph	....	Rt	1	0	1
Morley, William	....	Rt	1	0	1
Mucklow, Robert	....	Fr	1	1	0
Mucklow, Edward	....	Fr			
Reeve, General John	Leadenham-house	Fr	1	1	0
Reeve, Lieut.-Col. John	Leadenham-house	Fr	1	1	0
Robotham, William	Balderton	Fr	0	0	1
Robotham, John	....	Rt	0	1	1
Rycroft, Robert	....	Fr	0	0	1
Smith, Rev. Offley	....	Fr	1	1	0
Smith, Charles, esq.	Mablethorpe	Fr	1	1	0
Squires, John	....	Rt			
Winter, James	....	Fr	1	1	0

Metheringham.

Name of Elector.	Residence, if out of the Parish.	Qual.	T.	W.	P.
Allen, William	Lincoln	Fr	1	1	0
Atkin, Thomas	....	Fr	1	1	0
Baker, Richard	....	Fr	1	1	0
Buxton, Thomas	Metheringham-fen	Fr			
Bavin, Thomas	Ditto	Fr	0	0	1
Bavin, William	Ditto	Fr	0	0	1
Bavin, John	....	Fr	1	1	0
Bavin, Joseph	Metheringham-fen	Fr	0	0	1
Baker, Thomas	....	Fr	1	1	0
Belton, William Francis	....	Fr	1	1	0
Briggs, Uriah	....	Fr	1	1	0
Burbank, Henry	....	Fr	1	1	0
Burbank, Henry	Scopwick	Fr	1	1	0
Barnatt, John	Blankney-fen	Fr	1	1	0
Bosworth, John	Metheringham-fen	Fr	1	1	0

Metheringham—continued.

Name of Elector.	Residence, if out of the Parish.	Qual.	T.	W.	P.
Catton, Joseph	Blankney	Fr	1	1	0
Case, Rev. Isham	....	Fr	1	1	0
Cock, William	Metheringham-fen-side	Rt	1	1	0
Cock, William, jun.	Ditto	Fr	1	1	0
Chaplin, Thomas, esq.	Montague-square, London	Fr			
Clifton, Robert	Metheringham-fen	Fr			
Clifton, William	Ditto	Fr	1	1	0
Catton, William	....	Fr	1	1	0
Cartwright, Edward	Horncastle	Fr			
Edmonds, Moses	....	Fr	1	1	0
Ellis, John	Metheringham-fen	Fr	1	1	0
Elvidge, Joseph	....	Fr	1	1	0
Elvidge, Edward	Metheringham-fen-side	Rt	1	1	0
Elkington, William	Metheringham-grange	Rt	0	1	1
Gilbert, John Hill	Metheringham-lodge	Rt	1	1	0
Grebby, Cartwright	....	Rt			
Grimes, John	Pickworth, Rutland	Rt	1	1	0
Greenfield, John	....	Fr	1	1	0
Green, Richard	....	Rt	1	1	0
Greenwood, John	....	Fr	1	1	0
Harriss, John	Metheringham-fen	Rt	1	1	0
Hardy, William	....	Fr	1	1	0
Hayland, Thomas	....	Fr	1	1	0
Hiley, George	....	Fr	1	1	0
Henley, William	....	Fr	1	1	0
Hicks, Henry	Metheringham-barf	Rt	1	1	0
Hicks, William	....	Fr	1	1	0
Hutchinson, William	....	Fr	1	1	0
Longmate, William	Metheringham-fen	Fr	1	1	0
Marshall, William	Metheringham-heath	Rt	1	1	0
Marshall, William	St. Swithin's, Lincoln	Fr			
Marshall, John	St. Margaret's, Lincoln	Fr			
Newton, John	....	Fr	1	1	0
Onyon, William	15, Aldgate, London	Fr			
Osborn, Samuel	....	Fr	1	1	0
Pearson, George	Metheringham-fen	Fr	1	1	0
Read, Richard	....	Fr	1	1	0
Roberts, George	....	Fr	1	1	0

Metheringham—continued.

Name of Elector.	Residence, if out of the Parish.	Qual.	T.	W.	P.
Rycroft, John	....	Fr	1	1	0
Sharp, William	....	Fr	1	1	0
Sharp, William	....	Fr	1	1	0
Scoley, Thomas	....	Rt	1	1	0
Sharp, William	....	Fr			
Sharp, James	....	Fr	1	1	0
Smith, Thomas	....	Fr	1	1	0
Smith, John	....	Fr	1	1	0
Sharp, Joseph	....	Rt	1	1	0
Snow, James	Newark	Fr	1	1	0
Taylor, Thomas	Scopwick	Fr	1	1	0
Taylor, John	....	Fr	1	1	0
Tye, Gregory	Metheringham-fen	Le	1	1	0
Taylor, Joseph	....	Fr	1	1	0
Thorpe, Charles	....	Fr	1	1	0
Thompson, John	....	Fr	1	1	0
Tow, Timothy	Metheringham-fen	Fr	1	1	0
West, John	Miningsby	Fr	1	1	0
White, William	....	Fr	1	1	0
Wilson, William	Great Grimsby	Fr			
Willmott, William	....	Rt	1	1	0
Wray, Thomas	....	Rt	1	1	0
Winter, Thomas	....	Fr	1	1	0

Navenby.

Name of Elector.	Residence, if out of the Parish.	Qual.	T.	W.	P.
Armstead, Joseph	....	Fr	1	1	0
Armstead, William	....	Rt	1	1	0
Allen, John	Leadenham	Fr	1	1	0
Bird, Joseph	....	Rt			
Bates, Robert	....	Rt	1	1	0
Blackshaw, Robert	....	Fr	1	1	0
Bott, Charles	Blankney	Fr	1	1	0
Bottomley, Edward	....	Fr	0	1	1
Coddington, John	....	Fr	1	1	0
Cherry, John Rose	....	Fr	0	0	1
Cherry, Richard	....	Fr	1	1	0
Cooke, Robert	....	Rt	0	0	1
Doncaster, Rev. John, D.D.	Brighton	Fr			
Dexter, Thomas	....	Fr	0	0	1
Daubney, John	....	Fr	1	1	0

Navenby—continued.

Name of Elector.	Residence, if out of the Parish.	Qual.	T.	W.	P.
Daubney, Joseph	....	Fr	0	0	1
Daubney, James	....	Fr	1	1	0
Everitt, Joseph	....	Le	1	1	0
Evison, William	....	Rt	0	0	1
Frankish, John	Kirmington	Fr	1	1	0
Foottit, William	Hull	Fr			
Foottit, Christopher Carter	Newark	Fr	0	1	1
Gray, Charles	....	Rt	1	1	0
Hallam, Isaac	....	Fr	0	1	1
Heaton, Lawrance	....	Rt	1	1	0
Heanley, Marshall	Croft	Le	1	1	0
Hickenbotham, Joseph	Lincoln	Fr	1	1	0
Hales, Joseph	....	Fr	0	0	1
Hales, William	....	Fr	0	0	1
Hales, William	....	Fr	1	1	0
Hales, Clarke	....	Fr			
Housin, Daniel	Bathley	Fr	0	0	1
Lidget, William	....	Rt	1	1	0
Morley, Joseph	Hull	Fr			
Moore, Robert Coddington	Harmston	Fr			
Onyon, Henry	....	Fr	1	1	0
Onyon, Thomas	....	Fr	0	1	1
Pearson, Enoch	....	Rt	0	1	1
Pennington, Thomas Reville	....	Fr	0	1	1
Percy, the Honourable Charles Bertie	Guy's Cliff, Warwickshire	Fr			
Picker, Joseph	....	Rt	1	1	0
Pridgeon, William	....	Rt	1	1	0
Pridgeon, William N.	....	Rt	1	1	0
Priestly, John	....	Fr	0	0	1
Rollitt, William	....	Fr	0	1	1
Rooth, George	....	Rt	1	1	0
Rogers, John	Grantham	Fr	0	0	1
Sampson, John	....	Fr	1	1	0
Seeley, Robert	Lincoln	Fr	1	1	0
Simpson, George	....	Fr	0	1	1
Thorpe, John	....	Fr	1	1	0
Towers, Thomas	....	Fr	0	1	1
Wells, Joseph	....	Fr	0	1	1

Nocton.

Name of Elector.	Residence, if out of the Parish.	Qual.	T.	W.	P.
Beavin, Benjamin	Nocton-fen	Rt	0	0	1
Beavin, Thomas	Ditto	Rt	0	0	1
Cartwright, John	....	Rt	0	0	1
Goderich, The Viscount	Nocton-hall	Fr	0	0	1
Grayson, John	Nocton-fen	Rt	0	0	1
Howard, Robert	Nocton-rise	Rt	0	0	1
Howse, John	....	Rt	0	0	1
Mackinder, William	Meer-hall	Rt	1	1	0
Mills, John	Nocton-heath	Rt	0	0	1
Newton, Robert	Nocton-fen	Rt	0	0	1
Richardson, Thomas	....	Rt	0	0	1
Scoley, Robert	....	Rt	0	0	1
Toynbee, Charles	....	Rt	0	0	1
Wright, Robert	Nocton-heath	Rt	0	0	1
Woolhouse, Chapman George	Nocton-grange	Rt	0	1	1
Wilson, Rev. Edward	....	Fr	0	0	1

Potterhanworth.

Name of Elector.	Residence, if out of the Parish.	Qual.	T.	W.	P.
Anson, Rev. Arthur Henry	....	Fr			
Battle, John Richard	....	Rt	1	1	0
Bland, John Harrison	Flawborough, Notts	Fr	1	1	0
Briggs, John Headland	....	Rt	0	1	0
Briggs, George	....	Fr	0	1	1
Beavin, John	Ferry-house	Rt			
Dawson, Richard	Abury - hall, near Weare	Fr			
Dawson, William	Dunston-heath	Rt			
Daykins, William	....	Fr	1	1	0
Foster, William	Canwick	Fr	1	1	0
Gresham, Lawrence	....	Rt	0	0	1
Headland, William	....	Fr	0	1	1
Hird, David	....	Rt	0	1	1
Moore, Benjamin	....	Rt	0	0	1
Robinson, William	....	Rt	1	1	0
Saxe, Philip	....	Fr	1	1	0
Salter, Peter	....	Fr			
Walker, William	Dunholme	Rt	1	1	0
Willson, Anthony, esq.	South Rauceby	Fr			

Scopwick.

Name of Elector.	Residence, if out of the Parish.	Qual.	T.	W.	P.
Alvey, Richard	....	Rt	1	1	0

Scopwick—continued.

Name of Elector.	Residence, if out of the Parish.	Qual.	T.	W.	P.
Baker, John, jun.	....	Fr	1	1	0
Clarke, Charles	....	Rt	1	1	0
Catton, Richard	....	Fr			
George, Thomas	....	Fr	1	1	0
George, William	....	Fr	1	1	0
Harrison, John	....	Rt			
Oliver, Rev. George, D.D.	No. 7, Bank-street, Lincoln	Fr			
Pears, Edward	....	Rt	1	1	0
Pell, Paul Francis	....	Rt	1	1	0
Sewell, John Goulding	Candlesby	Fr			

Skinnand.

Name of Elector.	Residence, if out of the Parish.	Qual.	T.	W.	P.
Nicholls, Samuel, esq.	Chiswick Mall, Middlesex	Fr			
Scott, Rev. Francis Caleb	Chichester, Sussex	Fr			
Woolfitt, John	....	Rt			

Stragglethorpe.

Name of Elector.	Residence, if out of the Parish.	Qual.	T.	W.	P.
Chambers, Reuben	....	Rt	1	1	0
Parke, William	....	Rt	1	1	0
Tonge, Richard	....	Rt			

Washingborough.

Name of Elector.	Residence, if out of the Parish.	Qual.	T.	W.	P.
Burton, Frederick, esq.	S. Lindum-road, Lincoln	Fr			
Bontoft, Wright	....	Rt	1	1	0
Cooling, William	....	Fr	1	1	0
Clarke, John	....	Fr			
Carline, Richard, esq.	S. Flaxengate, Lincoln	Fr			
Ellis, John	Newton	Fr			
Durance, Joseph	Lindum-road, Lincoln	Fr			
Dixey, William	....	Rt			
Fairfax, Thomas, esq.	Newton Kyme, Yorkshire	Fr			
Fullard, William	Welton	Fr			
Green, John	....	Fr	1	1	0
Hatch, John	....	Rt	1	1	0
Hill, Robert Gardiner, esq. Surgeon	St. Peter's, Eastgate, Lincoln	Fr			
Hird, John	....	Rt	1	1	0
Howard, Henry	....	Fr			

Washingborough—continued.

Name of Elector.	Residence, if out of the Parish.	Qual.	T.	W.	P.
Kirk, Joseph	Dunston	Rt			
Marshall, John, esq.	Riseholme	Fr			
Mackinder, William	....	Fr			
Marshall, William, esq.	Lincoln	Fr	1	1	0
Parker, Zebedee	Nettleham	Fr			
Palin, Joseph	....	Rt	1	1	0
Rudgard, William, esq.	Lincoln	Fr			
Scorer, William	Burwell	Fr			
Sibthorp, Rev. Humphrey Waldo	....	Fr	1	1	0
Scoley, Matthew	....	Rt	1	1	0
Salter, Thomas	....	Fr	1	1	0
Stevenson, Thomas	Lincoln	Fr			
Taylor, Richard	Lincoln	Fr			
Taylor, John	Dunston	Fr	0	0	1
Tayles, Edward	Kinthorp	Fr			
Thornbury, David	....	Fr			
Thornbury, D. Featherby	...	Fr			
Wells, Atkin	....	Fr	1	1	0
Whelpton, George	Walpole, St. Peter, Norfolk	Fr			

Wellingore.

Name of Elector.	Residence, if out of the Parish.	Qual.	T.	W.	P.
Allix, Frederick William esq.	....	Rt			
Ashton, Matthew	....	Fr			
Bott, Charles	....	Fr	1	1	0
Barnes, John	Caythorpe-heath	Fr	0	1	1
Bailey, Thomas	Welbourn	Fr	0	1	1
Baxter, Charles	....	Fr	0	1	1
Chilton, James	....	Fr	1	1	0
Clarke, Richard	....	Fr	1	1	0
Dawson, Samuel	....	Fr	0	1	1
Duncomb, Thomas	Lincoln	Fr	1	1	0
Duncomb, John	....	Rt	1	1	0
Fox, Henry	....	Fr	0	1	0
Hales, John	....	Fr	1	1	0
Harrison, William	Spilsby	Fr	0	0	1
Hayward, Thomas	Wellingore-heath	Rt	1	1	0
Hilton, Robinson	Ditto	Fr	1	1	0
Hilton, William	Ditto	Fr	1	1	0

Wellingore.—continued.

Name of Elector.	Residence, if out of the Parish.	Qual.	T.	W.	P.
Hollingsworth, William	....	Rt	1	1	0
Horner, George	....	Fr	1	1	0
Mitton, Robert	....	Rt	0	1	1
Peacock, Rev. John	....	Fr	1	1	0
Preston, William	....	Fr	1	1	0
Reeve, Philip, esq.	No. 8, Lincoln's-inn, London	Fr			
Reeve, Ellis, esq.	No. 104, Portman-st., Gloucester-square, London	Fr			
Read, David	....	Fr	0	0	1
Scott, Samuel	....	Rt	1	1	0
Saywell, John	North Disney	Fr			
Stanhope, Charles	Leadenham	Fr	1	1	0
Worsdale, William	....	Fr	1	1	0

Welbourn.

Name of Elector.	Residence, if out of the Parish.	Qual.	T.	W.	P.
Brown, Rev. John	Batcombe, Somerset	Fr			
Brown, Francis, esq.	Elm Park, Rath-farnham, Ireland	Fr	0	1	1
Bush, Robert	....	Rt	0	0	1
Burtt, John	....	Rt	1	1	0
Booth, Joseph	....	Fr	0	1	1
Chambers, John	....	Fr	0	0	1
Disbrowe, Rev. Henry John	....	Fr	1	1	0
Harrison, Charles	Scopwick	Fr	1	1	0
Hodson, John	....	Fr	0	0	1
Minnitt, Henry	....	Fr	1	1	0
Minnitt, George	....	Rt	0	1	1
Palin, Francis	....	Rt	0	1	1
Rinder, Joseph	....	Rt	0	0	1
Shaw, David	....	Rt	0	0	1
Thompson, George	....	Rt	0	0	1

Sutterton.

Name of Elector.	Residence, if out of the Parish.	Qual.	T.	W.	P.
Gibney, Rev. John S.	St. Margaret's, Lincoln	Fr	1	1	0
Richter, Rev. Hy. Wm.	Silver-street, Lincoln	Fr	1	1	0

No. 4.—POLLING DISTRICT ASSIGNED TO GRANTHAM.

Allington.

Name of Elector.	Residence, if out of the Parish.	Qual.	T.	W.	P.
Breffit, Richard	West Allington	Rt	1	0	1
Bonser, William	Nottingham	Fr			
Bussell, Rev. Garrett J.	Appleton-gate, Newark	Fr	1	1	0
Caunt, Joseph	East Allington	Fr	1	0	1
Clay, Francis	Ditto	Rt	1	0	1
Eminson, John	Ditto	Fr			
Fox, John	Ditto	Fr	1	0	1
Hardy, Matthew	Ditto	Rt	0	0	1
Hubbard, Richard	Little Gonerby	Fr			
Hoyes, William	West Allington	Rt			
Lovitt, William	East Allington	Fr	0	0	1
Scrimshire, Robert	Ditto	Rt	1	0	1
Swift, Thomas	Lynby, Notts	Fr			
Welby, Rev. John Earle	Harston	Fr			
Welby, Rev. Montague Earle	West Allington	Fr	1	0	1
Winter, William	East Allington	Rt	0	0	1

Barrowby and Casthorpe.

Name of Elector.	Residence, if out of the Parish.	Qual.	T.	W.	P.
Ashwell, Michael	Barrowby	Fr	0	0	1
Bell, Eustace	Freeby, Leicestershsre	Fr	1	1	0
Brown, William	Grantham	Fr	1	1	0
Burnaby, Rev. Frederick George	Barkston, Leicestershire	Fr	1	1	0
Downing, William	Casthorpe	Rt	1	1	0
Downing, John	Barrowby	Rt	1	0	1
Essington, William	Ditto	Fr	1	1	0
Eminson, John	Ditto	Fr	1	0	1
Garton, William	Ditto	Fr	0	1	1
Garton, Francis John	Grantham	Fr	0	1	1
Gibson, Richard	Ditto	Fr	1	0	1
Huckerby, Joseph	Barrowby	Fr	1	1	0
Hutchinson, John	Foston	Fr			
Jenkinson, Daniel	Barrowby	Rt	1	1	0
Pinder, William	Ditto	Rt	1	1	0
Pearson, Arthur	Ditto	Fr	0	0	1
Pinder, Thomas	Ditto	Rt	1	0	1

Barrowby and Casthorpe—continued.

Name of Elector.	Residence, if out of the Parish.	Qual.	T.	W.	P.
Ragsdale, Mark	Barrowby	Fr	0	0	1
Ravell, Matthias	Bottesford	Fr	1	1	0
Reynolds, John	Ditto	Fr	1	1	0
Rimmington, Robert	Denton	Fr	1	0	1
Smith, John	Brether Hills	Rt	1	1	0
Stevens, Thomas	Buckminster	Fr	0	0	1
Singleton, William	Casthorpe	Rt	1	1	0
Simon, Robert	Muston	Fr			
Turner, Robert, esq.	Grantham	Fr			
Vincent, Francis, jun.	Barrowby	Rt	0	0	1
White, George, esq.	Grantham	Fr	*dead*		
Walker, William	Barrowby	Rt	1	1	0
White, Robert Azlack	Grantham *Solicitor*	Fr	1	1	0
Wade, Richard	Hungerton	Fr			
Wing, James Webb	Great Gonerby	Fr	1	0	1
Welby, Rev. George Earle	Barrowby	Fr	0	1	1

Barkston.

Name of Elector.	Residence, if out of the Parish.	Qual.	T.	W.	P.
Beecham, Robert	....	Rt			
Barker, Richard	Hough-on-the-Hill	Fr	1	1	0
Butler, Robert	Langworth	Rt	1	1	0
Cropley, William	....	Rt	1	1	0
Houblon, John Archer, esq.	Hallingbury-place, Essex	Fr	1	1	0
Hand, John	....	Fr	1	1	0
Holmes, William	....	Fr	1	1	0
Loveday, Charles	Barkston-mill	Rt	1	1	0
Minnitt, William	Barkston-heath	Rt	1	1	0
Millar, Edward	Barkston-becks	Fr	0	0	1
Power, Thomas Marlow	....	Rt	1	1	0
Reade, Rev. Richard	Dinon, Brittany, France	Fr			
Smith, John	....	Rt			
Shelbourn, George	Hough-on-the-Hill	Fr	1	1	0
Stanhope, John	....	Rt	1	1	0
Thompson, Thomas	....	Fr			

Bassingthorpe and Westby.

Name of Elector.	Residence, if out of the Parish.	Qual.	T.	W.	P.
Allsop, John	Bassingthorpe	Rt	1	0	1
Burgess, Richard	Westby	Rt	1	0	1
Evans, Rev. John Wm.	Builth, Brecknock	Fr			

Bassingthorpe and Westby—continued.

Name of Elector.	Residence, if out of the Parish.	Qual.	T.	W.	P.
Grummitt, Joseph	Westby	Rt	1	0	1
Gibson, John	Bassingthorpe	Rt	0	1	1
Scarborough, William	Westby	Rt	0	1	1
Wildgoose, Anthony	Bassingthorpe	Rt	0	1	1

Bennington and Bennington Grange.

Name of Elector.	Residence, if out of the Parish.	Qual.	T.	W.	P.
Atkin, William	....	Rt	0	0	1
Arnold, Thomas	Westborough	Fr	0	0	1
Andrews, Rev. Samuel Wright	Claxby	Co	1	0	0
Andrews, John Wood	....	Rt	1	0	1
Alcock, Thomas	Bennington-grange	Fr	1	0	1
Alcock, Samuel	....	Rt	0	0	1
Adams, Samuel	Dunholm	Co	0	0	1
Bemrose, John	....	Fr	0	0	1
Buck, Hart	Grantham	Co	0	0	1
Bemrose, Joseph	Gringley-on-the-Hill	Co		.	
Bradford, Robert	South Stoke	Fr	1	1	0
Buckland, Richard	....	Rt	1	0	1
Bradford, Joseph	....	Fr	0	0	1
Bradford, Andrew	Westborough-lodge	Co			
Christmas, Thomas	....	Rt	1	0	1
Coulby, Dickson	....	Fr	1	0	1
Campain, Samuel	....	Fr	0	0	1
Cook, Robert	Gainsborough	Co	0	0	1
Copley, William	Westborough	Fr	0	0	1
Daunt, William	....	Fr	0	0	1
Daunt, William, jun.	....	Fr	0	1	0
Dring, William	....	Fr	1	0	1
Fisher, Thomas	Cropwell Butler, Notts.	Fr	1	1	0
Grote, George, esq.	12, Saville-row, London	Fr	0	0	1
Gaby, Thomas	....	Co	1	0	1
Gaby, Thomas, jun.	....	Co	1	0	1
Geary, Rev. Robt. Wade	Colnworth Rectory, Bedfordshire	Fr			
Hackett, John	....	Rt	0	1	1
Halls, Rev. George	....	Fr	1	1	0
Harby, Thomas	....	Fr	1	0	1
Hardy, William	Foston	Fr			
Harby, John	....	Co	1	0	1
Harvey, James	....	Co	0	0	1

Bennington, and Bennington Grange—continued.

Name of Elector.	Residence, if out of the Parish.	Qual.	T.	W.	P.
Ingleton, John	....	Fr	0	0	1
Irving, William Bell	....	Fr	0	0	1
Jessopp, Robert	....	Co	1	0	0
Jackson, Robert	....	Fr	0	0	1
Johnson, Thomas	....	Rt	0	0	1
Johnson, Simon	....	Co	1	0	1
Kinning, Thomas	....	Rt	0	0	1
Leeson, John	24, Snenton-street, Nottingham	Co	0	0	1
Lynn, Richard, sen.	....	Co	1	0	0
Lynn, Robert	Newton	Fr	1	1	0
Lynn, John Cragg	Newton	Fr			
Lee, John	....	Co	0	0	1
Moore, Edward	....	Rt	1	1	0
May, Samuel	....	Co			
Miller, Robert	....	Rt	0	0	1
Newton, Richard	Kirkby Laythorpe	Fr	0	0	1
Pepper, Francis	....	Rt	1	1	0
Porter, Robert	Normanton	Co	1	1	0
Peatman, Thomas	....	Co	1	0	1
Patman, George	....	Fr	0	0	1
Page, Thomas	....	Fr	1	0	0
Pickworth, James	2, Woolmer-cottages, Hammersmith	Fr			
Royce, William	Buckminster	Co	0	0	1
Rimington, Daniel	....	Rt	1	0	0
Rimington, William	....	Co			
Roberts, Robert	....	Co	0	0	1
Rowbotham, Edmund	....	Co	0	0	1
Rushton, John	....	Co	1	0	1
Roe, Thomas	....	Rt	0	0	1
Short, John	....	Fr	0	0	1
Stafford, William	....	Fr	1	0	1
Staunton, Henry Charlton	Staunton Hall	Fr	1	1	0
Squiers, John	....	Fr	0	0	1
Seiles, Richard	....	Co	1	0	1
Simpson, George	....	Fr	1	0	1
Stephenson, Joseph	....	Rt	1	0	1
Stafford, Thomas	Marnham	Co	1	1	0
Taylor, John	Newark	Co			

Bennington, and Bennington Grange—continued.

Name of Elector.	Residence, if out of the Parish.	Qual.	T.	W.	P.
Welby, Rev. Montague Earle	Allington	Fr			
Wilson, William	....	Co	0	0	1
Wade, John	....	Co	0	0	1
Whitaker, John	....	Co	1	0	1
Whitaker, William	Grantham	Co	1	1	0
Whitaker, John	....	Fr	0	0	1
Whitaker, Robert	....	Rt	0	0	1
Wrath, John	....	Fr	1	0	1
Wilson, Robert	Dry Doddington	Co	0	0	1
Whitaker, Joseph	....	Rt	1	0	0
Wilkinson, Joseph	....	Rt	0	0	1

Belton.

Name of Elector.	Residence, if out of the Parish.	Qual.	T.	W.	P.
Cust, the Hon. Sir Edward	Leasowe Castle, Cheshire	Fr			
Cust, the Hon. Peregrine Francis	73, South Audley-street, Westminster	Fr	1	1	0
Cust, the Hon. and Rev. Richard	....	Fr	1	1	0
Hatfield, John	....	Rt	1	1	0
Long, John	....	Rt	1	1	0
Monks, William	Great Gonerby-grange	Rt	1	1	0
Richardson, Edward	....	Rt	1	1	0
Watts, Samuel	....	Rt	1	1	0

Bitchfield.

Name of Elector.	Residence, if out of the Parish.	Qual.	T.	W.	P.
Brereton, Rev. Abel Brett	Westby *Vicar*	Fr	1	0	1
Clarges, Sir Richard Goddard Hare, K.C.B.	London	Fr	1	1	0
Drury, Samuel	....	Rt	0	0	1
Hilton, Thomas	....	Rt	0	0	1
Inman, Rev. James Wm.	Grantham	Fr	1	1	0
Marriott, William	....	Rt	1	0	0
Nickolls, Edward	....	Rt	0	0	1
Wilkinson, Thomas	Grantham	Fr			

Boothby Pagnell.

Name of Elector.	Residence, if out of the Parish.	Qual.	T.	W.	P.
Hatfield, David	....	Rt	1	1	0
Litchford, John, esq.	Boothby-hall	Fr	1	1	0

Boothby Pagnell—continued.

Name of Elector.	Residence, if out of the Parish.	Qual.	T.	W.	P.
Newcome, Rev. William Charles	....	Fr	1	1	0
Robinson, William	....	Rt	1	1	0
Woodroffe, Charles	....	Rt	1	1	0
Ward, William	....	Rt	1	1	0

Braceby.

Brothwell, Joseph	....	Rt	1	1	0
Brothwell, Thomas	....	Rt	1	1	0
Lee, John	....	Fr	0	0	1
Leeson, William	....	Fr	1	1	0
Michelson, Thomas	....	Rt	1	1	0
Wood, John	....	Rt	1	1	0

Burton Coggles.

Aldwinckle, John	....	Rt	0	0	1
Burrows, Thomas	....	Rt	0	0	1
Lenton, George	....	Rt	0	0	1
Machin, John	....	Rt	0	0	1
Moor, William	....	Rt	0	0	1
Rippon, Thomas Luke	....	Rt	0	0	1
Sewards, William	....	Rt	0	0	1

Carlton Scrope.

Allix, Frederick William esq.	Willoughby	Fr			
Aldwinckle, John	Burton Coggles	Fr			
Craven, John	....	Fr	1	0	1
Foster, John	....	Rt	1	1	0
Foster, George	....	Rt	0	1	1
Manners, Thomas, esq.	Grantham *Solicitor*	Fr	1	0	1
Newton, John	....	Rt	0	0	1
Ripley, Benjamin	Normanton	Fr	0	1	1
Schneider, Rev. Henry	....	Fr	1	1	0
Sills, George	Honington	Fr	1	0	1
Silkstone, Thomas	....	Fr	1	1	0
Trevitt, William	....	Rt	0	1	1
Ward, William Frederick	....	Rt	0	0	1
Wolf, George	....	Fr			
Wyles, Joseph	Retford	Fr	1	0	1

Claypole.

Name of Elector.	Residence, if out of the Parish.	Qual.	T.	W.	P.
Andrews, William	Long Bennington	Fr	1	0	0
Andrews, Algernon John	Alverton	Fr	1	0	0
Astling, Elijah	....	Fr	0	0	1
Barnsdale, George	....	Rt	0	0	1
Barnsdale, Miles	....	Fr	0	0	1
Barnsdale, Lancelot	....	Fr	0	0	1
Birch, Henry	....	Rt	0	0	1
Birkitt, John	Barnby	Fr	0	0	1
Birkett, John	....	Rt	0	0	1
Baldock, Joseph	Cropwell Butler	Fr	1	1	0
Bunting, Baron	Sandy, Bedfordshire	Fr			
Beedham, William	Newark, Notts	Fr	0	0	1
Collin, Henry	....	Rt	0	0	1
Copley, John	....	Rt	0	0	1
Clark, John	Newark	Fr			
Collins, John	....	Fr	0	0	1
Curtis, Samuel	Norwell	Fr	1	1	0
Denison, John Evelyn, esq.	Ossington	Fr	0	0	1
Easam, Leonard	Norwell	Fr	1	1	0
Footitt, John	Brandon	Fr.	1	1	0
Grocock, William	....	Fr	0	0	1
Herring, Rev. Edmund	Norwell	Fr			
Harvey, Matthew	Balderton	Fr	1	1	0
Hebb, William	....	Fr	0	0	1
Hill, John	....	Fr	0	0	1
Hollins, Henry	Pleasley-works, Pleasley, Derbyshire	Fr			
Hubbard, George	....	Fr	0	0	1
Hoyes, Thomas	....	Fr	0	0	1
Jessop, John	....	Fr	0	0	1
Jackson, Henry	Newark	Fr	0	0	1
Jordan, Samuel	Honington	Fr	1	0	1
Lane, William	Bottesford, Leicestershire	Fr			
Longbottom, William	....	Fr	0	0	1
Lee, John Scrimshaw	....	Fr	0	0	1
Longbottom, William	Claypole-mill	Rt	0	0	1
Loughton, Philip	....	Fr	0	0	1
Moggs, Joseph	....	Rt	0	0	1

Claypole—continued.

Name of Elector.	Residence, if out of the Parish.	Qual.	T.	W.	P.
Nixon, John	Willoughby-on-the-Wolds	Fr			
Prew, Charles	. . . .	Rt	0	0	1
Prew, John	. . . .	Fr	0	0	1
Paling, William	Newark	Fr	1	0	1
Paulson, William	Mansfield	Fr			
Roberts, George	Newark, Notts	Fr	0	0	1
Revill, John	. . . .	Rt	0	0	1
Scholey, John	. . . .	Rt	0	0	1
Smith, Andrew	. . . .	Rt	0	0	1
Smith, John	Cropwell Bishop	Fr	1	1	0
Smith, Thomas	Sutton-upon-Trent	Fr	1	1	0
Spafford, John	. . . .	Fr	0	0	1
Summers, Michael, sen.	. . . .	Rt	0	0	1
Stevenson, James	Balderton	Fr	0	0	1
Surgey, Richard	. . . .	Fr	0	0	1
Streets, William	. . . .	Fr	0	0	1
Tallents, Godfrey, esq. *Sol*	Newark	Fr	1	1	0
Tallents, William Edward, esq. *Sol*	Newark	Fr			
Vickers, William	. . . .	Fr	0	0	1
Vickers, William, jun.	. . . .	Fr	0	0	1
Wadsworth, Thomas	. . . .	Fr			
Wilson, James	Newark	Fr			
Wadsworth, Thomas, jun.	. . . .	Fr	0	0	1
Warriner, John	. . . .	Rt	0	0	1
Whittaker, John	. . . .	Fr	0	0	1

Colsterworth and Woolsthorpe.

Name of Elector.	Residence, if out of the Parish.	Qual.	T.	W.	P.
Abbott, Charles	Colsterworth	Fr	1	0	1
Abbott, George	Ditto	Fr	0	0	1
Barber, Clark	Ditto	Fr	1	1	0
Barber, John	Ditto	Fr	0	0	1
Bright, Benjamin	Woolsthorpe	Fr	1	0	1
Bean, Richard	Skillington	Fr			
Briggs, Henry	Colsterworth	Fr	1	0	1
Burton, John	Ditto	Fr	1	0	1
Beeson, Bennett	Ditto	Rt	1	1	0
Doubleday, Thomas	Ditto	Fr	1	1	0
Goddard, Joseph	Ditto	Fr	0	0	1

Colsterworth and Woolsthorpe—continued.

Name of Elector.	Residence, if out of the Parish.	Qual.	.T.	W.	P.
Hack, Lionel	Stainby	Rt			
Handley, Henry	Woolsthorpe	Fr	1	1	0
Hawley, William	Burton Coggles	Fr	0	0	1
Hawley, George, jun.	Colsterworth	Fr	1	0	1
Ingle, Edward	Ditto	Fr	0	0	1
Lamb, William	Ditto	Fr	1	1	0
Mirehouse, Rev. William	Hanbrook-grove, Bristol	Fr			
Percival, George	Woolsthorpe	Fr	0	0	1
Porter, James	Colsterworth	Fr	0	0	1
Rippin, Thomas	Stretton, Rutland	Fr	1	0	1
Senescall, Richard	Colsterworth	Fr	0	0	1
Senescall, John	Woolsthorpe	Rt			
Sharpe, John	Colsterworth	Fr	1	0	1
Sharpe, Rev. R. M.	Ditto	Rt			
Taylor, Richard	Ditto	Fr	0	0	1
Tow, Thomas	Ditto	Rt	1	1	0
Thompson, Henry, jun.	Woolsthorpe	Rt	1	0	1
Thompson, Henry	Ditto	Fr	1	1	0
Thompson, John	Ditto	Fr	0	0	1
Townsend, John	Ditto	Fr	0	0	1
Taylor, Robert	Grantham	Fr	0	0	1
Worrall, William	Woolsthorpe	Fr	0	0	1
Wollerton, John	Ditto	Rt	1	1	0
Williamson, Thomas	Colsterworth	Rt	0	0	1

Denton.

Name of Elector.	Residence, if out of the Parish.	Qual.	.T.	W.	P.
Auger, John	....	Rt	1	1	0
Brice, Robert	Harston	Rt	1	1	0
Brewster, John	....	Rt	1	1	0
Collingwood, William Brewster	....	Rt	1	1	0
Downing, John	Casthorpe	Rt			
Greenwood, Edward	....	Rt	1	1	0
Geeson, William	....	Rt	1	1	0
Hand, Robert	....	Rt	1	1	0
Kingston, John	Woolsthope	Fr	1	1	0
Lane, Francis	....	Rt	1	1	0
Morris, John	....	Fr	1	1	0
Nicholls, John	Hungerton	Rt			

Denton—continued.

Name of Elector.	Residence, if out of the Parish.	Qual.	T.	W.	P.
Potchett,-Rev. George Thomas	....	Fr	1	1	0
Tyler, William	....	Rt	1	1	0
Welby, Sir Glynne Earle, bart.	....	Fr	1	1	0
Winter, Thomas	....	Fr	I	1	0

Doddington near Newark.

Name of Elector.	Residence, if out of the Parish.	Qual.	T.	W.	P.
Bennett, George	....	Fr	0	0	1
Bradford, Andrew	Westborough-lodge	Rt			
Bradley, George	Lenton Poplars, Nottingham	Fr			
Bennett, William	....	Fr	0	0	1
Cullin, William	....	Fr	0	0	1
Challands, William	Bottesford	Fr	1	1	0
Carver, John	....	Fr			
Cragg, Mark	....	Fr	0	0	1
Coltman, Edward	....	Rt	0	0	1
Cullin, George	....	Fr	0	0	1
Ellis, Richard	....	Fr			
Ewerdine, George	....	Rt	0	0	1
Freeston, Edward	....	Rt	0	0	1
Godfrey, Thomas Spragging, esq.	Balderton	Fr	0	0	1
Lowe, Robert Hornbuckle	Doddington, Littlegate	Rt	1	0	1
Lowe, William	Bassingfield, Notts	Fr			
Mills, William	....	Fr	0	0	I
Metheringham, John	....	Fr	0	0	1
Roberts, William	....	Fr	0	0	1
Roberts, Thomas	....	Rt	0	0	1
Sheppard, Richard Reckerby	Newark-on-Trent	Fr	0	0	1
Walster, Thomas	....	Rt	0	0	1
Withers, George	....	Fr	0	0	1
Wilson, William	Balderton-grange	Fr	0	0	1
White, John	....	Rt	0	0	1

Easton.

Name of Elector.	Residence, if out of the Parish.	Qual.	T.	W.	P.
Andrews, George	Easton-lodge	Rt	1	0	1
Cholmeley, Sir Montague John, bart.	Easton-house	Fr			

Easton—continued.

Name of Elector.	Residence, if out of the Parish.	Qual.	T.	W.	P.
Houghton, John	....	Rt	0	0	1
Newton, Thomas	....	Rt	0	0	1

Foston.

Name of Elector.	Residence, if out of the Parish.	Qual.	T.	W.	P.
Atkinson, Richard	....	Rt	1	0	1
Barnes, Edward	North Collingham	Co	1	1	0
Barrand, George	....	Co	0	0	1
Brown, John	....	Co	0	0	1
Barnsdale, Lancelot	Claypole	Co			
Brewster, Samuel	Westborough	Co			
Bullimore, Edward	....	Fr	0	0	1
Dolby, Joseph	....	Rt	1	0	1
Fowler, William	Allington	Co	0	1	1
Guy, John	Foston	Fr	0	1	1
Guy, Thomas	Honington	Co	1	0	0
Hindson, Daniel	....	Co	0	0	1
Hoyes, William	Allington	Fr	1	0	1
Holland, John	St. Neots	Co			
Holles, Thomas	....	Co	1	0	1
Hutchinson, John	....	Rt	1	0	1
Hodson, Thomas	Allington	Fr	1	0	1
Knight, John	....	Co	1	0	1
King, Abraham	....	Co	0	1	1
Leadenham, Edward	Alverton	Co	1	0	0
Massey, Thomas Hacket	Oxford-square, Paddington, Middlesex	Fr	0	0	1
Massey, Robert Marsden	Oxford-square, Paddington, Middlesex	Fr	0	0	1
Oliver, William	....	Rt	0	0	1
Poole, Winter Cupage	Little Gonerby	Co	1	0	1
Richards, James	....	Co	0	0	1
Rose, Thomas Berry	Allington	Co	0	0	1
Ridley, James Mosley	Newark	Fr	0	0	1
Seiles, John	Marston	Co	1	1	0
Steel, George	Lincoln	Co			
Winter, William	Allington	Co			
Winter, Daniel	Foston	Co	0	0	1
Weightman, Henry	Averham	Co	1	0	1
Winter, Robert	....	Co	1	0	1

Great Gonerby.

Name of Elector.	Residence, if out of the Parish.	Qual.	T.	W.	P.
Adcock, James	Grantham	Rt			
Brown, Thomas	....	Rt	1	1	0
Brewin, Francis	....	Fr	1	0	1
Brewster, Willinm	Grantham	Fr	1	1	0
Brown, Thomas	69, Gloucester-place, Portman-square, London	Fr			
Brown, William	Marston	Fr	1	1	0
Bennett, William	....	Fr	0	0	1
Cox, John	....	Rt	1	1	0
Eminson, Thomas	....	Fr	1	1	0
Eminson, Thomas John Timm	....	Fr	1	1	0
Fisher, Robert, esq.	....	Rt	1	1	0
Gamble, Richard	....	Fr	1	1	0
Graham, Joseph	....	Rt	1	1	0
Goodson, William	....	Fr	1	0	1
Green, Richard	Metheringham	Fr			
Hough, Edward Lynch	Grantham	Fr	1	1	0
Holmes, William	....	Rt	1	0	1
Holland, John	St. Neots	Fr	1	1	0
Harding, Thomas	....	Rt	1	1	0
Inman, Rev. William Charles	....	Fr	1	1	0
Kenney, Thomas	Hough-on-the-hill	Fr			
Kewney, George *Solicitor*	North Shields	Fr			
Kelham, Robert Kelham, esq.	Bleasby	Fr	1	1	0
Leeson, Thomas	....	Fr	1	0	1
Linnell, James	....	Rt	1	1	0
Lynn, Robert	Stroxton	Fr	1	1	0
Lord, Joseph	....	Rt	1	1	0
Marratt, Thomas	....	Rt	1	1	0
Moggs, Joseph	Claypole	Fr			
Nevitt, James	....	Fr	1	1	0
Ostler, John Lely, esq.	Grantham	Fr	0	1	1
Ogden, James	....	Rt	1	1	0
Poole, Joseph	....	Fr	1	0	1
Pindard, James	Little Gonerby	Fr			

Great Gonerby—continued.

Name of Elector.	Residence, if out of the Parish.	Qual.	T.	W.	P.
Pinner, George	....	Rt	1	1	0
Poole, William	....	Fr	1	1	0
Poole, James	....	Fr	1	1	0
Potchett, Rev. William	Grantham	Fr			
Pulling, Thomas, jun.	....	Rt	1	1	0
Pulling, Thomas, sen.	....	Rt			
Shelbourn, Thomas	....	Fr	1	0	1
Tenny, John Thomas	the land of Green Ginger, Hull	Fr	*Solicitor*		
Treadgold, John Reckerby	....	Fr	0	0	1
Treadgold, Thomas George	....	Fr	1	0	1
Webster, Jasper	Manthorpe	Rt	1	1	0
Wood, William	Grantham	Fr			
White, John, *Clerk*	Grayingham	Fr	1	1	0

Grantham.

Name of Elector.	Residence, if out of the Parish.	Qual.	T.	W.	P.
Andrews, Christopher Robert *Clerk*	Hough	Fr			
Amos, John	....	Fr	0	1	1
Andrews, Rev. J. N.	Baston	Fr	1	1	0
Bestwick, Richard Samuel	....	Fr	1	1	0
Brooks, James	....	Fr	0	0	1
Brewster, Edward	....	Fr	1	0	0
Bishell, Thomas	....	Fr	0	0	1
Brett, George	Little Gonerby	Fr	0	1	1
Burbidge, John Fowler	....	Fr	1	1	0
Brooks, Thomas	....	Fr	0	1	1
Caborn, John	Denton	Fr	1	1	0
Corbett, George	London	Fr			
Clark, Abraham	Little Gonerby	Fr	1	1	0
Clark, William	....	Fr			
Eminson, James	Great Gonerby	Fr	1	1	0
Flewker, John, esq. *Solicr*	Derby	Fr	1	1	0
Flewker, James	Derby	Fr			
Gamble, Richard	....	Fr	1	1	0
Greenwood, Edward	Denton	Fr			
Hardy, John	....	Fr	1	1	0
Healy, George *Sol*	....	Fr	0	0	1
Hunt, John	Little Gonerby	Fr	1	1	0
Holt, John	London	Fr	0	0	1
Houghton, Naaman	....	Fr	1	0	1

Grantham—continued.

Name of Elector.	Residence, if out of the Parish.	Qual.	T.	W.	P.
Hill, Henry	London	Fr			
Jeans, James William *F.R.S.*...		Fr	0	0	1
King, Robert	....	Fr			
Litchford, Robert *Sol*	Partney	Fr	*dead*		
Manton, Joseph	....	Fr	0	0	1
Morris, James	....	Fr	1	1	0
Morley, Thomas	....	Fr	0	1	1
Newham, John	....	Fr	0	0	1
Nicholson, Jeremiah	London	Fr			
Newbatt, Edward	Sleaford	Fr			
Potchett, Rev. William	....	Fr	1	1	0
Pape, John	....	Fr	1	1	0
Parkinson, William	London	Fr			
Quintin St. Matthew, Chitty Downes, Colonel 17th Lancers		Fr			
Ridge, Samuel	....	Fr	1	1	0
Rumsey, James	Leeds	Fr			
Scarborough, John	....	Fr	0	1	1
Summerby, William	....	Fr	0	0	1
Smith, William	....	Fr	1	1	0
Soper, Richard	Farringdon	Fr			
Tindall, John	Little Hale	Fr			
Turner, Robert *Esq*	....	Fr	0	0	1
Thompson, Henry	....	Fr	0	1	1
Thompson, Jabez	....	Fr	0	0	1
Wagstaffe, William Goodwin *Solicitor*	....	Fr	1	1	0
White, George, esq. *Solicitor*...		Fr	*dead*		
Wogdon, John	....	Fr	0	0	1
Wilson, George	Little Gonerby	Fr	0	1	1
Wiseman, Henry	....	Fr	1	0	1
Whichcote, Rev. Christopher	Aswarby	Fr			
Wood, William	....	Fr	1	1	0
Welby, Sir Glynne Earle, bart	Denton	Fr			

Gunby.

Name of Elector.	Residence, if out of the Parish.	Qual.	T.	W.	P.
Christian, Robert	Sewstern	Rt	0	0	1
Doubleday, Henry	North Witham	Rt	1	1	0

Gunby—continued.

Name of Elector.	Residence, if out of the Parish.	Qual.	T.	W.	P.
Lee, David	....	Rt	0	0	1
Rimington, Thomas	Sewstern	Fr			
Royce, Francis	....	Rt	0	0	1
Selby, Philip	....	Rt	1	1	0
Selby, Thomas	....	Rt	0	0	1
Smith, William	....	Fr	1	0	1

Harrowby.

Name of Elector.	Residence, if out of the Parish.	Qual.	T.	W.	P.
Burrows, William	....	Rt	1	0	1
Eaton, William *Mayor of*	Grantham	Rt	1	0	1
Gething, Edward	Hawton	Rt	1	1	0
Hardwicke, John	Grantham	Rt	0	0	1
Johnston, Robert Henry	Grantham *Solicitor*	Rt	1	1	0
Ryder, The Honourable Frederick, Dudley	Teklefield House, near Hitchin	Fr			

Haceby.

Name of Elector.	Residence, if out of the Parish.	Qual.	T.	W.	P.
Calcraft, Rev. John Neville	....	Fr	1	1	0
Lupton, Joseph	....	Rt	1	1	0
Muxlow, Audley	Dembleby	Rt	1	1	0

Harlaxton.

Name of Elector.	Residence, if out of the Parish.	Qual.	T.	W.	P.
Hemsley, Henry	....	Rt	0	0	1
Hardwick, Henry	....	Rt	1	0	1
Mirehouse, Rev. Henry	St. George's-hill, Somersetshire	Fr			
Mashiter, Octavius, esq.	Priests Romford	Fr			
Palethorpe, Richard	....	Rt	1	1	0
Palethorpe, John	....	Rt	1	0	1
Pullen, James	....	Fr	1	0	1
Robinson, Thomas	....	Rt	0	0	1
Rose, John	....	Rt	1	1	0
Scorror, John	....	Rt	0	0	1
Vincent, Thomas	....	Rt	1	0	1
Woodruffe, George	....	Rt			

Haydor, Aisby, and Oasby.

Name of Elector.	Residence, if out of the Parish.	Qual.	T.	W.	P.
Collishaw, John	Aisby	Rt	1	1	0
Deedes, Rev. Gordon Frederick	Haydor	Fr	1	1	0
Houblon, John Archer, esq.	Hallingbury-place, Essex	Fr			

Haydor, Aisby, and Oasby,—continued.

Name of Elector.	Residence, if out of the Parish.	Qual.	T.	W.	P.
Hoyes, William	Oasby	Rt	1	1	0
Hedworth, Thomas	Ditto	Rt	1	1	0
King, George	Culverthorpe	Rt			
Lane, Miles	Oasby	Rt	1	1	0
Parker, Thomas	Haydor-quarry	Rt	0	1	0
Smith, Thorpe	Oasby	Rt			
Selby, John	Aisby	Rt	1	1	0
Selby, Matthew	Ditto	Rt	1	1	0
Thompson, John Grundy Harvey	Haydor-lodge	Rt	0	1	1
Wakefield, Thomas	Oasby	Rt	1	1	0

Hough-on-the-Hill, Brandon, and Gelston.

Name of Elector.	Residence, if out of the Parish.	Qual.	T.	W.	P.
Andrews, Rev. Christopher Robert	Hough	Fr	1	1	0
Bailey, John Edward	Gelston	Rt	1	0	1
Barker, John	Ditto	Fr	1	1	0
Bell, John	Hough	Fr	1	1	0
Chapman, Thomas	Ditto	Fr	0	0	1
Carr, John Dunderdale	Gelston	Rt	1	1	0
Collin, Thomas	Ditto	Rt	1	1	0
Cucksey, Frederick Wm.	Hough	Rt	1	1	0
Freeston, William	Ditto	Fr	1	1	0
Hart, Francis, Esq.	Nottingham	Fr			
Kenney, Thomas	Hough	Fr	1	1	0
Lord, Richard	Ditto	Rt			
Lord, Thomas	Ditto	Rt	1	1	0
Lord, Richard, jun.	Ditto	Rt	1	1	0
Lilley, William	Brandon	Rt	0	0	1
Mitton, William	Hough	Rt	1	1	0
Minta, William	Ditto	Rt	1	1	0
Morley, William	Marston	Fr	1	1	0
Mason, William Minnitt	Wold Newton	Fr	1	0	1
Noel, Rev. Leland	Exton	Fr	1	0	0
Robinson, William, jun.	Brandon	Fr	0	0	1
Robinson, Frederick	Ditto	Fr	1	1	0
Robinson, A. Rudkin	Hough	Fr	0	1	1
Richardson, William	Ditto	Rt	1	1	0
Rowe, Edward	Ditto	Rt	1	1	0
Simpson, John	Ditto	Fr	0	0	1
Stevenson, William	Grantham	Fr	0	0	1

Hough-on-the-Hill, Brandon, and Gelston,—continued.

Name of Elector.	Residence, if out of the Parish.	Qual.	T.	W.	P.
Shelbourn, Edward	Ashridge	Rt			
Stuffin, William	Brandon	Fr	0	0	1
Stuffin, John	Gelston	Fr	0	0	1
Vere, James, esq.	United University Club House, Pall-mall East, Suffolk-street, Middlesex	Fr			
Watson, Joseph	Hough	Fr	0	0	1
Walton, Robert	Gelston	Fr	0	0	1
Wright, Joseph	Hough	Fr	1	0	0

Hougham.

Name of Elector.	Residence, if out of the Parish.	Qual.	T.	W.	P.
Broadhead, John	....	Rt	1	1	0
Brown, Robert Francis	....	Rt			
Briggs, Reuben	Horncastle	Fr	0	0	1
Farmer, William	....	Rt	1	1	0
Hickson, Richard	....	Rt	1	1	0
Manners, Thomas, esq.	Grantham	Fr			
Milnes, Robert, esq.	South Collingham	Fr			
Parke, Charles James	....	Rt	1	1	0
Parkins, William	....	Fr	1	1	0
Scott, Thomas	....	Rt	1	1	0
Thorold, Rev. H. Baugh	....	Fr	1	1	0

Honington.

Name of Elector.	Residence, if out of the Parish.	Qual.	T.	W.	P.
Billiatt, John	....	Rt	1	1	0
Coles, Rev. Thomas Henry, D.D.	....	Fr			
Sills, George	....	Rt			

Hungerton and Wyville.

Name of Elector.	Residence, if out of the Parish.	Qual.	T.	W.	P.
Dickenson, John	Wyville	Rt	1	0	0
Lord, Robert	Hungerton	Rt	1	0	0
Nicholls, John	Ditto	Rt	1	1	0
Rose, Thomas	Wyville	Rt	1	0	0
Staniland, George	Ditto	Rt	1	1	0
Tyler, William	Ditto	Rt	1	0	0
Woodruff, Richard	Hungerton	Rt	1	0	1

Little Humby.

Name of Elector.	Residence, if out of the Parish.	Qual.	T.	W.	P.
Bateman, Richard	Bicker	Rt	1	1	0
Bateman, John	... .	Rt	1	1	0

Little Humby—continued.

Name of Elector.	Residence, if out of the Parish.	Qual.	T.	W.	P.
Doughty, Richard	....	Rt	1	1	0
Doughty, William	....	Rt	0	0	1
Needham, Jeremiah	....	Rt	1	1	0

Ingoldsby.

Name of Elector.	Residence, if out of the Parish.	Qual.	T.	W.	P.
Alexander, Richard	....	Rt	0	0	1
Alexander, Anthony	....	Rt			
Curtis, William	....	Rt	0	0	1
Dawson, John	....	Rt	0	0	1
Hildyard, Rev. James	....	Fr	1	0	1
Hall, William	....	Rt	0	0	1
Howitt, John	....	Rt	0	0	1
Hack, Robert	Buckminster, Leicestershire	Rt	1	0	1
Mitton, William John	....	Fr	1	0	1
Needham, William	....	Rt	0	0	1
Pick, Austin	....	Rt	0	0	1
Palmer, William	....	Rt	0	0	1
Poole, John	....	Rt	0	0	1
Sharpe, John Watson	....	Rt	0	0	1
Thompson, James	....	Rt	0	1	1
Wood, James	....	Rt	1	0	1

Keisby.

Name of Elector.	Residence, if out of the Parish.	Qual.	T.	W.	P.
Anniss, John	....	Rt	0	0	1
Houghton, William	....	Rt	1	0	1
Houghton, Henry	....	Rt	1	0	1

Lenton and Hanby.

Name of Elector.	Residence, if out of the Parish.	Qual.	T.	W.	P.
Hoyes, William Keyworth	Hanby	Rt	1	0	1
Heathcote, Rev. Thomas	Lenton	Fr	0	0	1
Lawrence, Austin	Ditto	Rt	0	0	1
Lynn, John	Ditto	Rt	1	0	1
Pepper, John	Ditto	Rt	0	0	1
Rudkin, Henry	Hanby	Rt			
Scarborough, William	Ditto	Rt	0	0	1

Londonthorpe.

Name of Elector.	Residence, if out of the Parish.	Qual.	T.	W.	P.
Brackenbury, Richard	Londonthorpe-heath	Rt	1	1	0
Brackenbury, William	....	Rt	1	1	0
Eminson, Richard	....	Rt			
Garvey, Rev. Charles	Manthorpe	Fr			

Londonthorpe—continued.

Name of Elector.	Residence, if out of the Parish.	Qual.	T.	W.	P.
Palmer, Charles	Londonthorpe-mill	Rt	1	1	0
Potchett, Rev. William	Grantham	Fr			
Palmer, William Goode	Nottingham	Rt	1	1	0
Watson, Henry	. . . .	Rt	1	1	0

Marston.

Brown, Thomas	. . . .	Rt	1	0	1
Crow, John	. . . .	Rt	1.	1	0
Farmer, Thomas	. . . .	Rt	1	1	0
Farmer, James	ChapelTown, Yorks	Fr			
Goulson, Page	. . . .	Rt	1	1	0
Haughton, John	. . . .	Fr	1	1	0
Lane, Marshall	Denton	Fr	1	1	0
Leighton, William	. . . .	Rt	1	1	0
Mason, George Draper	. . . .	Rt	1	1	0
Treadgold, Robert	. . . .	Rt			
Watson, John	Grantham	Fr	1	1	0
Worth, William	. . . .	Rt	1	1	0

Manthorpe and Little Gonerby.

Barlow, Robert	Little Gonerby	Fr	0	0	1
Buzley, John George	Ditto	Fr	0	0	1
Burton, Thomas	Ditto	Fr	0	0	1
Buzley, William	Quadring	Fr			
Baker, William	Little Gonerby	Fr	1	1	0
Bushby, James	No.11,James'-place, St. John's-road, Hoxton	Fr			
Brett, George	Little Gonerby	Fr			
Chambers, Charles	Ditto	Fr	0	0	1
Coultas, James	Ditto	Fr	1	1	0
Cooper, Thomas	Ditto	Fr	0	0	1
Cooper, Thomas	Ditto	Fr	1	1	0
Cooper, Brittain	Ditto	Fr	1	1	0
Cooper, John	Grantham	Fr	1	1	0
Chesman, George Easton	Little Gonerby	Fr	1	0	1
Dixon, Thomas	Grantham	Fr	1	0	1
Draper, George	Little Gonerby	Fr			
Garvey, Rev. Charles	Manthorpe	Fr	1	1	0
Garratt, Robert	Little Gonerby	Fr	1	1	0

Manthorpe and Little Gonerby—continued.

Name of Elector.	Residence, if out of the Parish.	Qual.	T.	W.	P.
Green, Joseph	Little Gonerby	Fr	1	0	1
Green, John	Spittlegate	Fr	0	1	1
Healey, Anthony	Little Gonerby	Fr	0	0	1
Harding, Edward	Ditto	Fr	1	0	1
Holt, William George	Long Bennington	Fr			
Hutchinson, Simon	Manthorpe-lodge	Fr	1	1	0
Hobbs, Robert	Little Gonerby	Fr	1	0	1
Hutchins, Rev. Richard William	East Bridgford	Fr			
Howarth, George	Little Gonerby	Fr	0	0	1
Lloyd, John	Ditto	Fr	0	0	1
Musson, William	Fleet, in Holbeach	Fr	0	0	1
Mitton, Thomas	Marston	Fr			
Morley, William	Barkston	Fr	1	1	0
Morley, Thomas	Hougham	Fr	1	1	0
Morley, Charles	Marston	Fr	1	1	0
Morris, George	Spittlegate	Fr	0	0	1
Parker, John	Little Gonerby	Fr	0	0	1
Redhead, William	Spittlegate	Fr	1	0	1
Robinson, James	Little Gonerby	Fr	0	0	1
Robertson, Frederick Fowler	Bath	Fr			
Scoles, Charles	Grantham	Fr	1	0	1
Short, Richard	Little Gonerby	Fr	0	0	1
Soper, Richard	Farringdon	Fr			
Summerby, William	Grantham	Fr			
Taylor, William	Little Gonerby	Fr			
X Tempest, Rev. Thos. Peter	Ditto	Fr	0	0	1
Vere, James, esq.	United University ClubHouse,Suffolk-street,PallMallEast, Middlesex	Fr			
Walker, John	Grantham	Fr	0	0	1
Waite, James	Spittlegate	Fr			
Wand, William	Grantham	Fr	1	0	1
Ward, Richard	Marston	Fr	1	1	0
Wand, Charles	Grantham	Fr	0	0	1

Normanton.

Name of Elector.	Residence, if out of the Parish.	Qual.	T.	W.	P.
Chapman, Rev. Richard	Rectory	Fr	1	1	0
Cupit, Albert	￼.	Rt	1	1	0

X Roman Priest

Normanton
~~Manthorpe~~—continued.

Name of Elector.	Residence, if out of the Parish.	Qual.	T.	W.	P.
Minta, John	....	Rt	1	1	0
Minta, Thomas	....	Rt	1	1	0
Pulford, William	....	Rt	1	1	0
Pollard, Thomas	....	Rt	1	1	0
Shaw, Christopher	....	Rt	1	1	0
Shaw, Richard	....	Rt	1	1	0
Wadeson, Robert	....	Rt	1	1	0

Pickworth.

Name of Elector.	Residence, if out of the Parish.	Qual.	T.	W.	P.
Beasley, Thomas C. *Esq*	Harston	Fr	1	0	0
Carter, Thomas	....	Fr	0	1	1
Foottit, Richard	....	Rt	0	0	1
Manners, Thomas, esq.	Spittlegate	Fr	.		
Pauling, Stephen	....	Rt	1	1	0
Rimmington, Richard	Spittlegate	Fr	1	1	0
Rimmington, John	....	Rt	1	1	0
Seiles, John	....	Rt	1	1	0
Shields, Thomas	....	Rt	1	1	0
Skipworth, Rev. Thomas	....	Fr			
Tops, John	....	Fr	1	1	0

Great Ponton.

Name of Elector.	Residence, if out of the Parish.	Qual.	T.	W.	P.
Askew, James	....	Rt	0	0	1
Bellamy, Henry	....	Rt	0	0	1
Bellamy, Richard	....	Rt	1	0	1
Blankley, Thomas	Great Ponton-mill	Rt			
Blankley, Frederick	Great Ponton-mill	Rt	0	0	1
Dickinson, Thomas	Great Ponton-lodge	Rt	1	1	0
Dickinson, Jabez	....	Fr	1	0	1
Jackson, John	....	Rt	0	0	1
Knight, Richard	Stamford	Fr	1	0	0
Lee, Thomas	....	Rt	0	0	1
Lord, William	....	Rt			
North, Henry	Buckminster	Fr	0	0	1
Potchett, Rev. Brownlow	....	Fr	1	1	0
Porter, George	....	Fr	0	0	1
Sentance, George	....	Fr	0	0	1
Sentance, John	....	Rt	0	0	1
Wing, Samuel	....	Rt	1	0	1
Weston, Richard	....	Rt	1	0	1
Weston, Samuel	Great Ponton-lodge	Rt	0	0	1

Little Ponton.

Name of Elector.	Residence, if out of the Parish.	Qual.	T.	W.	P.
Atkin, John	....	Rt	1	1	0
Eminson, Thomas	....	Rt	1	1	0
Fane, Vere, esq.	Little Ponton Hall	Rt	1	1	0
Wyles, Thomas	....	Rt	0	1	1
Worsley, Rev. Pennyman Warton	....	Fr	1	1	0
Wyles, Lawrence	....	Rt	0	1	1

Ropsley.

Name of Elector.	Residence, if out of the Parish.	Qual.	T.	W.	P.
Ayre, James	....	Fr	0	1	0
Brothwell, Turnball	Edenham	Fr			
Coke, Rev. John Henry	....	Fr	1	1	0
Clay, William	....	Fr	1	1	0
Collishaw, Richard	Ropsley-heath	Rt	1	1	0
Dennis, John	Sapperton	Fr	1	1	0
Ducker, James	Grantham	Fr			
Eeles, James	....	Fr	1	1	0
Green, William	....	Fr			
Guylee, William	....	Rt	1	1	0
Guylee, William, jun.	....	Rt	1	1	0
Hill, George	....	Rt	1	0	1
Hill, Richard	Ropsley-heath	Rt	1	1	0
Hazlewood, Oliver Hunt	Stamford	Fr			
Howett, Thomas	....	Rt	1	1	0
Isaac, Richard	Aisby	Fr			
Lane Edward	....	Rt	1	1	0
Lane, John	Grantham	Fr	0	0	1
Lane, Joseph	Boothby	Rt	1	1	0
Lewin, Richard	....	Fr	0	0	1
Machears, John	....	Fr	0	1	1
Moor, George	....	Fr	1	1	0
Moor, Frederick	....	Rt	1	1	0
Parker, Henry	....	Rt	1	1	0
Robinson, Thomas	....	Fr	1	1	0
Ross, Henry	....	Fr	0	1	1
Selby, Thomas	....	Rt	1	1	0
Summerfield, George	....	Fr			
Sewards, Francis	Great Gonerby	Fr	1	1	0
Tyler, William	Ancaster	Fr	0	1	1
Wilson, John	Grantham	Fr	1	0	1
Wright, Thomas	....	Fr			

Ropsley—continued.

Name of Elector.	Residence, if out of the Parish.	Qual.	T.	W.	P.
Wass, John	....	Rt	1	1	0
Welbourn, Christopher Edward,	....	Fr	1	1	0

Sapperton.

Bland, Rev. W. Handley	Braceby	Fr	1	1	0
Foster, Henry	....	Rt	1	1	0
Sardeson, John	....	Rt	1	0	1
Wass, Elijah	....	Rt	1	1	0

Sedgebrook.

Ashwell, Michael Sherring	Barrowby	Rt	1	1	0
Brewster, Edmund	....	Rt	1	1	0
Burroughs, Mark	....	Rt	1	1	0
Folkett, Samuel	....	Fr	1	1	0
Monks, William Allen	....	Rt	1	1	0
Robinson, George	....	Rt	1	1	0
Robinson, Richard	....	Rt	1	1	0
Simons, Joseph	....	Fr	1	1	0
Wilson, Rev. Alfred William	Sedgebrook Rectory	Fr	1	1	0

Somerby, Great Humby, and Cold Harbour.

Alcock, John	Spittlegate	Rt	1	0	1
Ashbourne, George	Croxton Lodge	Fr	0	0	1
Andrew, William	Somerby	Rt	1	0	1
Ashbourne, John	Wykeham	Fr	1	0	0
Ayre, John	Somerby	Fr	1	1	0
Bellamy, Thomas	Ditto	Rt	1	1	0
Chapman, Rev. William Emerson	Edenham	Fr	1	0	1
Harris, William	Somerby	Rt	1	1	0
Key, Robert	Ditto	Rt	1	1	0
Matkin, John	Great Humby	Rt	1	1	0
Nixon, Thomas	Great Humby Mill	Rt	0	1	1
Roberts, John	Grantham	Rt	1	1	0
Simpson, George	Cold Harbour	Rt	1	1	0
Sneath, Thomas	Somerby	Rt	1	1	0

Spittlegate, Houghton, and Walton.

Akrill, George	Spittlegate	Fr	0	0	1
Askew, Charles	Grantham	Fr	1	0	1

Spittlegate, Houghton, and Walton—continued.

Name of Elector.	Residence, if out of the Parish.	Qual.	T.	W.	P.
Bakes, William	Spittlegate	Fr	1	0	1
Barnes, John	Ditto	Fr	1	1	0
Bedford, William	Little Gonerby	Fr	1	0	1
Boyall, Richard John	Grantham	Rt	1	1	0
Briggs, James	Ditto	Fr	1	0	1
Burbidge, John Fowler	Ditto	Fr			
Briggs, William	Spittlegate	Fr	1	0	1
Briggs, John	Ditto	Fr	1	1	0
Catlin, Robert	Grantham	Fr	0	0	1
Collingwood, John	Ditto	Fr	.		
Cross, John	Wisbeach	Fr			
Collingwood, James Henry	Grantham	Fr	0	0	1
Ceppi, Dazzio	Ditto	Fr	1	1	0
Dixon, David	Ditto	Fr	0	1	1
Ducker, James	Spittlegate	Fr			
Edwards, John	Ditto	Fr	0	0	1
Everitt, John	Ditto	Fr	0	0	1
Faulkner, Charles	Grantham	Fr	0	1	1
Flower, John	Newark	Fr	1	1	0
Green, John	Grantham	Fr			
Greenwood, James	Spittlegate	Fr	1	0	1
Holton, John	Croxton	Fr			
Holt, Charles	Spittlegate	Fr	1	1	0
Hind, Joseph	Ryhall	Fr	1	0	1
Hole, Samuel, esq.	Caunton-manor	Rt	0	0	1
Hodson, John	Spittlegate	Fr	1	0	1
Hornsby, Richard	Ditto	Fr	1	0	1
Jesson, Rev. Frederick	Ditto	Fr	1	0	1
Johnston, Robert Henry *S.*	Grantham	·Fr			
Kirton, John	Little Gonerby	Fr	1	0	1
King, John Poore *Solicit.*	Grantham	Fr	0	0	1
King, Philip Henry	Ditto	Fr			
Litchford, Robert *Solicit.*	Partney	Fr	*dead*		
Manners, Thomas, esq. *Sol.*	Spittlegate	Fr			
Mitchell, Thomas Henry	Ditto	Fr	1	0	1
Nixon, Edward	Great Ponton	Fr			
Nixon, Charles	Ditto	Fr	1	0	1
Norton, William Fletcher Norton, esq.	Elton	Fr			
Ormond, Richard	Spittlegate	Fr	1	0	1

Spittlegate, Houghton, and Walton—continued.

Name of Elector.	Residence, if out of the Parish.	Qual.	T.	W.	P.
Pawson, George	Grantham	Fr	0	1	1
Pepper, Thomas	Ditto	Fr	0	0	1
Parker, John	Ditto	Fr	1	0	1
Redhead, George	Manthorpe-cum-Little Gonerby	Fr	1	0	1
Roberts, John	Spittlegate	Fr	1	0	1
Russell, Christopher George	Little Gonerby	Fr	0	0	1
Seaman, Isaac, sen.	Marchwood Southampton	Fr			
Sexton, William	Grantham	Fr	0	0	1
Shelbourne, William	Spittlegate	Fr	1	0	1
Smith, James	Harlaxton	Fr	1	1	0
Smith, William	Spittlegate	Fr	1	0	1
Scarborough, Thomas	Grantham	Fr	0	0	1
Smith, Edward	Ditto	Fr	0	0	1
Scarborough, Wilson	Ditto	Fr	1	0	1
Smith, William	Ditto	Fr			
Siddey, George	Spittlegate	Fr	1	0	1
Taylor, Thomas	Grantham	Fr	1	1	0
Taylor, William	Spittlegate	Fr	0	0	1
Tinkler, Thomas	Ditto	Fr			
Thompson, Jabez	Grantham	Fr			
Whyman, William	Spittlegate	Fr			
Weaver, William	Ditto	Fr	0	0	1
Wakefield, Thomas Hawkins	Grantham	Fr	1	1	0
Walton, William Skelton	Bourn	Fr			
Willcock, Luke	Spittlegate	Fr	0	0	1
Wilcox, George	Ditto	Fr	1	0	1
Walkington, William	Grantham	Fr	1	1	0
Waite, James	Spittlegate	Fr	1	0	1
Wyles, Laurence	Grantham	Fr	1	1	0

Stroxton.

Name of Elector	Residence	Qual.	T.	W.	P.
Blankley, Robert	....	Rt			
Hind, William Richard	....	Rt	1	1	0
Voce, Edward	....	Rt	1	1	0

Stubton.

Name of Elector	Residence	Qual.	T.	W.	P.
Clark, Francis	....	Rt	0	0	1

Stubton—continued.

Name of Elector.	Residence, if out of the Parish.	Qual	T.	W.	P.
Clarke, William	. . . .	Rt	0	0	1
Copley, Timothy	. . . .	Rt	0	0	1
Hodgkinson, William	Cotham	Fr			
Nevile, George, esq.	. . . .	Fr	0	0	1
Rastall, Rev. Robert	Winthorpe	Fr			
Rowbottom, Joseph	. . . .	Fr	0	0	1
Robinson, Matthew	. . . .	Rt	0	0	1
Stevenson, Henry	. . . .	Rt	0	0	1

Skillington.

Name of Elector.	Residence, if out of the Parish.	Qual	T.	W.	P.
Bean, Richard	. . . .	Fr	0	0	1
Bennett, William	. . . .	Rt	0	0	1
Briggs, Robert	Horncastle	Fr			
Cottingham, James	Grantham	Fr	1	1	0
Cottingham, Richard	Ditto	Fr	0	0	1
Christian, Thomas	. . . .	Rt	0	0	1
Christian, Robert	Barrow, Rutland	Fr	1	0	0
Glassup, Joseph	Buckminster	Rt	0	0	1
Hawley, Warrener	. . . .	Rt	1	1	0
Kitchen, Anthony	. . . .	Rt	1	1	0
Mackay, Rev. Sween Macdonald	. . . .	Fr	1	1	0
Newton, William	. . . .	Rt	1	0	1
Pickering, John	. . . .	Rt	1	1	0
Tyler, John	. . . .	Rt	0	0	1
Waddington, William, jun.	. . . .	Rt	1	0	0

Stoke Rochford.

Name of Elector.	Residence, if out of the Parish.	Qual	T.	W.	P.
Beeson, Bennett	Stoke-old-park	Rt	1	1	0
Bradford, Robert	Stoke-lodge	Rt			
Cartwright, Rev. Richard Belton	Stoke-rectory	Fr			
Turnor, Christopher, esq.	Stoke-house	Fr	1	1	0

North Stoke.

Name of Elector.	Residence, if out of the Parish.	Qual	T.	W.	P.
Bamber, William	Stoke-grange	Rt	1	1	0
Bagshaw, Henry	Stoke-pasture	Rt	1	1	0

Stainby.

Name of Elector.	Residence, if out of the Parish.	Qual	T.	W.	P.
Culpin, George	. . . .	Rt	1	0	1
Drayton, William	. . . .	Fr	1	0	1

Stainby—continued.

Name of Elector.	Residence, if out of the Parish.	Qual	T.	W.	P.
Dysart, the Earl of	Buckminster Hall	Fr			
Hack, William	Buckminster	Rt	1	0	1
Hack, Lionel	....	Rt	0	0	1
Jackson, William	....	Rt	0	0	1
Osborne, Rev. George	....	Fr	1	1	0
Penford, Thomas	....	Rt	0	0	1
Rudkin, John	....	Rt	0	0	1
Spriggs, John	....	Rt	1	1	0
Weston, William	....	Rt	0	0	1
Weston, Stephen	....	Rt	0	0	1

Syston.

Name of Elector.	Residence, if out of the Parish.	Qual	T.	W.	P.
Atkin, William	Gipple	Rt	1	1	0
Clarke, Samuel	....	Rt	1	1	0
Dolby, William Ashton	....	Rt	1	1	0
Gilbert, Rev. George	Grantham	Fr	1	1	0
Hardy, George	Jericho	Rt	1	1	0
Thorold, Sir John Charles bart.	Syston Hall	Fr	1	1	0

Twyford.

Name of Elector.	Residence, if out of the Parish.	Qual	T.	W.	P.
Barber, Charles Henry	Colsterworth	Fr	1	0	1
Doubleday, Robert	Ditto	Fr	1	0	1
Ferneley, William	....	Fr	1	0	1
Gery, Hugh Wade, Esq.	Bushmead-priory, Bedfordshire	Fr			
Hawley, George	....	Fr	1	0	1
Hibbitt, John	....	Fr			
Harris, William	Woolsthorpe	Fr	1	1 .	0
Lazonby, Paul Henry Clerk	Somerby, near Grantham	Fr	1	1	0
Lynn, John	Stainby	Fr			
Porter, William	....	Rt	0	1	1
Priest, William	....	Fr	0	0	1
Willerton, Robert Taylor	Corby	Fr			

Welby.

Name of Elector.	Residence, if out of the Parish.	Qual	T.	W.	P.
Avery, William	....	Fr	1	1	0
Avery, Francis	....	Rt	1	1	0
Barber, George	....	Rt	1	1	0
Cheetham, John	....	Fr	1	1	0

Welby—continued.

Name of Elector.	Residence, if out of the Parish.	Qual.	T.	W.	P.
Freeman, John	....	Rt	1	1	0
Moulds, George Henry	....	Rt	1	1	0
Otley, Rev. Charles Bethel	....	Fr	1	1	0
Sharpe, William	....	Rt	1	1	0
Sharpe, Frederick	....	Rt	1	1	0
Smith, John	....	Rt	1	0	1
Wilkinson, Joseph	....	Fr	1	1	0
Watson, John	....	Rt	1	0	0
Wyles, Joseph	Grantham	Rt	1	0	1

Westborough.

Name of Elector.	Residence, if out of the Parish.	Qual.	T.	W.	P.
Bradford, Andrew	Westborough-lodge	Rt	0	0	1
Broughton, John	....	Fr	0	0	1
Copley, Richard	....	Rt	0	0	1
Gilbert, James	....	Rt	0	0	1
Hall, Rev. Robert	....	Fr			
Hall, Matthew	Car Coultson	Fr	1	1	0
Johnson, Robert	....	Rt	0	0	1
Lee, Robert	....	Fr			
Lee, John	Little Gonerby	Fr	0	0	1
Minta, Henry	Doddington	Rt	1	1	0
Potts, John	....	Rt	0	0	1
Wilson, George	Kilvington	Fr	0	0	1
Wilson, William	Flawbro'	Fr			
Wilson, James	Hawton	Fr	0	1	1

North Witham and Lobthorpe.

Name of Elector.	Residence, if out of the Parish.	Qual.	T.	W.	P.
Barber, Samuel	North Witham	Rt	1	0	1
Bryan, John	Lobthorpe	Rt	0	0	1
Caparn, Richard Hare	North Witham	Rt	1	0	1
Doubleday, Edward	Duddington	Fr	1	1	0
Doubleday, Henry	North Witham	Rt			
Hardy, John	Witham Common	Le			
Nixon, John	Bridge Casterton	Fr			
Neilson, Rev. Horatio	North Witham	Fr	1	1	0
Preston, Edward	Stretton	Fr	0	0	1
Senescall, Thomas	Lobthorpe	Rt	0	0	1
Seddon, William	North Witham	Rt	0	0	1
Scott, William	Lobthorpe-lodge	Rt	0	0	1
Smith, Jeremiah	Stretton	Fr	0	0	1
White, George	Lobthorpe	Rt			
Young, James	Kingerby	Fr			

South Witham.

Name of Elector.	Residence, if out of the Parish.	Qual.	T.	W.	P.
Abbott, William	....	Fr	0	0	1
Adcock, Josiah	....	Fr	1	1	0
Brian, Thomas	Lobthorpe	Fr	0	0	1
Boss, William	Wymondham	Fr	1	1	0
Bright, Benjamin Priest-man	Sewstern	Fr			
Collin, Parker	Swayfield	Fr	0	0	1
Coverley, Lawrence	....	Fr			
Cooper, John	....	Rt	0	0	1
Dring, George	....	Fr	1	0	1
Dring, William	....	Fr	1	1	0
Dunmore, Robert	....	Fr	0	0	1
Eaglesfield, William	Greetham, Rutland	Fr	1	0	1
Fowler, John	....	Fr	1	0	1
Fludyer, William, esq.	Ayston	Fr	1	1	0
George, Richard Whitehead	St. Mary's, Stamford	Fr	1	1	0
Hardy, George	Thistleton	Fr	1	1	0
Hilton, John	....	Fr	1	0	0
Hardy, John	North Witham	Fr			
Harris, John	Little Bytham	Fr			
Lank, James	....	Fr	1	1	0
Linney, John	Thistleton	Fr	1	0	0
Pearson, William	....	Rt	0	0	1
Priestman, John	....	Fr	0	0	1
Rayson, Thomas	Westbray-lodge, King's Cliffe	Fr	1	1	0
Scarborough, James	....	Rt	0	1	1
Spriggs, John	....	Fr	1	0	1
Selby, Robert	....	Rt	1	0	1
Thorpe, Edward	Tinwell	Fr	1	1	0
Tollemache, Rev. Ralph. William Lionel	....	Fr	1	1	0
Wyles, Thomas	Little Ponton	Fr			
Wildman, William	....	Fr	1	1	0
Whyman, Dan. Ebenezer	....	Fr	1	0	1
Walker, Joseph	....	Fr	0	0	1
Wootton, John	....	Fr	1	0	1

Woolsthorpe, near Belvoir.

Name of Elector.	Residence, if out of the Parish.	Qual.	T.	W.	P.
Clarke, John	Bescaby	Fr	1	1	0

Woolsthorpe, near Belvoir—continued.

Name of Elector.	Residence, if out of the Parish.	Qual.	T.	W.	P.
Dickenson, John	Woolsthorpe-lodge	Fr	1	1	0
Hand, John Downing	....	Rt	1	1	0
Kemp, Eustace	....	Rt	1	1	0
Lovitt, Richard	....	Rt	1	1	0
Palmer, Rev. Philip Hall	....	Fr	1	1	0
Prince, Joseph	Barrowby Stenwith	Fr			
Thompson, Edward	Somerby	Fr			

No. 5.—POLLING DISTRICT ASSIGNED TO SWINDERBY.

Bassingham.

Name of Elector.	Residence, if out of the Parish.	Qual.	T.	W.	P.
Alvey, Thomas	Armthorpe, Yorkshire	Fr	0	1	0
Ashley, William Edward	Newark	Fr	0	0	1
Bartholomew, William	....	Rt	1	1	0
Beedham, William	....	Fr			
Blow, Thomas	....	Fr	0	0	1
Bradley, Gervaise	Carlton-le-Morland	Fr	0	1	0
Brocklebank, John	Carlton-le-Morland	Fr	1	1	0
Burnside, Rev. John	Plumptree, Notts	Fr			
Boaler, Joseph	Worksop	Fr			
Challens, Thomas	....	Fr	1	1	0
Cottingham, John	Snarford	Fr	0	0	1
Cucksey, Frederick William	Hough-on-the-Hill	Fr			
Donson, William	....	Fr	1	1	0
Dalton, Robert	....	Fr	1	1	0
Daubney, John	Navenby	Fr			
Fryer, Francis	Coddington	Fr	0	0	1
Freeman, John	....	Fr	0	1	0
Fytche, John Lewis, esq.	Thorpe Hall	Fr			
Goodwin, Francis	North Hykeham	Fr			
Gresham, William	Lincoln	Fr	0	0	1
Hodgkinson, Frederick Scott	Clipstone	Fr			
Hammond, John	....	Fr			
Hart, Charles	....	Fr	0	1	0
Holmes, Joseph	....	Fr	1	1	0
Harris, John	....	Fr	0	0	1

Bassingham—continued.

Name of Elector.	Residence, if out of the Parish.	Qual.	T.	W.	P.
Holmes, William	....	Fr	1	1	0
Hollis, William	....	Fr	0	0	1
Johnson, Thomas	....	Rt	1	1	0
Knight, Thomas	Broughton	Fr	1	1	0
Marfleet, Edward	Boothby	Fr			
Marfleet, Charles Barber	....	Fr	1	1	0
Marshall, George	Newark	Fr	0	0	1
Martin, John	....	Fr	0	1	1
Morley, Richard Newcomb	....	Rt	1	1	0
Newbut, Joseph	....	Fr			
Newton, Thomas	....	Fr	1	1	0
Parnell, John Jessop	Waltham Abbey	Fr			
Pickard, John	....	Rt	0	1	1
Pacey, John	....	Rt	0	0	1
Reynolds, Pool	....	Fr	0	0	1
Rogers, Joseph	....	Fr	1	1	0
Rogers, Samuel	Faldingworth	Fr			
Rogers, George	....	Fr	0	1	1
Rogers, Charles	....	Fr	0	1	0
Rogers, John	....	Fr	1	1	0
Read, William	....	Fr	0	1	1
Rogers, Matthew	16, Cheapside, London	Fr			
Robinson, Thomas	....	Fr	1	1	0
Robinson, William	....	Fr	1	1	0
Sewards, John	....	Rt	1	1	0
Smith, John	....	Fr	0	1	1
Storr, William	....	Fr	0	0	1
Storr, Edward	....	Fr	0	0	1
Singleton, David	....	Fr	0	1	0
Stuart, George	....	Fr	1	1	0
Tuxford, James	Thurlby	Fr			
Theaker, William	Carlton-le-Morland	Fr			
Taylor, William	Baumber	Fr	0	0	1
Uffindall, William	....	Fr	1	1	0
Weightman, Hugh	....	Fr	1	1	0
Woolhouse, Joseph	Ingham	Fr			
Worsdall, Albine	....	Fr	0	1	1
Worsdall, John	....	Fr	0	1	1

Boultham.

Name of Elector	Residence	Qual.	T.	W.	P.
Dalton, Henry	....	Rt	1	1	0

Boultham—continued.

Name of Elector.	Residence, if out of the Parish.	Qual.	T.	W.	P.
Ellison, Lieut - Colonel Richard	Boultham-hall	Fr	1	1	0
Ellison, Henry, esq.	Teddington, Middlesex	Fr			
Jackson, William	Lincoln	Rt	1	1	0
Johnson, Benjamin	....	Rt	1	1	0
Newmarsh, Rev. Henry	Hessell, near Hull	Fr			
Pearson, James	Lincoln	Rt	1	1	0
Thurman, John	....	Rt	1	1	0
Watson, James	Lincoln	Rt	1	1	0

Carlton-le-Morland.

Name of Elector.	Residence, if out of the Parish.	Qual.	T.	W.	P.
Anderson, John	South Collingham	Fr	0	0	1
Bailey, John	....	Fr	1	1	0
Brocklebank, William	....	Fr			
Brocklebank, Joseph	....	Fr			
Booth, Conyers	....	Rt	1	1	0
Drury, John	Gamston	Fr	1	1	0
Dunn, Thomas	Brant Broughton	Fr			
Goy, Matthew	St. Martin's, Lincoln	Fr	0	0	1
Hall, Samuel	....	Fr	0	1	1
Hayward, John	St. Martin's, Lincoln	Fr	1	1	0
Hayward, William Knight	....	Rt			
Hill, George John	....	Co	1	1	0
Holmes, Joseph	Brant Broughton	Co	1	1	0
Hutchinson, John	....	Co			
Keep, William	....	Rt	0	1	1
Merrill, Joseph	Gainsborough	Co	0	0	1
Pigott, John	....	Fr	1	1	0
Stevenson, Benjamin	Bassingham	Fr	0	1	0
Swann, James Butler	Heapham	Fr			
Taylor, James	....	Rt	1	1	0
Tonge, Morris	....	Rt	1	1	0
Wade, John	....	Fr	1	1	0
Willoughby, Rev. George Percival	....	Fr	1	1	0

Doddington, near Lincoln.

Name of Elector.	Residence, if out of the Parish.	Qual.	T.	W.	P.
Clements, John	....	Rt	1	1	0
Jarvis, Rev. Charles Macquarie George	....	Fr	1	1	0

Doddington, near Lincoln—continued.

Name of Elector.	Residence, if out of the Parish.	Qual.	T.	W.	P.
Jarvis, George Knollis, esq.	Doddington-hall	Fr			
Marriott, John	....	Rt			
Marriott, Joseph	....	Rt	1	1	0
Mimmack, John	....	Rt			
Nesbitt, John	....	Rt	1	1	0
Noden, Samuel	....	Rt	1	1	0
Pickworth, Benjamin	....	Rt	1	1	0
Starkey, George	....	Rt	1	1	0
Wilkinson, George	....	Rt	1	1	0

Eagle, Eagle-Hall, and Eagle Woodhouse.

Name of Elector.	Residence, if out of the Parish.	Qual.	T.	W.	P.
Argyle, Benjamin	Eagle-hall	Fr	0	0	1
Barlow, Samuel	Eagle	Co	1	1	0
Brown, John	Ditto	Rt	0	1	0
Cater, Gervaise	St. Martin's, Lincoln	Fr	1	1	0
Colton, Thomas	North Collingham	Co	1	1	0
Colton, Thomas Boot	Eagle-hall	Rt	1	1	0
Cuts, William	Eagle	Co	0	1	0
Crosby, John	Ditto	Fr	0	1	0
Doncaster, Thomas	Newark	Co	0	1	0
Drury, Samuel	Eagle	Fr	0	1	0
Drury, John	Housham	Co			
Daft, George	Eagle	Co	1	1	0
Fenton, John	Ditto	Co			
Huddleston, George	Lincoln	Fr	1	1	0
Hittersay, James	Skirbeck, Boston	Co	1	1	0
Hittersay, John	Brough, Notts	Co	1	1	0
Ingilby, The Rev. Henry John	Ripley-castle, York- shire	Fr			
Lambert, Esau	Eagle	Co	1	1	0
Maltby, William	Ditto	Co	0	0	1
Merryweather, Thomas	Ditto	Co	1	1	0
Nevile, Henry, esq.	Walcot	Fr			
Patchett, Thomas	Eagle	Co	1	1	0
Petch, William	Searby	Co	0	0	1
Pennington, John	Eagle Woodhouse	Rt	1	1	0
Porter, William	Eagle	Fr	0	0	1
Simpson, Robert	Hackthorne	Co			
Smith, John	Eagle	Co	1	0	1
Snow, William	Lincoln	Co			

Eagle, Eagle Hall, and Eagle Woodhouse—continued.

Name of Elector.	Residence, if out of the Parish.	Qual.	T.	W.	P.
Smith, Alfred	Gainsborough	Co			
Smith, William Thomas	Eagle	Co	0	0	1
Spencer, George	Ditto	Co	1	1	0
Taylor, John	Ditto	Fr			
Welch, William	Wigsley	Fr			
Waddington, George	Eagle	Fr	0	1	0

Haddington.

Name of Elector.	Residence, if out of the Parish.	Qual.	T.	W.	P.
Brown, William	....	Rt	1	1	0
Lambe, Edward	....	Rt	1	1	0
Wood, William	....	Rt	1	1	0

North Hykeham.

Name of Elector.	Residence, if out of the Parish.	Qual.	T.	W.	P.
Bartholomew, John	....	Rt	1	1	0
Bellamy, John	....	Fr	1	1	0
Bemrose, John	....	Co	1	0	1
Bemrose, Robert	....	Fr	1	0	1
Blow, Samuel	St. Benedict's, Lincoln	Fr	0	0	1
Cooper, Edward Allington	Horncastle	Fr			
Clarke, Richard	....	Rt	0	1	1
Collingwood, John	....	Fr			
Coult, Robert	....	Fr	1	1	0
Coult, John	....	Fr	1	1	0
Coult, Samuel	....	Co	1	1	0
Coupland, George	Swinderby	Co	0	0	1
Dickinson, Thomas	....	Rt	1	1	0
Faulkner, Philip Richard	Newark *Sol*	Fr			
Garvey, Rev. Richard	Vicar's-court, Lincoln	Fr	1	1	0
Gibson, Robert	....	Co	1	1	0
Glenn, John Hyslop	3, Magpie-square, Lincoln	Fr	0	0	1
Goodwin, John	....	Co	1	1	0
Goodwin, Francis	....	Fr			
Gibson, Willie	Thorpe-on-the-Hill	Co	1	1	0
Grubb, John	Swinethorpe	Co			
Glasier, George	St. Martin's, Lincoln	Co			
Glasier, Samuel	South Hykeham	Co			
Grubb, James	....	Fr	1	1	0
Hall, Rev. John	Horncastle	Fr			
Heanley, Robert	....	Fr	1	1	0

North Hykeham—continued.

Name of Elector.	Residence, if out of the Parish.	Qual.	T.	W.	P.
Hiley, John	....	Co	1	0	1
Johnson, William	....	Fr	1	1	0
Johnson, Joseph	....	Fr	1	1	0
Johnson, James	....	Fr	0	1	1
Johnson, Edward	....	Rt	1	1	0
King, John	....	Fr	1	1	0
Longmate, William	....	Fr	0	1	0
Lascelles, John	....	Rt	1	1	0
Long, Henry Benjamin Holmes	East-gate, Lincoln	Fr	1	1	0
Marshall, William	....	Co	1	1	0
Oates, Frederick William	Barlings *2y.*	Fr	0	0	1
Palmer, Edward Richard Hopper Griffith, *Clerk*	Blind-street, Horn-castle ×	Fr			
Padley, Rev. Augustus F.	East-gate, Lincoln	Fr	1	1	0
Robinson, Rev. William	Blind-street, Horn-castle	Fr			
Richardson, Walter	Tring Railway Station	Fr			
Roe, John	....	Rt	0	1	1
Shuttleworth, John	....	Fr	1	1	0
Shuttleworth, Thomas	....	Co	1	1	0
Thorpe, William	St. Botolph's, Lincoln	Fr	1	1	0
Trotter, Theodore	....	Rt	1	1	0
Welbourn, John	....	Fr	1	1	0

South Hykeham.

Name of Elector.	Residence, if out of the Parish.	Qual.	T.	W.	P.
Gratton, David	....	Rt	1	1	0
Glasier, Samuel	....	Rt	1	1	0
Roe, Robert	....	Rt	1	1	0
Roe, George Roadley	....	Rt	1	1	0
Smith, George	....	Rt	1	1	0

Norton Disney.

Name of Elector.	Residence, if out of the Parish.	Qual.	T.	W.	P.
Astling, Henry	....	Rt	1	1	0
Burnaby, Thomas Fowke Andrew, esq. *Sol*	Newark	Fr	1	1	0
Blundy, Thomas	....	Rt	1	1	0
Gilbert, John	....	Rt	1	1	0
Grosse, Thomas	....	Rt	1	1	0
Hitch, Robert	....	Rt	1	1	0
Kirk, William	....	Rt	1	1	0

× Vicar of Nackt Somercotes

Norton Disney—continued.

Name of Elector.	Residence, if out of the Parish.	Qual.	T.	W.	P.
Lynn, William	....	Rt	1	1	0
Lynn, John	....	Rt	1	1	0
Lynn, Robert	....	Rt	1	1	0
Rogers, William	....	Rt	1	1	0
Sewards, John	....	Rt	1	1	0

North Scarle.

Name of Elector.	Residence, if out of the Parish.	Qual.	T.	W.	P.
Atkinson, Robert	....	Co	0	1	0
Atkinson, Wilson John	North-street, Lisson-grove, London	Co	1	1	0
Atkinson, Joseph	....	Co	1	1	0
Brown, William	....	Rt	1	1	0
Broughton, John	....	Co	0	0	1
Butler, Poole William	Hicklington, Yorkshire	Co			
Beardsall, John	....	Co	1	1	0
Bottomley, William	....	Co	1	1	0
Branston, Joseph	Newark	Co	0	1	0
Brown, Thomas	....	Co	1	1	0
Checkley, Joseph	Girton	Co	1	1	0
Cooley, John	Spalford	Co	0	0	1
Croft, John	....	Co	0	0	1
Croft, John, jun.	....	Co	0	0	1
Croft, William	....	Co	1	0	1
Collingham, George	....	Co	1	1	0
Caudwell, Joseph	Norwell Woodhouse	Fr			
Curtis, John	....	Rt	1	0	1
Dewick, Samuel	....	Co	0	0	1
Dixon, William	....	Fr	0	0	1
Dixon, Joseph	Brodholme	Rt	1	1	0
Dakins, Frederick	....	Co	0	1	1
Frith, George,	4, Spring-gardens, Terrace, London, and Standard-hill, near Nottingham	Fr			
Fotherby, John	....	Fr			
Falkner, Philip Richard, esq.	Newark	Co			
Gross, Thomas	Norton Disney	Rt			
Halgarth, Samuel	....	Co	1	1	0

North Scarle—continued.

Name of Elector.	Residence, if out of the Parish.	Qual.	T.	W.	P.
Hopkinson, John	....	Co	0	0	1
Hunt, William	....	Fr	0	1	1
Hardy, Thomas	Thorney, Notts.	Co	1	0	0
Lawrence, Joseph	Grantham	Co	1	1	0
Linley, John Banks	....	Co			
Marshall, George	....	Fr	0	1	1
Moody, John	....	Co	0	0	1
Nell, Richard	Little Gonerby	Fr			
Pacey, William	Garthorpe, Leicester-shire	Co			
Parr, William	....	Co	1	1	0
Proctor, George	Newark	Fr			
Preston, James	Eagle-hall	Fr			
Rait, David Creighton	Woodlands-cottage, near Glasgow	Co			
Rawson, Joseph	....	Co	1	0	1
Rawson, William	Eagle	Co	0	0	1
Roe, William	....	Rt	0	0	1
Roe, Thomas	....	Co	1	0	1
Savage, Robert	....	Co	1	1	0
Selby, Samuel	....	Co			
Sockett, Rev. Thomas	Petworth, Sussex	Fr			
Sketchley, Samuel	Newark	Co	*dead*		
Slingsby, George	....	Rt	0	0	1
Smith, John	Lincoln	Fr	1	1	0
Stow, William	....	Fr			
Taylor, David	....	Rt	0	1	0
Thorpe, Christopher	....	Co	0	0	1
Thompson, William	Appleton-gate, Newark	Co	1	1	0
Tustin, William	....	Co	0	1	1
Uffindall, William	Bassingham	Co			
Wakefield, William	....	Rf	1	1	0
Walker, Matthew	....	Fr	1	1	0
Wells, John	....	Co	1	1	0
Wright, Richard	....	Co	1	1	0
Watson, Thomas	....	Co	1	1	0
Wright, John	....	Fr	1	1	0
Wright, James	....	Co			
Wightman, John	Elsebey, near Retford	Co			

North Scarle—continued.

Name of Elector.	Residence, if out of the Parish.	Qual.	T.	W.	P.
Wells, William	....	Fr	0	0	1
Younghusband, Edward	Edgmanton	Fr	1	1	0

Skellingthorpe.

Name of Elector	Residence	Qual.	T.	W.	P.
Alison, Charles	Lincoln	Rt	0	0	1
Armstrong, Rev. Edward Pakenham	Ditto	Fr			
Boot, J. Hopkinson, M.D.	New Sleaford	Fr	0	1	0
Carline, Richard, esq.	Lincoln	Fr	1	1	0
Coupland, Richard	Waddington	Fr	0	0	1
Curtis, William, jun.	Hykeham	Fr	0	1	0
Gask, Robert	....	Rt	1	1	0
Holmes, Reynolds	....	Rt	1	1	0
Harrison, Richard	....	Fr			
Harrison, Joseph	....	Rt	1	1	0
Lascelles, Ralph	....	Rt	0	1	0
Straw, Frederick	....	Rt	1	1	0
Stevenson, John Booth	....	Rt	1	1	0
Shuttleworth, Edmund	....	Rt			
Scarborough, Robert	....	Rt	1	1	0
Taylor, Thomas	....	Rt			
Wilson, Francis	....	Rt	1	1	0

Stapleford and part of Flawferd.

Name of Elector	Residence	Qual.	T.	W.	P.
Clayworth, John	....	Rt	1	1	0
George, Timothy	....	Rt	1	1	0
Handley, Rev. William	Winthorpe	Fr	0	1	1
Handley, John, esq.	North Muskham	Fr			
Holmes, George	....	Rt	1	1	0
Oliver, Joseph	....	Rt	1	1	0
Oliver, Thomas	....	Rt	1	1	0
Oliver, Thomas, jun.	....	Rt	1	1	0
Thompson, James	....	Rt	1	1	0
Tonge, Charles	Branston	Fr			
Tonge, Joseph	....	Fr	1	1	0
Walton, William	....	Rt	1	1	0

Swinderby and Morton.

Name of Elector	Residence	Qual.	T.	W.	P.
Bean, John	....	Rt	0	0	1
Bainbridge, Thomas	Saint Martin's Lincoln	Fr	0	1	0
Bingham, Henry Corles	Broadstairs, Kent	Fr	1	1	0

Swinderby and Morton—continued.

Name of Elector.	Residence, if out of the Parish.	Qual.	T.	W.	P.
Camomile, Joseph	Winthorpe, Notts	Fr	0	1	0
Chambers, James	....	Rt	1	1	0
Clayworth, Joseph	South Scarle	Fr	1	1	0
Crocker, Reuben	....	Fr	0	0	1
Clarke, Walter John, *Vicar*		Fr	1	0	1
Cropper, William	Holme, Notts	Fr			
Curtis, George Patchett	....	Rt	1	1	0
Colton, John	Brough, South Collingham	Fr	1	1	0
Dalton, William	....	Rt	1	1	0
Dalton, John	....	Rt			
Doubleday, George	Newark	Fr	0	1	1
Eastland, John	Walpole, St. Andrews, Norfolk	Fr			
Gamble, G. Harrison	Winthorpe, Notts	Fr	0	1	1
Glazier, Richard	....	Fr	1	0	1
Jackson, David	....	Rt	1	1	0
Johnson, William	....	Fr	1	1	0
Jalland, Boswell Middleton *Esq*	Holderness, House, Hull	Fr	0	0	1
Jarratt, William	Appleford, Bedfordshire	Fr			
Mayor, Joseph, *Clerk*	South Collingham	Fr	1	1	0
Milns, Robert	South Collingham	Fr	1	1	0
Newton, Charles	....	Fr	0	1	1
Nettleship, Joseph	....	Rt	1	1	0
Noden, John	....	Rt	1	1	0
Paulson, William	....	Fr	1	0	0
Pilgrim, Thomas	Morton	Rt	1	1	0
Pyburn, John	....	Fr	1	1	0
Raven, John	....	Fr	1	1	0
Revill, William	Fiskerton	Fr			
Short, John	....	Rt	1	1	0
Simpson, Robert	Hackthorne	Fr	0	0	1
Smith, John	....	Rt	1	1	0
Smith, William	....	Fr	1	1	0
Snow, John	....	Fr	1	1	0
Talbot, Robert	....	Fr	1	1	0
Taylor, Timothy	....	Fr	0	0	1
Taylor, Francis	....	Fr	0	0	1

Swinderby and Morton—continued.

Name of Elector.	Residence, if out of the Parish.	Qual.	T.	W.	P.
Taylor, George	....	Rt	0	1	0
Thompson, George	....	Rt	1	0	1
Wildsmith, Robert	....	Rt	0	1	1
Woolley, William	North Collingham	Fr	0	1	1
Wright, William	North Collingham	Fr	1	1	0

Swinethorpe.

Name of Elector.	Residence, if out of the Parish.	Qual.	T.	W.	P.
Burnaby, Thomas Fowke Andrew, esq. *Sol*	Newark	Rt			
Curteis, Major Edward Barrett	Leasam, Rye, Sussex	Fr			
Dixon, Joseph	Harby	Rt	0	0	1
Grubb, John	....	Rt	1	0	1
Harpham, John	....	Rt	0	0	1

Thurlby.

Name of Elector.	Residence, if out of the Parish.	Qual.	T.	W.	P.
Bromhead, Sir Edmund Gonville, bart.	Thurlby-hall	Fr	1	1	0
Coult, Thomas	....	Fr			
Clayton, Thomas	....	Rt			
Clayton, William	....	Rt	1	1	0
Collingham, William	....	Rt	1	1	0
Fisher, John	....	Rt	1	1	0
Greenfield, William	....	Rt	1	1	0
Harston, John	....	Rt	1	1	0
Harston, William	....	Rt	1	1	0
Haywood, William	....	Rt	1	1	0
Rogers, George Marshall	....	Rt	1	1	0
Southern, William	New Sleaford	Co	1	1	0
Weightman, Agur	Bassingham	Rt	1	1	0

Thorpe-on-the-Hill.

Name of Elector.	Residence, if out of the Parish.	Qual.	T.	W.	P.
Apthorp, Rev. George Frederick	Vicar's-court, Lincoln	Fr	1	1	0
Bainbridge, Nathan	86, St. Mark's-lane, London	Fr			
Baston, John	Harmston	Fr			
Chapman, Richard	....	Fr	1	1	0
Day, William	....	Fr	0	0	1
Dixon, Charles	....	Fr	1	1	0
East, Henry	....	Rt	1	1	0

Thorpe-on-the-Hill—continued.

Name of Elector.	Residence, if out of the Parish.	Qual.	T.	W.	P.
Fenelay, Richard	....	Rt			
Foster, Henry	Sapperton	Fr			
Fotherby, Thomas	....	Fr	1	1	0
Gibson, John	....	Fr			
Gibson, John	....	Fr	1	1	0
Hansard, Robert	....	Fr	1	1	0
Hunt, William	Normanby, by Spital	Fr	1	1	0
Martinson, Joseph	....	Fr	1	0	0
Newton, John	....	Fr	1	1	0
Nicholson, John	....	Fr	1	1	0
Pickwell, Matthew	....	Rt	0	1	0
Pepperdine, Lemuel	High-street, Lincoln	Fr	1	1	0
Rigge, Rev. George	St. Nicholas, Lincoln	Fr	1	1	0
Roper, William	....	Fr	0	1	1
Stevenson, John	Lincoln	Fr			
Sewards, Thomas	....	Rt	1	1	0
Spafford, Thomas	....	Rt	1	1	0
Taylor, William	....	Rt	1	1	0
Taylor, Richard	....	Rt	1	1	0
Wheatcroft, William	....	Rt	1	1	0
Wilson, Matthew, esq.	Casewick-hall, Yorkshire	Fr			
Wainwright, Thomas	Haddington	Fr	1	1	0
Willmott, Benjamin	Harby, Notts	Fr			

Whisby.

Name of Elector.	Residence, if out of the Parish.	Qual.	T.	W.	P.
Crossley, John	....	Rt	0	0	1
Hebblewhite, James	....	Rt	0	0	1
Moss, Richard	....	Rt	0	0	1
Miles, Joseph	....	Rt	0	0	1
Rawson, Mark	....	Rt	0	0	1
Ward, Edward	....	Rt	0	0	1

END OF PARTS OF KESTEVEN.

PARTS OF HOLLAND.

No. 1.—POLLING DISTRICT ASSIGNED TO BOSTON.

POLLED AT BOSTON.

Algarkirk.

Name	Residence				
Armstrong, John	Algarkirk-fen	Rt	1	1	0
Adams, William *Clerk*	Throcking, Hertfordshire	Fr			
Beridge, Rev. Basil	....	Fr	1	1	0
Coulson, William	Hart's Grounds	Fr	0	0	1
Cowham, Thomas	....	Rt	1	0	1
Cowham, Richard	....	Fr	1	1	0
Clough, John Noble	Gayton-le-fen	Fr			
Crawford, Samuel	....	Fr	1	0	1
Clark, William	Algarkirk-fen	Fr	1	1	0
Crawford, James	Sutterton	Fr	1	1	0
Clifton, William	Donington	Fr			
Chaplin, William	Tathwell, near Louth, Lincolnshire	Fr	1	1	0
Chaplin, Frederick	Tathwell, near Louth, Lincolnshire	Fr	1	1	0
Doncaster, John, D.D.	Oakham, Rutland	Fr			
Dean, Edward	....	Rt	1	1	0
Eley, Joseph Marshall	....	Fr			
Eley, Thomas	....	Fr	1	1	0
Eyre, Thomas	....	Fr	1	1	0
Gutteridge, Thomas	Algarkirk-fen	Fr	0	0	1
Hides, George William	Algarkirk-fen	Rt	1	1	0
Hanks, Frederick Joseph	....	Fr	1	1	0
Kirby, George	Sutterton	Fr			
Leedale, John Bates	....	Fr	1	1	0
Lee, John	....	Rt	1	1	0
Leak, John	....	Rt	1	1	0
Lloyd, Rev. Henry Robert	Vicar of Owersby-cum-Osgodby	Fr	1	1	0
Marshall, Benjamin	....	Fr	1	1	0

Algarkirk—continued.

Name of Elector.	Residence, if out of the Parish.	Qual.	T.	W.	P.
Millns, William	Lyndhurst, Notts	Fr			
Mullins, Barry O'Meare	4, Severn-place, Holdgate, York	Fr			
Munk, Edward	Nottingham	Fr			
Parker, William	....	Rt	1	1	0
Palmer, Samuel	....	Rt	1	1	0
Pearce, Richard	....	Rt			
Pocklington, Samuel	Sutterton	Rt	1	1	0
Pocklington, Joseph	Algarkirk-fen	Rt	1	1	0
Pretty, Joseph	....	Rt	1	0	1
Pick, Joseph	Algarkirk-fen	Rt	1	1	0
Pearce, Joseph	Agarkirk-fen	Rt	1	1	0
Palmer, William	....	Rt	1	1	0
Robinson, Francis	....	Rt	1	1	0
Robinson, George	Owersby	Fr			
Rogerson, Joseph	....	Rt	1	1	0
Scott, Sir Claude Edward bart.	29, Bruton-street, London	Fr	0	1	0
Sewell, John, jun.	Algarkirk-fen	Rt	1	1	0
Taylor, Michael	Algarkirk-fen	Rt	0	0	1
Taylor, Hides	Algarkirk-fen	Fr	1	1	0
Turner, Saul	Bracebridge Heath	Fr			
Temple, John	....	Rt	1	1	0
Tooley, John	....	Fr	1	1	0
Ulyatt, Thomas	Algarkirk-fen	Rt	0	0	1
Ulyatt, Edward Woods	Algarkirk-fen	Fr	0	0	1
Westmoreland, William	Algarkirk-fen	Rt	1	1	0
Westmoreland, George	....	Rt	1	1	0
West, Thomas	....	Fr	1	1	0
Ward, Jonathan	Algarkirk-fen	Rt	1	1	0
Ward, Richard	Algarkirk-fen	Rt	1	1	0
Weatherhogg, Thomas	....	Fr	1	1	0
Whittaker, David	....	Fr			

Benington.

Name of Elector.	Residence, if out of the Parish.	Qual.	T.	W.	P.
Adlard, John	....	Fr	1	0	0
Abbott, Absalom	Boston	Rt	0	0	1
Black, Edward	....	Fr			
Black, Thomas	Boston	Fr	1	1	0
Cammack, Richard	....	Fr	0	0	1

Benington—continued.

Name of Elector.	Residence, if out of the Parish.	Qual.	T.	W.	P.
Calthrop, James	....	Fr	0	0	1
Chapman, Dickinson	....	Fr	0	0	1
Cammack, Richard, jun.	....	Fr			
Ealand, John	....	Fr	1	1	0
Ealand, Robert Fawcett	....	Rt	1	1	0
Futter, John	....	Fr	1	0	1
Harrison, Anthony	....	Rt	1	1	0
Hallam, Henry *Esq*	London	Fr		·	
Hoyles, William	....	Rt	1	1	0
Hubbert, George	Butterwick	Fr	1	1	0
Hodgson, John	Sousthorp	Fr	1	1	0
King, Henry	Boston	Fr	1	1	0
Lindsey, Charles, *Archd.*	Monkstown	Fr			
Meredith, Philip, jun.	Tathwell	Fr			
Nicholson, William	....	Fr	0	0	1
Overton, William	....	Fr			
Reeson, John	....	Fr	0	0	1
Russell, John	....	Rt	1	1	0
Russell, Thomas	....	Fr	1	1	0
Royle, William	....	Fr	0	0	1
Robbins, John	....	Fr	1	1	0
Rogers, Henry *Esq*	Stagenhoe Park, Herts	Fr			
Roe, John	....	Fr			
Swan, Rev. Francis	Sousthorp	Fr	1	1	0
Swain, William	Leverton	Fr	1	1	0
Swain, William	....	Rt	1	1	0
Sawer, William	....	Rt	0	0	1
Smith, Thomas	....	Fr			
Smith, William	....	Fr	1	0	1
Taylor, William	Witham-place, Boston	Fr	0	0	1
Taylor, John	....	Fr	0	0	1
Toynton, John	....	Rt	0	0	1
Tether, John	....	Fr	0	1	0
Taylor, Jonathan	....	Fr	0	0	1
Walls, Rev. Joseph	Boothby *dead*	Fr			
Wortley, John	....	Fr	1	1	0
Woodward, John	....	Fr			
Waldegrave, D. Burton	....	Fr	0	0	1
Waldegrave, J. Stephen	....	Fr	0	0	1

Boston.

Name of Elector.	Residence, if out of the Parish.	Qual.	T.	W.	P.
Adams, Wm. H., esq.	....	Fr	1	1	0
Akrill, John	....	Fr	1	0	1
Alison, John	....	Fr	1	0	1
Allitt, John	Langton, Lincolnshire	Fr			
Arnall, Joseph Cooke	....	Fr	1	1	0
Artindale, James	....	Rt			
Asling, Edward Brelsford	....	Fr	0	0	1
Aspland, Charles	....	Fr	1	1	0
Atkin, William Gideon	....	Fr	1	1	0
Abbott, John	March, Cambridge-shire	Fr			
Anderson, Charles	....	Fr	0	0	1
Artindale, T. Stainton	....	Fr	1	1	0
Bailey, John Skinner	Croydon, Surrey	Fr			
Bacon, Thomas, jun.	....	Fr	0	0	1
Ball, Richard	....	Fr	0	1	1
Bargewell, Matthew	Freiston	Fr	0	0	1
Barton, George Samuel	....	Fr	1	1	0
Barwick, Enoch	....	Fr	0	0	1
Barwick, Enoch	....	Fr	0	0	1
Barwick, Jabez	....	Fr	0	0	1
Baxter, William	....	Fr	1	0	1
Bedford, John	....	Fr			
Beetham, John Tidy	Bunney, Notting-hamshire	Fr			
Bellamy, George	....	Fr			
Benson, Edward	....	Fr			
Benton, John	Boston, West	Fr	1	1	0
Billyard, William	....	Rt	0	0	1
Billyard, Nathaniel	Huddersfield, Yorkshire	Fr	0	0	1
Blakey, John Boyes	Sibsey	Fr	0	0	1
Blow, Lawrence	Thorpe, Lincolnshire	Fr	1	1	0
Bowles, William Pepper	*Sel*	Fr	1	0	1
Brader, Richard	....	Fr	0	0	1
Brady, Thomas	....	Fr			
Briggs, Robert John	1, Clarendon-street, Clarendon-square, London	Fr	1	0	1
Brown, William	Bardney, Lincolnshire	Fr	0	1	1

Boston—continued.

Name of Elector.	Residence, if out of the Parish.	Qual.	T.	W.	P.
Brown, William	....	Fr	1	0	1
Brown, Thomas	....	Fr	1	1	0
Brumby, John	....	Fr	1	1	0
Burton, Joseph	....	Fr	0	0	1
Bell, John	Newark	Fr	0	0	1
Bontoft, James William	....	Fr			
Baker, John Henry	....	Fr	0	0	1
Ball, Bothamley	....	Fr	0	0	1
Bates, Henry	....	Fr	1	1	0
Beverley, Joshua	....	Fr	1	1	0
Booth, Benjamin	....	Fr	1	0	1
Bradley, William	....	Fr	1	0	1
Cole, John	....	Fr	1	1	0
Caistor, John	....	Fr	0	0	1
Cartwright, Tobias	Fordington	Fr			
Cartwright, Edward	Horncastle	Fr	1	1	0
Cheeseman, William	....	Fr	0	0	1
Clarke, Henry Hodson	....	Fr	1	0	1
Clark, Charles	Skirbeck	Fr			
Clarkson, Luke	....	Fr	1	1	0
Clayton, Daniel Gregory	....	Fr	1	1	0
Cooke, John	....	Fr	0	0	1
Cooke, Frederick, esq.	....	Fr	1	1	0
Cooke, Thomas Smalley	....	Fr	0	0	1
Cooke, William	Eastwood	Fr			
Conington, Henry James,	....	Fr	1	0	1
Crapley, William	....	Fr	0	0	1
Carter, Benjamin	....	Fr	0	0	1
Collis, Thomas	....	Fr			
Clarke, William Housely	....	Fr	1	1	0
Cartwright, George	Well	Fr	1	1	0
Cooper, Charles	....	Fr	1	0	1
Cottam, John	....	Fr	0	0	1
Darley, Thomas	....	Fr	1	0	1
Darwin, John	....	Fr	1	0	1
Daubney, R. Heaford	Market Rasen	Fr	1	1	0
Dickinson, R. Cousens	Melton Mowbray	Fr			
Duke, James Sir, bart.,	43, Portland-place, London	Fr			
Dring, Arnall	....	Fr	1	1	0

Boston—continued.

Name of Elector.	Residence, if out of the Parish.	Qual.	T.	W.	P.
Eno, Hildred	Sibsey	Fr	0	0	1
Evison, Thomas	Hemingsby, Lincolnshire	Fr	0	0	1
Fendelow, John	....	Fr	1	0	0
Fendelow, John	....	Fr	0	0	1
Fixter, Thomas	Old River Bottom, an extra parochial place, parish of Boston	Fr	0	0	1
Foster, Nathaniel Thomas	Wainfleet St. Marys	Fr	1	1	0
Fothergill, Miles	....	Fr	1	0	1
Fydell, S. Richard, esq.	Morcot, Rutland	Fr			
Firman, Frederick, *Clerk*	....	Fr	1	1	0
Gent, Richard	....	Fr	1	0	1
Gilliatt, William	Martin, Lincolnshire	Fr			
Goodbarne, John Rogers	....	Fr			
Gresham, William	....	Fr	1	1	0
Griffin, Howard	West Ashby				
Groom, Farndon	....	Fr	0	0	1
Groom, Joseph	Wisbeach St. Peter's	Fr	0	0	1
Golsworthy, James *Bapt* Sutterton *Preacher*		Fr			
Gregory, Robert	10, Lambeth-terrace, Lambeth	Fr			
Garfit, Thomas	....	Fr	1	0	1
Goodacre, Richard	....	Fr			
Garnham, Jacob	....	Fr	0	0	1
Grant, James	Fishtoft	Fr	0	0	1
Greenwood, Thomas, jun.	Kirton	Fr	0	0	1
Haddon, Joseph	....	Fr	0	0	1
Hall, William	....	Fr	1	0	1
Hancock, John	Bollingbroke	Fr			
Handley, Thomas	....	Fr	1	0	1
Harmstrong, John	Lincoln	Fr	0	0	1
Hartley, Holiday Wm.	....	Fr	0	0	1
Hartley, George	....	Fr	0	0	1
Hartley, James Armitage	....	Fr	1	1	0
Harvey, Thomas	....	Fr	0	1	1
Harrison, Thomas	....	Fr	0	0	1
Harvey, James	....	Fr	1	1	0
Harwood, Thomas	Skirbeck	Fr			
Hemstock, William	....	Fr	1	1	0

Boston—continued.

Name of Elector.	Residence, if out of the Parish.	Qual.	T.	W.	P.
Hildred, Benjamin Ablitt	....	Fr	1	1	0
Hill, John	York-place, City Road, London	Fr			
Hobson, John	....	Fr	1	0	1
Hodgson, T. Brough	....	Fr	1	1	0
Holland, John	....	Fr	0	0	1
Hollway, John H., esq. Gunby, Lincoln-shire		Fr	1	1	0
Holmes, John	....	Fr	1	1	0
Horner, Edmund	....	Fr			
Horton, William	....	Fr	1	0	1
Hairby, James, M.D.	Hundleby	Fr	1	1	0
Hall, John	....	Fr			
Hanson, Joshua Westland	Alford	Fr	0	0	1
Hobson, Butler Hairby	....	Fr	1	0	1
Hopkins, F. Lyon, esq.	....	Fr	1	1	0
Hyde, Benjamin,	Louth	Fr	0	0	1
Hawe, William	....	Fr	0	0	1
Higgs, Arthur Tanner	Kirton	Fr	1	1	0
Hodgson, Shadworth Hollway,	....	Fr			
Hutchinson, William	Wisbech	Fr			
Hall, George Henry	....	Fr	0	0	1
Harrison, Robert	....	Fr	0	0	1
Holmes, Edward	....	Fr	0	0	1
Ingram, Herbert,	Acton, Middlesex	Fr	voted		
Ingram, Edward	....	Fr	1	0	1
Jacob, Jonathan	Huntingdon	Fr			
Jackson, Robert	Skirbeck	Fr			
Jebb, Charles William	....	Fr	1	0	1
Johnson, Martin	Brigg and Lincoln	Fr			
Jones, David	....	Fr	1	1	0
Jessup, Charles	Haven Bank	Fr			
Jones, Alley Thomas	1, Clifford's Inn, London	Fr			
Killingworth, Benjamin	....	Fr	1	0	1
King, Samuel	....	Fr	1	0	0
King, Henry	....	Fr			
Kitchen, William	Skirbeck	Fr	1	1	0
King, Thomas	Skirbeck Quarter	Fr	0	0	1

Boston—continued.

Name of Elector.	Residence, if out of the Parish.	Qual.	T.	W.	P.
Leedham, John	....	Fr	0	0	1
Lewin, William	....	Fr	1	1	0
Lewin, William	....	Fr			
Lewin, William Henry	....	Fr			
Lewis, Joseph	....	Fr			
Loft, John, *Clerk*	~~Market Stainton~~ *Wyham*	Fr			
Lucas, John Walsam	....	Fr	0	0	1
Lyne, George Brittin	....	Fr	0	0	1
Lynn, John	....	Fr			
Lewis, John, *Clerk*	Spalding	Fr	1	1	0
Lill, Frederick	....	Fr	0	0	1
Lamiman, Benjamin	....	Fr	0	0	1
Mackinder, Henry George	Langtoft, Lincolnshire	Fr			
Mann, James	....	Fr	1	0	1
Mann, John Peperdine	Stamford	Fr	1	1	0
Marshall, Henry, *Sol*	....	Fr	1	0	0
Marshall, James	Kingston-upon-Hull	Fr			
Mears, William	....	Fr	1	0	0
Mears, Robert	....	Fr	0	0	1
Meggitt, Thomas	....	Fr	0	0	1
Millington, J. B., esq. *Sol*	....	Fr			
Miller, George	....	Fr	1	0	1
Miller, William	....	Fr	0	0	1
Mimmack, John	....	Fr	1	0	1
Morphew, G. V.	....	Fr	0	0	1
Morton, T. N. *Clerk*	....	Fr			
Morton, Robert	....	Fr	1	0	1
Moore, George	Ropsley	Fr			
Muschamp, William	....	Fr	1	1	0
Maltby, John	....	Fr	0	0	1
Mackinder, Harwood	Langton	Fr	1	1	0
Mackinder, Robert	Langton	Fr	1	1	0
Mountain, Henry	Skirbeck	Fr	0	0	1
Miggitt, George	....	Fr	0	0	1
Norfolk, William	....	Fr	0	0	1
Norfolk, Thomas	....	Fr	0	0	1
Noble, John, *Eqr*	....	Fr	0	0	1
Oldfield, James	Skirbeck	Fr			
Ostler, George	Skirbeck	Fr	1	1	0

Boston—continued.

Name of Elector.	Residence, if out of the Parish.	Qual.	T.	W.	P.
Ogle, William *Physician* ~~Edinburgh, 125,~~ *Pimlico* ~~George-street~~		Fr	1	1	0
Ogle, John Furniss, *Clerk* ~~Flamborough~~		Fr	*abroad*		
Oldham, Joseph	....	Fr	0	0	1
Palmer, William	Stickney	Fr	0	0	1
Palmer, James	....	Fr	1	0	1
Pape, Simpson Goy	....	Fr	1	0	1
Pape, John Lealand	....	Fr	1	0	1
Partridge, Charles	Grantham	Fr	0	0	1
Pell, William Bennett	Tupholme, Lin-colnshire	Fr			
Peniston, Michael	Lincoln	Fr	0	0	1
Pepper, Kingston Savery	Westville	Fr	1	1	0
Philips, Henry Wilson	....	Fr	1	1	0
Parrott, George William	....	Fr	0	0	1
Plant, Thomas	....	Fr	1	1	0
Pinches, George	....	Fr	1	1	0
Pocklington, Cabourn	....	Fr	1	1	0
Pollington, John	....	Fr	0	0	1
Poppleton, James	....	Fr	1	1	0
Porter, John	....	Fr	1	1	0
Porter, John, jun.	....	Fr	1	1	0
Pownall, Charles Colyear Beaty, ~~esq.~~ *Vicar of*	Milton Ernest, Bedfordshire	Fr	1	1	0
Procter, George	Leeds	Fr			
Pattenden, G. Edwin, Rev.	....	Fr	1	0	1
Pearson, John	....	Fr	1	0	1
Proctor, Charles	Bentley-street, Brad-ford, Yorkshire	Fr	1	1	0
Procter, Samuel	Church-street, Brad-ford, Yorkshire	Fr	1	1	0
Procter, Henry	3, Courland Grove, Clapham, Surrey	Fr	1	0	1
Pell, John	Scopwick	Fr	1	1	0
Poppleton, J. M.	....	Fr	0	0	1
Rainford, Robert	....	Fr	0	0	1
Rawson, John, esq.	Skirbeck	Fr	0	0	1
Rawling, Ropert Cooper	Threadneedle-st.	Fr			
Renney, John	....	Fr	0	0	1
Reynolds, Robert	....	Fr	1	0	1

Boston—continued.

Name of Elector.	Residence, if out of the Parish.	Qual.	T.	W.	P.
Reynolds, James	Romford-street, Nelson-street, Oxford Road, Manchester	Fr			
Robson, Charles	....	Fr	0	0	1
Robson, George	....	Fr	0	0	1
Rogers, William	....	Fr	1	0	1
Routen, William	....	Fr	0	0	1
Rowland, Benjamin	....	Fr			
Richardson, Edmund	Louth *Clerk*	Fr	1	0	1
Robinson, John	....	Fr	1	1	0
Richardson, William	....	Fr			
Ranyell, Robert, jun.	....	Fr	1	1	0
Ranyell, Thomas	....	Fr	1	1	0
Rice, Charles, *Sol*	....	Fr	1	1	0
Ranson, John	....	Fr	0	0	1
Roe, John	5, Grove-place, Southampton-st,, Camberwell	Fr			
Ruff, John	....	Fr	0	0	1
Sanders, Edward, *Esqre*	~~Gainsborough,~~ *Cheltenham* Lincolnshire	Fr	*dead*		
Searby, Benjamin	Firsby, Lincolnshire	Fr	1	1	0
Searle, John	....	Fr	0	0	1
Seeley, Charles, *Esqre*	Lincoln	Fr			
Sewel, George, jun.	....	Fr			
Sewell, St. John	....	Fr	0	0	1
Sewell, Ruben	....	Fr			
Sharp, John	....	Fr	0	0	1
Shaw, Isaac	Wakefield *dead*	Fr			
Shepherd, Joseph	....	Fr	0	0	1
Shipley, Henry	....	Fr	0	0	1
Simpson, John	Skirbeck	Fr	0	0	1
Small, Joseph Harpham	....	Fr			
Smith, Thomas	Spilsby	Fr			
Smith, James	....	Fr	1	0	1
Smithee, William	....	Fr	0	0	1
Snaith, Thomas, *M.Y.*	Horncastle	Fr	0	0	1
Southwell, William	....	Fr	0	0	1
Spikins, Edward	....	Fr			
Staniland, Meaburn, *Sol*	Skirbeck Quarter	Fr			

Boston—continued.

Name of Elector.	Residence, if out of the Parish.	Qual.	T.	W.	P.
Staniland, Meaburn, *Sol*	Skirbeck Quarter	Fr			
Stennett, Thomas	....	Fr	0	0	1
Storr, Thomas	....	Fr	1	1	0
Swinn, John	....	Fr	0	0	1
Sykes, William	Skirbeck	Fr	0	1	1
Scott, William	....	Fr	1	0	1
Smith, Edward	Skirbeck	Fr	1	1	0
Simpson, Benjamin Soulby, *Sol*	....	Fr	1	1	0
Sayles, Frederick Alban	Lincoln	Fr	0	0	1
Storr, Jonathan	....	Fr	1	1	0
Spurr, George	....	Fr	1	1	0
Stanwell, William	....	Fr	0	0	1
Smith, Thomas	Skirbeck	Fr	1	1	0
Small, Thomas	....	Fr	1	0	1
Scarfe, William	....	Fr	0	0	1
Smith, George Ward	....	Fr			
Smith, James	....	Fr	1	1	0
Stevens, Isaac Thomas	....	Fr	0	0	1
Taylor, John	....	Fr	1	0	1
Thimbleby, Henry	Paris	Fr			
Thomas, John Holiday	....	Fr			
Thompson, Edward	....	Fr	1	0	1
Thompson, Francis	....	Fr			
Thompson, George	Skirbeck	Fr	1	1	0
Thorpe, Thomas Wells	....	Fr	1	0	1
Topley, James	....	Fr	1	0	1
Torry, Parkinson	East Skirbeck	Fr			
Tuxford, James Ed. jun.	....	Fr	0	0	1
Tuxford, Peter	Clarth-street, Jubilee-place, Commercial-road, London	Fr			
Towl, Joseph	....	Fr	0	0	1
Torry, William Henry	29, Granville-square, Pentonville, London	Fr			
Tuxford, Peter Ingram	Great Grimsby	Fr	0	0	1
Underwood, William	Cleveland Park, Cambridgshire	Fr			
Vent, John	Quarndon, Leicestershire	Fr			
Waite, George	....	Fr	0	0	1
Wallis, James	Stickney	Fr	0	0	1

Boston—continued.

Name of Elector.	Residence, if out of the Parish.	Qual.	T.	W.	P.
Warsap, Henry	....;	Fr	1	0	1
Warwick, William	....	Fr	1	0	1
Wellman, Charles, jun.	Sutterton	Fr			
Wheatcroft, John	....	Fr	1	1	0
Whelbourne, John	....	Fr	1	0	1
Whelbourne, Benjamin	....	Fr	0	0	1
Whitechurch, Reuben	Melton Mowbray	Fr *Sol*			
White, George, *Sol*	Grantham	Fr *dead*			
White, F. Thirkill, esq. *Sol*	.....	Fr	1	1	0
Whitworth, Charles	....	Fr	0	0	1
Willamott, William	....	Fr	0	0	1
Williamson, John	....	Fr	0	0	1
Williamson, Thomas	St. Nicholas, Lincoln	Fr			
Wilson, John	....	Fr	1	1	0
Wingfield, John Muxloe	Market Overton	Fr			
Winter, John Holland	....	Fr	0	0	1
Wise, Thomas	....	Fr			
Wise, Thomas, jun.	....	Fr	1	1	0
Wood, Benjamin Ward	....	Fr	1	1	0
Woods, William	Dogdyke	Fr			
Woodcock, William	....	Fr	1	0	1
Wright, Charles	....	Fr	1	0	1
Wright, Charles, jun.	Skirbeck	Fr	0	0	1
Wright, Edward	....	Fr			
Wrangle, Charles	....	Fr	0	0	1
Wrangle, William	....	Fr	0	0	1
Watts, John	....	Fr	1	0	1
Wright, John, esq.	Spilsby	Fr	1	1	0
Waltham, Joseph	....	Fr	1	0	1
Warrener, William	....	Fr	0	0	1
Wells, William	....	Fr			
Wells, Frederick	....	Fr	1	1	0
Wright, William	Skirbeck	Fr	1	0	1
Wingate, George	....	Fr	0	0	1
Ward, John	....	Fr	0	0	1
Watson, John Woodcock	....	Fr	1	0	1
Williamson, William	....	Fr	0	0	1
Wright, William Turner	....	Fr			

Brothertoft.

Name of Elector.	Residence, if out of the Parish.	Qual.	T.	W.	P.
Cornwell, Thomas	....	Fr	1	1	0

Brothertoft—continued.

Name of Elector.	Residence, if out of the Parish.	Qual.	T.	W.	P
Cook, Daniel	....	Rt	1	1	0
Fletcher, Robert	North-forty-foot-bank	Fr	1	1	0
Fox, Jonathan	....	Fr	1	1	0
Gee, Thomas, esq.	....	Fr	1	1	0
Ingram, Herbert, *Esqr*	Acton, Middlesex	Fr			
Mowbray, John	Friskney	Rt			
Mells, William	....	Rt	1	1	0
Oldrid, John Henry, *Clerk*	Boston	Fr	1	0	1
Peart, John	....	Rt	1	1	0
Rogers, Henry, esq.	Stagenhoe Park, Herts.	Fr	1	1	0
Wright, Ichabod, *Esqr*	Mapperly	Fr			
Wakefield, John	North-forty-foot-bank	Fr	1	1	0
Wright, Henry	Kirton Fen	Fr	0	1	0
Wilkinson, John	North-forty-foot-bank	Fr			
Waddington, William	....	Rt	1	0	0

Butterwick.

Name of Elector.	Residence, if out of the Parish.	Qual.	T.	W.	P
Adams, Jonatham	Stickney	Co			
Asher, William	....	Fr	1	1	0
Brough, John	....	Fr	0	0	1
Bolland, William	....	Fr	1	0	1
Brooks, Samuel Edward	Sleaford *and minis*	Fr	1	1	0
Brown, Edward	....	Fr	1	0	1
Carlton, Robert	....	Fr	0	0	1
Calthrop, John George, *&*	Boston	Fr	1	1	0
Calthrop, Thomas	....	Fr	1	1	0
Collins, Hubert	....	Rt	0	0	1
Chapman, John	....	Fr	1	0	1
Forinton, William	....	Fr	1	1	0
Hanks, Edmund	....	Fr	1	0	1
Hanks, Edward	....	Fr	1	0	1
Hanks, George	....	Co	1	0	1
Ireland, Robert Ingamells	....	Fr	1	1	0
Jacklin, Joseph	....	Co	1	0	1
Jacklin, Miles	....	Fr	1	0	0
Johnson, Jonathan	....	Fr	0	0	1
Jackson, John *Clk*	....	Fr	1	1	0
Kent, Thomas	....	Fr	1	0	1
Lee, James	Scrivelsby	Fr	0	0	1

Butterwick—continued.

Name of Elector.	Residence, if out of the Parish.	Qual.	T.	W.	P.
Ling, Samuel	....	Fr	1	0	0
Martin, George	....	Fr	1	1	0
Mowbray, John	....	Fr	1	1	0
Marshall, Joseph	....	Rt	1	1	0
Orrey, Barton	Frieston	Fr	1	0	1
Paddison, Peter	....	Fr	0	0	1
Paddison, Edward	....	Fr	0	0	1
Parnham, Peter	....	Rt	1	0	0
Silvester, William	....	Fr	1	1	0
Stennett, William	....	Fr	1	0	0
Stennett, Stockdale	....	Fr	1	0	1
Spurr, George	Boston	Fr			
Sharp, William	....	Fr	1	1	0
Stringfellow, Henry	....	Rt	1	1	0
Turner, Samuel	....	Fr	1	0	1
Upsall, John	....	Fr	1	0	1
Welberry, William	....	Rt	1	1	0
Welberry, Joseph	Frieston	Fr	0	0	1
Westland, Samuel	....	Fr	1	0	1

Fishtoft.

Name of Elector.	Residence, if out of the Parish.	Qual.	T.	W.	P.
Ashby, William	....	Fr	1	1	0
Allbones, Michael	....	Fr	1	0	1
Allen, John	....	Fr	1	1	0
Bailey, John	....	Rt	0	1	1
Barber, Thomas	....	Fr	1	1	0
Barber, John	....	Fr			
Barber, Charles	....	Fr	1	1	0
Bellamy, William	....	Fr	1	1	0
Buffham, John	Midville	Fr	1	1	0
Barber, Henry	....	Fr	1	0	1
Collins, William	....	Fr	0	0	1
Danby, Charles	....	Rt	0	1	1
Dickens, Thomas	Skirbeck	Fr	0	0	1
Hornbuckle, Thomas	Boston East	Fr			
Hebblewhite, Overton	Cambridge	Fr			
Holdsworth, Rev. Henry	Rectory House, Fishtoft	Fr	1	1	0
Hodgson, Robert	....	Fr	1	1	0
Horrey, Barton	....	Rt	1	1	0

Fishtoft—continued.

Name of Elector.	Residence, if out of the Parish.	Qual.	T.	W.	P.
Ingoldby, John	Boston	Fr	0	1	0
Johnson, George	....	Fr	1	1	0
Jebb, Samuel Henry *Sol*	Boston	Fr	1	0	1
Jackson, George	....	Rt	1	0	1
Kennington, John	New Sleaford	Fr			
Lawrence, George	....	Rt			
Mountain, Joseph	....	Rt			
Mowbray, George	....	Rt	1	0	1
Maddison, Thomas	....	Fr	1	0	1
Mowbray, William Physic	....	Rt	1	1	0
Orrey, John	....	Fr	1	1	0
Payne, Joseph	....	Fr	1	1	0
Rogers, Richard *Esqre*	SaintPaul's,Walden Hertfordshire	Fr			
Rawson, John *Esqre*	Skirbeck	Fr			
Reeson, Jacob	....	Fr	1	0	1
Rilet, Plant	....	Rt	1	0	1
Reeson, Francis	....	Fr	1	0	0
Saul, William	Sibsey	Fr			
Simmonds, John Cabourn	....	Rt			
Simpson, Joseph	....	Fr	1	1	0
Sharp, William	....	Fr	0	0	1
Teat, Thomas	....	Fr			
Talks, Thomas	Frieston	Fr	1	0	1
Ward, John	Boston	Fr	1	1	0
Winteringham, William	....	Fr	0	0	1
Watmough, William	Skirbeck	Fr			
Watmough, Alfred	....	Rt	0	1	0
Wilkinson, George	....	Rt	1	1	0

Fosdyke.

Name of Elector.	Residence, if out of the Parish.	Qual.	T.	W.	P.
Baker, Richard	Hough-on-the-Hill	Fr			
Burnett, John West	....	Fr	1	1	0
Bett, William	Howel	Fr	1	1	0
Bett, William, jun.	....	Rt			
Bowles, William	Coningsby	Fr	1	0	1
Bellars, John Thomas	....	Rt			
Billyard, Richard	....	Fr	0	0	1
Cartwright, John	North-forty-foot-bank	Fr	1	0	1
Cartwright, Robert	South Thoresby	Fr			

Fosdyke—continued.

Name of Elector.	Residence, if out of the Parish.	Qual.	T.	W.	P.
Chambers, John	Fosdyke-fen	Fr	1	1	0
Clement, Robert	....	Fr	0	1	0
Craven, Christopher	....	Rt	1	1	0
Chambers, Robert	Stragglethorpe and Lincoln	Fr			
Craven, Brewster	Wigtoft	Fr			
Clark, John	North-forty-foot-bank	Fr	0	1	0
Day, William	North-forty-foot-bank	Fr			
Elsom, William	....	Rt	1	1	0
Fairweather, Joel	Old Witham Marsh	Fr	1	1	0
Hall, William	....	Fr	1	1	0
Hall, William	North-forty-foot-bank	Fr	1	1	0
Hammond, Charles	Fosdyke-fen	Fr			
Harrison, Joseph	....	Rt			
Hilton, James	North-forty-foot-bank	Fr	1	1	0
Head, Matthew	....	Fr	1	1	0
Ireland, Thomas	....	Rt	1	1	0
Jackson, John	Fosdyke-fen	Rt	1	1	0
Jackson, Middleton John	Fosdyke-fen	Rt			
Kemp, Jonathan	....	Fr	1	1	0
Kemp, Charles	....	Fr	1	1	0
Kemp, Jarvis	....	Fr	1	1	0
Lawrence, William	Dunsby	Rt			
Lawrence, William Munton	Dunsby	Rt			
Lovell, Charles Pentin	Boston Main-ridge	Fr	0	0	1
Marshall, William	....	Fr	1	0	1
Meeds, John Abraham	Coningsby	Rt	1	0	1
Muse, John	Sutterton	Fr			
Ogden, James	Fosdyke-bridge	Rt	1	1	0
Parker, Joseph	Boston	Fr			
Parker, Joseph	Boston	Fr	0	0	1
Pick, Thomas	Fosdyke-fen	Fr			
Pick, Thomas, jun.	Fosdyke-fen	Rt	0	1	1
Pearson, Matthew	Algarkirk	Fr	1	0	1
Redford, Richard	....	Fr	1	1	0
Russell, Rev. John	Kirton-fen	Fr			
Redding, John	....	Fr	1	1	0
Silvester, Robert	Fosdyke-fen	Fr			
Simon's, Thomas	Pelham's Land	Rt			
Starmer, Samuel	Old Witham Marsh	Fr			

Fosdyke—continued.

Name of Elector.	Residence, if out of the Parish.	Qual.	T.	W.	P.
Shipley, Joseph	North-forty-foot-bank	Fr			
Smith, John	....	Rt	1	0	1
Smith, John	....	Fr			
Stennett, Thomas	North-forty-foot-bank	Fr	0	0	1
Taylor, John	....	Fr	1	0	0
Twigg, Samuel	North-forty-foot-bank	Fr	1	1	0
Townsend, Richard	Long Sutton	Fr	0	0	1
Talkes, Henry	Roman-bank, Fosdyke	Fr	1	1	0
Wells, James	North-forty-foot-bank	Fr			
Wells, Joseph	North-forty-foot-bank	Fr	0	0	1
Wells, Philip	Fosdyke-fen	Fr			
Wilson, Thomas	....	Fr	1	1	0
Wilkinson, John	Fosdyke-fen	Fr	0	0	1
Whittaker, Richard	North-forty-foot-bank	Rt	1	0	1
Whittaker, James	North-forty-foot-bank	Fr	1	1	0
Ward, Thomas	....	Fr			

Frampton.

Name of Elector.	Residence, if out of the Parish.	Qual.	T.	W.	P.
Andrew, William Adkin	Boston	Fr	1	0	1
Barker, Francis	Ditto	Fr	1	1	0
Blancher, George	....	Fr	1	0	1
Benton, John	Holbeach	Rt	1	0	1
Benton, Charles	....	Rt	1	1	0
Benton, William	Frampton-fen	Rt	1	1	0
Birkitt, John	Kirton	Fr	0	0	1
Brown, John	....	Rt	1	1	0
Burrell, Joseph Peach	....	Fr	1	1	0
Bacon, Thomas	....	Rt	0	0	1
Boothby, Henry	....	Fr	1	1	0
Burrell, Thomas	....	Rt	1	0	1
Billyard, Richard	....	Rt	0	1	1
Burman, William	Kirton	Fr	1	1	0
Burrell, Matthew	....	Rt	1	1	0
Brinkley, William	West End	Fr	1	0	1
Blythe, Robert	Wyberton West End	Fr			
Brown, John	Wyberton-fen	Fr	0	0	1
Cumberworth, Searson	Swineshead	Fr			
Clark, George	Frampton-fen	Rt	1	1	0
Casswell, John Queen-borough	....	Rt	1	1	0

Frampton—continued.

Name of Elector.	Residence, if out of the Parish.	Qual.	T.	W.	P.
Cecil, William	....	Rt	1	1	0
Dodd, Charles	....	Rt	1	1	0
Dickenson, James	....	Fr	1	1	0
Dodd, Henry Caleb	....	Rt	1	1	0
Ellis, William	Wyberton	Fr	0	0	1
Goose, Daniel	....	Fr	1	0	1
Goose, James	....	Fr			
Goodger, John	Boston	Fr	0	0	1
Goodacre, Samuel	....	Rt	1	1	0
Hardy, Richard	....	Fr	0	1	1
Horn, George	....	Rt	1	1	0
Harlock, William	....	Fr	1	0	0
King, George	....	Rt	0	0	1
Kitching, William Henry	....	Rt	1	1	0
Lighton, James	....	Fr	1	1	0
Lighton, James	....	Fr	1	0	1
Moore, Major C. T. J.	Frampton Hall	Fr	1	1	0
Mumby, Thomas	....	Rt	1	0	1
Marlow, Thomas	Sausthorpe	Fr			
Plumtree, George	Boston	Fr			
Pearson, John	....	Rt	1	1	0
Robinson, Francis	....	Rt	1	1	0
Ridley, William	....	Fr	1	1	0
Redshaw, Charles	....	Fr	1	1	0
Rylett, Timothy	....	Fr	1	0	1
Redshaw, Benjamin	....	Fr	0	0	1
Rawson, John	Skirbeck	Fr			
Smith, John	....	Fr	0	1	1
Shaw, George	....	Rt	1	1	0
Sharp, John, sen.	London	Fr	1	1	0
Simonds, William	Kirton	Fr			
Smith, Charles	....	Fr	1	1	0
Sharp, John, jun.	....	Rt	1	1	0
Shaw, Thomas	....	Fr	1	1	0
Thorpe, Richard Wells	Wyberton	Rt			
Tunnard, Rev. John	Frampton House	Fr	1	1	0
Toyne, Charles	....	Fr	0	0	1
Ward, George	....	Rt	0	1	1
Willey, John	....	Fr	1	1	0
Watson, Thomas Steed	Wisbeach *Sol*	Fr			

Frampton—continued.

Name of Elector.	Residence, if out of the Parish.	Qual.	T.	W.	P.
Watson, William	Frampton Sandholme	Rt	1	0	0
Woodcock, Joseph	....	Fr	1	1	0
Woodcock, John	....	Fr	1	0	1
Wright, John	....	Co	1	0	1
Watson, James	....	Fr	1	1	0
Walker, Benjamin	....	Fr	1	0	1
Wadsley, Thomas	....	Rt	0	0	1
Yerburgh, Rev. Richard	Sleaford	Fr			
Young, John	....	Rt	0	0	1

Freiston.

Name of Elector.	Residence, if out of the Parish.	Qual.	T.	W.	P.
Artindale, Capps	Coningsby	Fr			
Artindale, James	....	Rt	1	1	0
Baker, Henry	....	Rt	1	1	0
Bolland, Thomas	....	Fr	0	0	1
Bell, James	....	Rt	0	0	1
Bourn, John	....	Fr	0	0	1
Butler, Richard	....	Fr	1	1	0
Blanchard, John King	....	Fr	0	0	1
Boyce, Samuel	....	Fr	1	0	1
Buffham, John	....	Fr	1	0	1
Buffham, William	Skirbeck	Fr	1	0	1
Brummitt, John	Boston	Fr			
Bringeman, Thomas	....	Rt	1	1	0
Barnett, Thomas	....	Fr			
Buttress, John	....	Fr	1	1	0
Clark, Joseph	Wainfleet, All Saints	Fr	1	1	0
Coltman, Thomas, esq.	Hagnaby	Fr			
Clayton, Nathaniel	Butterwick	Fr	1	0	1
Coupland, John George	....	Fr	1	1	0
Clark, Rushby	....	Fr			
Cary, Richard Dawson	Frith Ville	Rt	1	0	1
Casswell, J. Q.	Butterwick	Fr			
Casswell, George	Butterwick	Fr	1	0	1
Chapman, John	Hawthorn-hill, Coningsby	Fr			
Dean, William, sen.	....	Fr	0	0	1
Dean, William, jun.	....	Fr	0	0	1
Day, Joseph	....	Fr	1	1	0
Edman, John	Bardney	Fr	0	1	1

Frieston—continued.

Name of Elector.	Residence, if out of the Parish.	Qual.	T.	W.	P.
Eley, John, jun,	....	Fr	1	0	1
Faunt, John	....	Fr	1	1	0
Faunt, John	Croft	Fr	0	0	1
Francis, Henry	....	Rt			
Flowers, George	....	Fr	1	0	1
Fletcher, Charles	....	Fr	1	1	0
Goslin, James	....	Fr	0	0	1
Hildred, Benjamin	....	Fr	1	0	1
Hoyes, John	....	Fr	1	1	0
Hildred, William	....	Fr			
Homer, Rev. Thomas	....	Fr	1	1	0
Hawksworth, Robert	....	Fr	1	1	0
Holmes, George	....	Rt	1	1	0
Jessop, Thomas Fletcher	....	Fr	1	1	0
Johnson, William	....	Fr	1	1	0
Jackson, Henry	....	Fr	1	1	0
Kirby, Thomas	....	Rt	0	0	1
Kirkby, Henry	....	Fr	1	0	1
Kitching, Francis	....	Fr.	1	1	0
Kirkby, Henry Charles	Aswardby	Fr	0	0	1
Kirkby, Frederick	....	Rt	1	0	1
Kirkby, William	....	Rt	1	0	1
Linton, John, Lieut. Col.	Buckden, Huntingdonshire	Fr	1	1	0
Lawis, Francis	....	Fr	1	0	1
Lawis, John	....	Fr	1	1	0
Maidens, Thomas Cousins	Brinkhill	Fr	1	0	1
Meredith, Philip, jun.	Tathwell	Fr	1	1	0
Michelson, Charles	....	Rt			
Morton, Thomas Ashton	Boston	Fr	1	1	0
Maidens, Robert	East Kirkby	Fr	1	1	0
Marshall, Samuel France	Skirbeck	Rt	0	0	1
Millington, John Boyfield	....	Fr			
Moore, Charles Thomas John, esq.	Frampton Hall	Fr			
Nell, William	Louth	Fr	1	1	0
Norman, George	....	Rt	0	0	1
Oldham, Thomas	....	Fr	1	1	0
Orrey, James	....	Fr	1	1	0

Freiston—continued.

Name of Elector.	Residence, if out of the Parish.	Qual.	T.	W.	P.
Orlebar, Robert Shipton, *Esq.*	Crawley House, Woburn, Beds.	Fr			
Orlebar, John Shipton, *Esq.*	Crawley House, Woburn, Beds.	Fr			
Porter, Edward Clark	Boston	Rt	1	1	0
Porter, William	Skirbeck	Fr *dead*			
Porter, Richard	....	Fr	0	0	1
Pollexfen, Stephen	Thornton	Fr	1	1	0
Plummer, Thomas	....	Fr	0	0	1
Plummer, William	....	Fr			
Paddison, Henry	....	Fr	0	0	1
Parrott, Edman	....	Fr	1	0	0
Reeson, George Howard	Benington	Fr	0	0	1
Rawson, John	Skirbeck	Fr			
Redgate, Thomas B., esq.	Weston, Notts. *Sol*	Fr	1	1	0
Swift, William Anthony	....	Fr	1	1	0
Staples, William	....	Fr			
Saul, William	Sibsey	Fr	1	1	0
Sharp, Grantham	....	Fr	1	0	1
Staples, John	....	Fr	1	1	0
Sawer, Shepherd	Boston	Fr	1	1	0
Tilson, Silvester	....	Fr	1	1	0
Talton, John	....	Rt	1	1	0
Vamplew, Robert	....	Fr	1	1	0
Westland, Richard	....	Fr	1	0	1
Welberry, Samuel	....	Fr	1	0	1
Waite, Brown Edmund	Sibsey	Rt	1	1	0
Wilson, Joseph	....	Fr	1	0	1
Whitchurch, Nathaniel	Melton Mowbray	Fr			
Wise, William	....	Fr	1	1	0
Welberry, Edward	....	Rt	1	1	0
Walker, John	Spilsby	Fr	0	0	1
Widall, Edley	....	Fr	1	0	1
Young, Henry	....	Rt	1	0	1

Kirton.

Name of Elector.	Residence, if out of the Parish.	Qual.	T.	W.	P.
Adams, Rev. William	Throcking, Hertfordshire	Fr	1	1	0
Aspland, Joshua	Kirton Holme	Fr	1	1	0
Atkin, Thomas	Kirton Sea-dyke	Fr	0	0	1

Kirton—continued.

Name of Elector.	Residence, if out of the Parish.	Qual.	T.	W.	P.
Atkinson, Joseph	....	Rt	1	1	0
Aspland, David Curtis	....	Rt	1	1	0
Aspland, Henry	....	Rt			
Bucknell, Joseph	Kirton Sea-dyke	Fr	1	0	1
Brooks, Thomas	Kirton Low-fen	Rt	1	0	1
Birkitt, John	....	Fr	1	0	1
Birkitt, Richard	....	Fr	0	0	1
Brewster, William Gibson	Kirton Holme	Fr	0	0	1
Bontoft, William	....	Fr	0	1	1
Borman, Allen	....	Fr			
Bull, Daniel	....	Rt	1	1	0
Booth, George	....	Rt	1	1	0
Bliss, James	....	Fr	1	1	0
Bowles, William	....	Fr	0	1	1
Cammack, Thomas	Kirton Holme	Rt	1	1	0
Cartwright, Robert	Owersby	Fr			
Cade, Thomas, sen.	....	Rt	1	0	1
Chesman, David	Kirton Holme	Fr	0	1	1
Cooke, George	Kirton Skeldyke	Fr	0	0	1
Cartwright, Thomas	Kirton-fen	Fr			
Cade, David	Coningsby	Fr			
Craven, Charles	Boston East	Fr	0	0	1
Codling, Thomas	....	Fr	0	0	1
Coupland, Eno	....	Fr			
Cartwright, Thomas	....	Fr	0	1	1
Dalby, William Birkitt	....	Fr	0	0	1
Durance, William	Kirton-fen	Fr	0	1	1
Dickenson, William	Kirton End	Fr	0	0	1
Dawson, Parker	....	Fr	1	1	0
Dawson, John	....	Fr	0	1	0
Dixon, Robert	Kirton-fen	Fr			
Dowse, John	Kirton Skeldyke	Fr			
Dickenson, Joseph	Kirton End	Fr	1	0	1
Dickenson, W. R.	Wilton Crescent, London	Fr			
Dale, John	....	Fr			
Day, John	Kirton End	Fr	0	0	1
Dudding, John	City of Lincoln	Fr	1	1	0
Dickenson, Richard	....	Fr			
Dixon, John	....	Rt	1	0	1

Kirton—continued.

Name of Elector.	Residence, if out of the Parish.	Qual.	T.	W.	P.
Eastgate, John	Kirton Holme	Fr	1	1	0
Eagle, John	....	Fr	1	1	0
Elmhirst, William, esq.	West Ashby	Fr	1	1	0
Evans, John	....	Fr	0	0	1
Favil, Samuel	Kirton End	Fr	1	1	0
Fountain, John	Kirton-fen	Rt	0	0	1
Frankling, Thomas	Kirton Drain-side	Fr	0	0	1
Fuller, Benjamin	Germans, Buckinghamshire	Fr			
Fuller, Benjamin	Gresham, Buckinghamshire	Fr			
Garfit, William *Esq*	Boston	Fr	*dead*		
Goodaker, Edward	Kirton Skeldye	Fr	0	0	1
Gorin, William	Kirton End	Fr	1	1	0
Green, Charles	....	Rt	1	1	0
Green, Joseph	Kirton-fen	Rt	1	1	0
Gooby, William	....	Rt			
Good, Ezekiel	....	Fr	1	0	1
Greetham, Joseph	....	Rt	1	1	0
Gery, Robert W., *esq Clk*	Colnworth, County Bedford	Fr	1	1	0
Hubbard, Thomas Cook	Witham-on-the-hill	Fr			
Holland, Rev. William	Huntingfield Rectory	Fr			
Hackney, John	Kirton End	Fr	1	0	1
Higdon, William	....	Fr	1	1	0
Holland, Thomas	....	Fr			
Hammond, Christopher	Kirton-fen	Fr	1	0	1
Hammond, John	Kirton-fen	Rt	0	1	1
Harness, James	Kirton Mears	Rt	1	1	0
Hammond, Edward	Fosdyke	Fr	1	1	0
Holland, John	Boston	Fr	0	0	1
Harlock, William	Frampton	Fr			
Hodgson, Joseph	Kirton Skeldyke	Rt	1	0	1
Hobson, William	Kirton-fen	Rt	0	0	1
Hand, William	Kirton-fen	Rt	1	1	0
Harwood, Thomas	....	Fr	0	0	1
Hall, George	....	Fr	1	1	0
Hutchinson, John	....	Fr	1	0	0
Hutchinson, Robert	....	Fr	1	1	0
Hutchinson, Thomas	....	Fr	0	1	1

Kirton—continued.

Name of Elector.	Residence, if out of the Parish.	Qual.	T.	W.	P.
Ireland, William	....	Fr	0	1	1
Jackson, Myers	....	Fr	1	1	0
Jeffrey, Benjamin	Kirton End	Fr	1	1	0
Ketton, Robert	Kirton Mears	Fr	1	1	0
Kirk, James	Boston	Fr			
Kent, John	....	Fr	1	1	0
Knight, William	....	Fr	0	0	1
Lupton, Thomas	....	Fr	0	1	1
Layton, Thomas	Kirton End	Fr	1	1	0
Leake, Edward	Kirton Sea-dyke	Fr	0	0	1
Langley, John	....	Fr			
Ludlow, Rev. William	Kirton Vicarage	Fr	1	1	0
Lawrence, William Exton	....	Rt	1	1	0
Mason, Henry	Kirton Mears	Rt	1	1	0
Mason, John	....	Fr	0	0	1
Medley, William	Kirton Drain-side	Fr	0	0	1
Marjerison, Samuel	Bradford, Yorkshire	Fr			
Moore, C. T. J.	Frampton Hall	Le			
Morley, Robert	Kirton Drain-side	Rt	1	0	1
Meeds, William	Kirton-fen	Fr	1	1	0
Millhouse, John	Kirton-end	Fr	0	0	1
Meredith, Henry	Kirton-holme	Fr	1	1	0
Meredith, Henry	Kirton-holme	Fr	1	1	0
Millhouse, John	Kirton-house	Fr	0	0	1
Marlow, Francis	....	Fr	0	1	0
Martin, David	Wainfleet	Rt			
Martin, George	....	Rt	1	1	0
Millington, John Boyfield	Boston	Fr			
Marshall, Benjamin	Kirton	Rt	1	0	1
Naylor, William	Kirton Town	Fr	1	0	1
Nidd, John	Boston	Fr	1	0	1
Nidd, Richard	....	Fr	1	0	1
Nainby, Charles Manby	Peterborough	Fr			
Nunneley, John	Boston	Fr			
Ownsworth, Robert	Kirton-fen	Rt	0	1	1
Overton, George	....	Fr	0	0	1
Overton, William	Kirton-holme	Fr	0	0	1
Pick, Thomas	Kirton-fen	Fr	1	1	0
Pick, John	....	Rt	0	0	1
Parr, Richard	London	Fr			

Kirton—continued.

Name of Elector.	Residence, if out of the Parish.	Qual.	T.	W.	P.
Priestley, George	Kirton-town	Fr	1	1	0
Preston, James	Wigtoft-fen	Fr			
Parker, Anthony	Kirton-holme	Rt	1	0	0
Parker, James	Kirton-holme	Fr	1	0	0
Palian, John	....	Fr			
Pearson, John, jun., esq.	Tanbridge, Surrey	Fr			
Pye, Henry, esq. *Sd*	Louth	Fr	1	1	0
Page, John	Eydon, Northamptonshire	Fr			
Pilmore, John	Kirton-end	Fr	1	1	0
Pacey, Rev. H. Butler,	Aston, Hertfordshire	Fr *X.X.*			
Pulson, John	....	Rt	1	0	1
Porter, William	....	Fr	0	1	1
Rastall, William	....	Fr	0	1	1
Richardson, William	London	Fr			
Reeson, Gilbert	....	Rt	0	1	1
Rodgers, William	....	Fr	1	0	1
Reynolds, Henry Harrison	....	Fr	0	0	1
Roberts, William Smith	No.11,King-street, Kingsland-road, Parishof St.Leonard, County of Middlesex	Fr			
Russell, Rev. John	Kirton-fen	Fr	1	1	0
Rayner, Henry	....	Fr			
Stratton, William	LittleBerkhamstead, Hertfordshire	Fr			
Slator, Thomas	Boston	Fr	1	1	0
Sutton, Thomas, sen.	Kirton Drain-side	Fr	1	0	1
Smeeton, Samuel	....	Fr			
Sellars, Richard	Kirton-fen	Rt	1	1	0
Smith, Charles	....	Fr			
Stanley, William	....	Fr	0	0	1
Slight, Samuel	Skirbeck	Fr	1	1	0
Sharpe, Thomas	Pelham's Land	Rt	1	1	0
Smith, Robert	Kirton-fen	Fr			
Smith, William	....	Rt	1	1	0
Stennett, Richard	Carrington	Fr	1	1	0
Sawyer, Joseph	Kirton-fen	Rt	1	1	0
Soulby, Edward Harding	Revesby	Fr			
Savage, Frederick Bellamy	Lincoln	Fr	0	1	1

Kirton—continued.

Name of Elector.	Residence, if out of the Parish.	Qual.	T.	W.	P.
Simpson, Rev. W. H.	Falkingham	Fr	1	1	0
Smeeton, Samuel, jun.	....	Rt			
Simmonds, William	....	Fr			
Sutton, Thomas	....	Fr	1	1	0
Setchell, John	....	Rt	1	1	0
Tunnard, Joseph	Kirton Skeldyke	Fr	1	0	1
Thorp, Richard	....	Fr	1	1	0
Tidd, John	Kirton Bucklegate	Fr	0	1	1
Thompson, Charles	....	Rt	1	1	0
Tewson, Edward	Boston	Fr	1	0	1
Toynton, William	Butterwick	Fr	0	0	1
Vickers, William	Kirton-end	Fr	1	1	0
Vickers, Thomas	....	Fr	1	0	1
Vessey, Erastus	....	Fr	0	0	1
Wilkinson, William	Kirton-holme	Rt	0	0	1
Welberry, Robert	Kirton-end	Fr	0	1	1
Warner, Charles	....	Fr	1	1	0
Watson, Thomas Steed	Wisbech	Fr			
Walter, William	Edlington	Rt	1	1	0
Wileman, William	....	Fr	0	0	1
Ward, Richard	Kirton-fen	Rt			
Wakefield, Thomas	Kirton-fen	Fr	1	1	0
Wright, George	Claxby	Fr			
Wadsley, James	Kirton-fen	Fr	1	1	0
Watson, John	Kirton-end	Rt	1	1	0
Weldon, William	....	Fr	0	1	1
Wain, Joseph	Kirton-holme	Fr	1	1	0
Westmoreland, Moses	Kirton-fen	Rt	1	1	0
Wainer, William	....	Fr	0	0	1
Ward, James	South Kyme	Fr			
Woods, Henry Jackson, sen.	....	Fr	0	1	1
Woods, Henry Jackson	....	Fr	0	1	1

Leake.

Name of Elector.	Residence, if out of the Parish.	Qual.	T.	W.	P.
Allen, John	....	Fr	1	1	0
Arnall, John	....	Fr	1	1	0
Appleby, John	....	Fr	1	1	0
Alliwell, William	....	Fr	1	1	0
Ashlin, John	Firsby	Fr	0	1	1
Arnall, James	....	Rt	1	1	0
Brooks, John	Welton	Fr			

Leake—continued.

Name of Elector.	Residence, if out of the Parish.	Qual.	T.	W.	P.
Barfoot, Henry	*Vicar*	Fr	1	1	0
Brookes, Charles	....	Rt	1	1	0
Bringeman, John	....	Rt	1	1	0
Buffham, John	....	Fr	1	1	0
Betts, George	....	Fr	1	·1	0
Burton, William	....	Fr			
Blenkarn, Thomas	Leverton	Rt	1	1	0
Blenkarn, William	....	Fr	1	1	0
Butler, Richard	....	Fr	1	1	0
Beverley, John Thomas	Boston	Fr	1	1	0
Brooks, John	Welton	Rt	1	1	0
Cowham, John	....	Fr	1	0	1
Conington, Rev., John	~~Navenby~~ *Southock* Fr		0	0	1
Cook, Joseph	AnthonyGowt,extra parochial	Fr	1	1	0
Cullen, William	....	Fr	1	1	0
Curtis, Grave *Rowland* Gallingham, near Chatham		Fr			
Clarke, Samuel	....	Fr	1	0	1
Collins, Jabez	....	Rt	1	1	0
Creasey, Joseph	Friskney	Fr			
Clarke, John	Leverton	Fr			
Clarke, Robert	....	Fr	1	1	0
Cawdwell, Joseph	Frith-ville	Fr	1	1	0
Clarke, Richard	Leverton	Fr			
Cotney, William	....	Fr			
Cook, Joseph	....	Fr	1	1	0
Clater, Henry	Thorp	Rt	1	1	0
Dinnis, James	London	Fr			
Dunham, James	....	Fr	1	0	1
Dodds, Samuel	....	Fr	1	1	0
Dawson, George	Boston	Fr			
Dix, John	....	Fr	1	1	0
Drury, John	....	Fr	1	1	0
Dorrington, Baxter Manassah	Strubby nr. Alford	Fr			
Daubney,Heaford William	Great Grimsby *Sol*	Fr			
Dabb, John	....	Fr	1	1	0
Elmhirst, Edward	Shawall,Countyof Leicester	Fr			
Eno, John	....	Fr	1	0	1

Leake—continued.

Name of Elector.	Residence, if out of the Parish.	Qual.	T.	W.	P.
Fowler, Samuel	....	Fr			
Fountain, William	....	Rt			
Fountain, Henry	....	Fr	1	1	0
Gray, Jonathan	....	Fr	1	1	0
Griffin, George	West Ashby Thorpe	Fr	0	0	1
Grayson, Thomas	....	Fr	1	1	0
Graburn, James	Saleby	Fr	1	1	0
Haddock, Samuel	....	Fr	1	1	0
Haywood, Thomas	Wellingore, near Lincoln	Fr			
Hansord, Temple	....	Fr	1	1	0
Hildred, William	....	Rt	1	1	0
Hotchen, Thomas	....	Rt	1	1	0
Hayward, John Sol	St. Martin's, City of Lincoln	Fr			
Horton, Geo George	....	Fr	1	0	1
Hastings, Solomon	....	Fr	1	0	0
Howard, William	....	Fr	1	1	0
Ingamells, James	East Ville	Fr			
Jackson, Samuel	....	Rt	1	1	0
Johnson, Edward	....	Fr	1	0	1
Johnson, Stephen Maurice Theophilus, esq.	Spalding	Fr			
Kirton, Henry	Revesby	Fr	1	1	0
King, John	....	Fr	1	1	0
Lilley, Richard	....	Fr	1	1	0
Mills, John	....	Rt	1	1	0
Mells, William	Sibsey	Fr	1	1	0
Mills, Richard	....	Fr	1	1	0
Millington, Boyfield John	Boston Sol	Fr			
Merrifield, Seare Thomas	Wainfleet Sol	Fr	1	1	0
Markham, Robert	....	Fr	1	1	0
Mayse, William	....	Fr	1	1	0
Maidens, John	....	Fr	1	1	0
Nunneley, John	Boston	Fr	0	0	1
Plant, Adams	....	Fr	1	1	0
Plant, James	....	Fr	1	1	0
Palmer, Edward	....	Fr	1	1	0
Reeson, James	....	Fr	1	1	0
Rose, Edward	....	Rt	1	1	0
Reeson, William	....	Fr	1	1	0

Leake—continued.

Name of Elector.	Residence, if out of the Parish.	Qual.	T.	W.	P.
Rose, Joseph Peal	....	Rt	1	1	0
Robinson, Gilbert	....	Fr	1	1	0
Richardson, William	....	Fr			
Richardson, John	....	Fr	1	1	0
Richardson, Charles	....	Fr			
Reeson, Doughty William	....	Fr			
Robinson, Christopher	....	Fr	1	1	0
Rollinson, Elijah	Butterwick	Fr	0	0	1
Rushby, John	....	Fr	1	1	0
Soulby, Harding Edward	Revesby	Fr	1	1	0
Smith, Joseph	....	Fr	0	0	1
Sharp, Richard	....	Fr	1	1	0
Swain, Benjamin	....	Rt	0	0	1
Smith, John	....	Fr	1	1	0
Sykes, David	Croft	Fr			
Saul, George	Wrangle	Fr	1	1	0
Saul, William	Sibsey	Fr	1	1	0
Staniland, Meaburn	Boston	Fr			
Stephenson, Robert	Boston	Fr	1	0	1
Sands, John	....	Fr	1	1	0
Sharp, Morton Henry	....	Fr	1	1	0
Sykes, Thomas	Croft	Fr			
Spence, Rev. Joseph	East Keal	Fr	1	1	0
Smith, William	East Ville	Fr	1	1	0
Todd, William	....	Rt			
Torgoose, John	....	Fr	1	1	0
Thompson, John	....	Fr	1	1	0
Torry, Parkinson	East Skirbeck	Fr	1	0	0
Toynton, Joseph	....	Fr	1	0	1
Taylor, Richard	....	Fr	0	1	1
Tipping, Matthew	....	Rt	0	0	1
Thimbleby, Thomas	Spilsby	Fr	1	1	0
Walker, William	....	Fr	1	1	0
Watson, William	....	Rt	1	1	0
Welsh, William	....	Rt	1	1	0
Weylard, Powell H., esq.	Foxleas Lyndhurst, Hants	Fr			
Woods, John	....	Rt	1	1	0
Wilson, Miles	....	Rt	1	1	0
Williams, Abel	Leverton Outgate	Fr	1	1	0

Leake—continued.

Name of Elector.	Residence, if out of the Parish.	Qual.	T.	W.	P.
Whiting, John	Benington	Fr	1	1	0
Wright, William	....	Fr	0	0	1
Waltham, George	....	Fr	1	1	0
Wray, Francis John, *Ellr* Horsington *dead*		Fr			
Woods, John	....	Fr	1	1	0
Would, William	Belchford	Fr	0	0	1
Watkin, the Rev. John Woodland	Horsington	Fr	0	0	1
Wing, Webb James	Little Gonerby	Fr			
Wing, Webb James	Great Gonerby	Fr			
Wilson, Joseph	....	Fr	1	1	0
Young, Edward	....	Fr	1	1	0
Young, John	....	Fr	1	1	0
Young, Clark	....	Fr	0	0	1

Leverton.

Name of Elector.	Residence, if out of the Parish.	Qual.	T.	W.	P.
Barker, William	....	Rt	1	1	0
Burgess, Hunstan	....	Fr	0	0	1
Bettinson, John	....	Fr	1	0	1
Barton, William	....	Fr	0	1	1
Brown, Thomas	....	Fr	1	0	1
Brown, Solomon	....	Rt	1	0	1
Barker, William Jackson	....	Fr	1	0	1
Boucher, Thomas	....	Fr	0	1	0
Cammack, James	....	Rt	1	1	0
Clark, John	....	Rt	1	0	1
Cammack, James	....	Rt	0	0	1
Clark, Richard	....	Fr	1	0	1
Clark, Charles Codling	....	Rt	1	1	0
Dawson, Joseph Winter	....	Fr	0	0	1
Dracass, John	....	Fr	1	0	1
Dodds, William	....	Fr	1	0	1
Euby, Mark	....	Fr	1	1	0
Fixture, William	....	Fr	0	0	1
Fox, William	....	Fr	0	0	1
Fields, Charles	....	Fr	0	0	1
Fant, John	Freiston	Fr	1	0	1
Gask, William	....	Rt	1	1	0
Gainsley, Michael	....	Fr	1	1	0
Haywood, John	the Parish of St. Martin, Lincoln	Fr			

Leverton—continued.

Name of Elector.	Residence, if out of the Parish.	Qual.	T.	W.	P.
Harrison, William	Benington	Fr			
Hayward, John	Saint Mark's, Lincoln	Fr			
Hayward, Thomas	Wellingore, County of Lincoln	Fr			
Johnson, John	……	Fr	0	0	1
Johnson, D. E.	Grantham	Fr	1	0	1
Jackson, John	Butterwick	Fr			
Lacey, John	……	Fr	0	0	1
Leggott, William	……	Rt	1	1	0
Lightfoot, Joseph	……	Fr	0	0	1
Lakins, John	……	Rt	0	0	1
Lee, John Clakton	Scrivelsby	Fr	0	0	1
Nicholson, Luke	Benington	Fr			
Newmarch, Rev. C. F.	Leverton Rectory	Fr	0	0	1
Paul, Bloom William	……	Fr			
Robinson, William	……	Rt	0	1	0
Rogers, Thomas	Stagenhoe Park, Parish of Saint Paul, Hertford	Fr			
Rensher, Robert	Staythorpe, near Newark, Notts.	Fr	1	1	0
Sharp, William	……	Fr	0	0	1
Smith, James	……	Fr	1	1	0
Slight, James	……	Fr	1	1	0
Smith, William	……	Fr	0	1	1
Tenant, Thomas, esq.	21, Blenheim Terrace, Leeds, Yorks.	Fr	1	1	0
Tenant, Rev. William	No. 3, Cowley-st., St. John's the Evangelist, Westminster	Fr	1	1	0
Wedd, Peter	West-street, Boston	Fr	1	1	0
Ward, Joseph	……	Fr	0	0	1
Wilson, George	Leake	Fr	1	0	1
xWilliams, Edward	Wrangle *dead*	Fr	1	1	0
Williams, Kime	……	Fr	1	1	0
Williams, Lambrick	……	Fr	0	0	1

Skirbeck.

Name of Elector.	Residence, if out of the Parish.	Qual.	T.	W.	P.
Arnold, Thomas Graham	SaintMartin'sStamford Baron	Fr			

Skirbeck—continued.

Name of Elector.	Residence, if out of the Parish.	Qual.	T.	W.	P.
Bramley, John	Toynton All Saints Allotment	Rt			
Bothamley, Benjamin	Boston	Fr	1	1	0
Buttou, Henry	Boston	Fr			
Burgess, John	Boston	Fr	0	0	1
Bowser, William	....	Rt	1	0	1
Buchanan, Alfred Daniel	RedLion-st.,Boston	Fr	1	0	1
Burton, Thomas	....	Fr	0	1	1
Conington, Richard, *Clerk*	Boston	Fr	1	0	1
Cook, Thomas Smalley	Boston	Fr			
Conington, John	University College, Oxford	Fr			
Clarke, Charles	....	Fr	1	1	0
Clarke, Joseph	....	Fr	0	0	1
Cooke, Thomas	Boston	Fr	0	0	1
Chapman, William	Revesby	Fr	1	1	0
Dennison, Frederick	Boston	Fr	1	0	1
Elsom, John	Boston	Fr	0	0	1
Eliff, John	....	Fr	1	1	0
Groom, William	Boston	Fr	0	0	1
Goe, Field Flowers *Sol*	Louth	Fr	1	0	1
Gilson, Robert Henry	....	Fr	1	0	1
Garn, John	Caroline-st., Boston	Fr	0	0	1
Gazeley, Robert Count	Compton, Berks	Fr			
Hall, Thomas	Boston	Fr	1	0	1
Hall, John	Boston	Fr	0	0	1
Hall, John	Wide Bargate, Boston	Fr			
Harrard, Joseph	....	Fr	0	0	1
Harwood, Henry *Sol*	Boston	Fr	0	0	1
Jebb, Samuel Henry *Sol*	Boston	Fr			
Johnson, William Wade	Boston East	Fr	0	0	1
Joyce, William	Boston	Fr	1	0	1
Lancaster, James	Boston	Fr	1	1	0
Lawrance, Richard	....	Fr	1	0	1
Little, John Caruthers	South-place,Boston	Rt	1	1	0
Mountain, Joseph	Boston	Rt			
Maddison, Thomas	High Toynton	Rt			
Morton, William Rastall	....	Fr	1	0	1
Newton, Samuel	Boston	Rt	1	0	1
Oldfield, James	....	Fr	1	0	1
Ostler, John	....	Fr			

Skirbeck—continued.

Name of Elector.	Residence, if out of the Parish.	Qual	T.	W.	P.
Ostler, James	....	Rt	1	1	0
Phillips, Thomas	....	Fr	0	0	1
Pocklington, Henry	Cheyney-st., Boston	Fr			
Pocklington, Henry	Boston	Fr	1	1	0
Rogers, John	Coningsby	Fr	1	1	0
Rogers, Henry, jun.	Stagenhoe Park, in Walden, Herts.	Fr			
Rose, George	Sutton St. Mary's	Fr	0	0	1
Rawson, John	....	Fr			
Rawson, John Rinder	....	Fr	0	0	1
Saunders, John Gower	Lynn Regis	Fr	1	1	0
Snaith, John	Boston	Fr	0	0	1
Sykes, Jacob	....	Rt	1	1	0
Simpson, Thomas	Boston	Fr	1	0	1
Smith, William Henry	Sleaford	Fr	0	0	1
Stevenson, James	Boston	Fr	1	0	1
Stainton, John	....	Fr	0	0	1
Stephenson, Charles Tooley	Maddison's-row, Skirbeck	Fr	0	0	1
Soulby, William	Stickney	Fr			
Temple, William	Boston West	Rt			
Tuxford, William Wedd	Boston	Fr	0	0	1
Thorpe, John	....	Rt	0	0	1
Thompson, Abraham	....	Fr	0	0	1
Torry, Parkinson	Spilsby-road, Skirbeck	Fr			
Talkes, John	Gourley's-row, Lincoln	Fr			
Temple, Thomas	Boston	Rt	0	0	1
Tuxford, William	Boston Market-place	Fr	0	0	1
Tuxford, Webb	....	Fr	0	0	1
Tuxford, Weston	Boston Market-place	Fr	0	0	1
Tuxford, Joseph Shepherd	....	Fr	0	0	1
Vinters, William	....	Fr	1	0	1
Watmough, William	....	Fr	0	1	0
Wiseman, Robert	....	Fr	0	1	1
Winter, William	....	Fr	1	0	1
Winter, Matthew Lee	Boston West	Fr	1	0	1
Winter, George	....	Fr	1	1	0
Williamson, John	Fishtoft	Rt	1	0	1
Wilson, John	Saint John's-row, Boston	Fr			

Hamlet of Skirbeck Quarter.

Name of Elector.	Residence, if out of the Parish.	Qual.	T.	W.	P.
Baxter, George	....	Fr	0	0	1
Barrack, John	Boston	Fr	0	0	1
Clark, Henry	....	Fr			
Claypon, Bartholomew	Hampstead	Fr			
Claypon, Joseph	Hampstead	Fr			
Dawson, Samuel	....	Fr	0	0	1
Hobster, Stephen	....	Fr	1	1	0
Kittmer, Thomas	Sutton Saint James	Fr	1	1	0
Leak, John Chapman	....	Fr	0	0	1
Munk, Henry	Skirbeck	Fr	0	0	1
Oldman, John	....	Fr	1	0	1
Osborne, Joseph	....	Fr	1	0	1
Pigot, William	Findern, Derbyshire	Fr			
Potter, Henry	....	Fr			
Preston, Sir R., Bart.	Bath	Fr			
Roy, Robert Evelyn	Skirbeck	Fr	1	1	0
Stainbank, Robert William	....	Fr	0	0	1
Stainbank, Robert	....	Fr			
Sooby, Matthew	Gainsborough	Fr			
Triphook, Thomas	Stevenage, Hertfordshire	Fr			
Tuck, John	....	Rt	1	0,	1
Vyner, H., esq.	St. James' Square, London	Fr	0	0	1
West, William	Wyberton	Fr	1	0	1
Wilson, Edward	Skirbeck	Fr	0	0	1
Wilson, Robert George	Boston	Fr			
Watmough, Ernest	Skirbeck	Fr			
Wilson, Edward, jun.	....	Rt	1	1	0

Sutterton.

Name of Elector.	Residence, if out of the Parish.	Qual.	T.	W.	P.
Abbott, John	....	Rt			
Allenby, Thomas	Spalding	Fr			
Adams, Rev. William	Throcking, Herts.	Fr			
Ashby, Thomas	Wormgate, Boston	Fr	0	0	1
Barnsdale, George	....	Fr	1	0	1
Barton, John	....	Rt	1	1	0
Barty, Charles	....	Fr	0	1	1
Bissill, Edward	Spalding	Fr			
Bourn, Thomas	....	Rt	1	1	0
Brewster, Samuel	....	Fr	1	0	1
Brewster, John	....	Fr	1	1	0

Sutterton—continued.

Name of Elector.	Residence, if out of the Parish.	Qual.	T.	W.	P.
Brittain, John	....	Fr	1	0	1
Brock, John	Wigtoft	Fr	1	1	0
Bycroft, William	....	Fr	1	0	1
Butterfield, Joseph	....	Co	1	1	0
Brown, Robert	....	Fr			
Cash, William	....	Fr	1	1	0
Challans, Timothy	....	Fr	1	1	0
Cropley, William	Beckingham	Fr			
Curtois, Peregrine S.	Langrick Ferry	Fr	1	0	1
Cutforth, John	....	Rt			
Crow, Edward	Great Creaton, Northamptonshire	Fr			
Dickenson, John	....	Fr	1	1	0
Dobney, Thomas	....	Rt			
Dowse, Thomas	Sutterton-fen	Fr	1	1	0
Dowse, Thomas	....	Rt			
Dring, Richard	....	Rt	1	1	0
Ebb, John	....	Fr	1	1	0
Evans, John	....	Fr	1	0	1
Evison, William	....	Rt	1	1	0
Ebb, Edward	....	Rt	1	1	0
Farrow, John	Sleithwaite, Yorks.	Fr			
Fossitt, John	....	Fr	0	0	1
Fossitt, Frederick	....	Fr	0	0	1
Fisher, Robert	Gonerby	Fr			
Faulkner, Samuel	....	Fr	1	1	0
Faulkner, Charles	....	Fr	1	1	0
Gaunt, James	....	Fr	1	0	1
Gilding, Matthew	....	Fr	0	0	1
Gadd, Benjamin	....	Fr	1	1	0
Greetham, Robert	....	Fr	0	0	1
Gibney, Rev. John S.	St. Margaret's, Lincoln	Fr			
Gray, Samuel	....	Fr	0	0	1
Garnham, William	....	Rt			
Garner, Cornelius	....	Fr	0	0	1
Hall, Charles	....	Rt	1	0	1
Hanks, John	....	Fr	0	0	1
Healey, Robert	....	Fr	1	1	0

Sutterion—continued.

Name of Elector.	Residence, if out of the Parish.	Qual.	T.	W.	P.
Heathcote, John *Esq.*	Conington Castle, Hunts.	Fr			
Heathcote, Robert B. *Clk*	Chingford, Essex	Fr	0	0	1
Hydes, George	South Kyme	Fr			
Hunt, Thomas	....	Fr			
Hutton, William *Esqe*	Gate Burton	Fr	0	0	1
Hudson, John	....	Fr	0	1	1
Holmes, John Joseph	Sutterton-fen	Fr	0	0	1
Ireland, Thomas	Fosdyke	Fr			
Jepson, Rev. William N.	Lincoln	Fr	1	1	0
Jebb, John Joshua *Sol*	Boston	Fr			
Kent, Rev. John	Lincoln	Fr			
Kent, George Davis *Clk*	Lincoln	Fr			
Kirby, George	....	Fr	1	1	0
King, William	Sutterton-fen	Rt	1	0	1
Lawson, Henry	Boston	Fr	1	1	0
Lee, Charles	Leeds, Yorkshire	Fr			
Maltby, William	....	Rt	1	1	0
Maltby, John	....	Co	1	0	1
Mason, William	....	Fr			
Metcalf, David	Leeds, Yorkshire	Fr			
Moore, Joseph *Sol*	Lincoln	Fr			
Nussey, George	Leeds, Yorkshire	Fr			
Palmer, John	Stamford	Fr			
Parker, William	....	Fr	1	0	1
Patchett, John	Sutterton-fen	Fr	1	1	0
Pearson, John, esq,	Tandridge, Surrey	Fr	1	1	0
Peacock, Anthony, esq.	South Rauceby	Fr	*the candidate*		
Pell, George	....	Fr	1	1	0
Pepper, Valentine	Carrington	Rt	1	0	1
Pinion, William	Sutterton-fen	Fr	0	1	1
Pocklington, Roger	....	Fr	1	0	0
Pooles, Isaac	....	Fr	1	1	0
Richardson, Charles	....	Rt	0	0	1
Ritcher, Rev. William	Silver-street, St. Peter at Arches, Lincoln	Fr			
Richardson, John	....	Rt	1	1	0
Rose, William	....	Fr	1	1	0
Robinson, George	Sutterton-fen	Fr	1	1	0

Sutterton—continued.

Name of Elector.	Residence, if out of the Parish.	Qual.	T.	W.	P.
Richardson, Charles	....	Fr			
Seaman, Richard	Frampton	Fr			
Scargall, William	Boston	Fr	1	0	1
Scarborough, Tickler T.	Spalding	Fr			
Sellars, Thomas	Sutterton-fen	Rt			
Sharpe, James	....	Rt	1	1	0
Shaw, George	Frampton	Rt			
Spencer, Rev. John	East Keal	Fr	1	1	0
Stainbank, Robert	Skirbeck Quarter	Fr			
Sivers, William	....	Fr	0	0	1
Southern, John Casswell	....	Fr	1	1	0
Southern, George H.	....	Fr	1	1	0
Thorold, Richard, esq.	Weelsby House	Fr			
Thorpe, James Cole	Otby	Fr	1	1	0
Tooley, Samuel	....	Fr	1	0	1
Trafford, Edward	....	Rt	1	1	0
Thornhill, George, esq.	Deddington, Hunts.	Fr	1	1	0
Wadsley, Thomas	....	Fr	1	1	0
Wadsley, George	....	Rt	1	1	0
Wadsley, John	Sutterton-fen	Fr	1	1	0
Waltham, Robert	....	Fr	0	1	1
Ward, Joseph	Sutterton-fen	Fr	0	0	1
Wanty, Henry	Lynn	Co	1	1	0
Wellman, Charles	....	Fr	1	1	0
Willson, Rev. John	Wigtoft Vicarage	Fr			
Ward, James	South Kyme	Fr			
Wadsley, John	Boston	Fr	1	1	0

Wrangle.

Name of Elector.	Residence, if out of the Parish.	Qual.	T.	W.	P.
Alenson, Cornelius Margison	....	Fr	1	1	0
Alford, John	Friskney	Rt	1	1	0
Ashby, Thomas	....	Fr	1	1	0
Baldestone, John	....	Fr	1	1	0
Bontoft, Matthew	....	Fr			
Bothamley, William	....	Fr	0	1	1
Bell, John	Spalding	Fr	0	0	1
Brufton, John	....	Fr	1	0	1
Bycroft, William, jun.	....	Fr	1	1	0
Bucknell, Edward	....	Fr	1	1	0
Brackenbury, J. L. *Sol*	Alford	Fr	1	1	0

Wrangle—continued.

Name of Elector.	Residence, if out of the Parish.	Qual.	T.	W.	P.
Clark, William Gask	……	Rt			
Codd, David	……	Fr	0	1	1
Collins, George	……	Fr	1	1	0
Cook, Thomas	……	Fr	1	1	0
Chapman, Robert, sen.	……	Fr	1	1	0
Chapman, Robert, jun.	……	Fr	1	1	0
Chapman, Robert, jun.	Wrangle Common	Rt	1	1	0
Cowham, William	……	Fr	1	1	0
Dunn, George	Beckingham, Newark	Fr			
Donnor, John	……	Rt	1	1	0
English, John	……	Fr	1	1	0
Exton, Edward	……	Rt	1	1	0
Edwards, Timothy	……	Fr	1	1	0
Evison, William Merrill	……	Fr	1	1	0
Emery, George	……	Fr	0	0	1
Foster, Thomas	……	Fr	1	1	0
Gant, John	Friskney	Fr	0	0	1
Gask, William, sen.	……	Rt	1	1	0
Goodrick, John	Claxby, Alford	Fr			
Greenfield, Martin, sen.	……	Fr			
Greenfield, John	……	Fr	0	1	1
Greenfield, Martin, jun.	……	Fr	0	1	1
Gilbert, John	Grimoldby	Fr	0	0	1
Haynes, Thomas	……	Fr	0	1	1
Hoyles, Francis	Friskney	Fr	1	0	1
Hill, James	……	Rt	0	0	1
Huggard, James	……	Fr	1	1	0
Harrison, John	……	Rt	1	1	0
Horton, George, sen.	……	Fr	1	1	0
Hoyles, William Lowe	……	Fr	0	0	1
Hurton, Samuel	……	Fr	1	1	0
Humble, Samuel	……	Fr	1	1	0
Keal, Oldham, sen.	……	Rt			
Kitching, David	……	Rt	1	1	0
Keal, Oldham, jun.	Leake	Fr	0	1	1
Kime, Joseph	Skirbeck	Fr	1	0	1
Lilley, William, jun.	……	Fr	1	1	0
Lilley, Joseph	……	Fr	1	1	0
Lilley, John	……	Fr	1	1	0
Linton, Rev. James	Hemingford Abbots, Huntingdonshire	Fr	1	1	0

Wrangle—continued.

Name of Elector.	Residence, if out of the Parish.	Qual.	T.	W.	P.
Morley, Rev. William	Raithby, Parsonage	Fr	1	1	0
Muntos, William	Leake	Fr	1	1	0
Mason, John	Leake	Fr	1	1	0
Massingbird, Rev. Francis Charles	Ormsby Rectory, Alford	Fr	1	1	0
Needham, George	....	Fr	1	1	0
Newton, John	....	Rt	1	1	0
Page, Thomas	Upwell, Norfolk	Fr			
Pearson, John	....	Fr	0	1	0
Plant, James	Sibsey	Fr			
Parker, John, jun.	....	Rt	1	1	0
Pinder, John	Friskney	Fr	1	1	0
Reeson, Thomas	....	Fr	0	0	1
Rawson, William	....	Fr			
Rinder, Joseph, sen.	East Keal	Fr	1	1	0
Rinder, John	Skendleby	Fr			
Rinder, Joseph, jun.	Welbourne	Fr			
Rawson, John	Skirbeck	Fr			
Robinson, Zachariah	Leake	Fr	1	1	0
Royle, Saywell	....	Fr	0	0	1
Savage, Benjamin	....	Fr			
Short, John Hassard Esqr. Stanbrook House, Brighton		Fr			
Swain, Charles	....	Fr	1	1	0
Simpson, Elijah	....	Fr	1	1	0
Snowden, John	....	Fr	1	1	0
Simpson, Charles	....	Fr	1	0	0
Simpson, Elijah, jun.	....	Fr	1	1	0
Simpson, George	Friskney	Fr			
Simpson, Hansard	....	Fr	1	1	0
Simpson, Thomas	....	Fr	1	1	0
Smith, William	....	Fr	1	1	0
Swift, Richard	....	Fr			
Southwell, Robert	Friskney	Fr	0	0	1
Stephenson, Joseph	....	Fr			
Thompson, Rev. Sir Henry, Bart.	Farneham, Southampton	Fr			
Torgoose, William	....	Rt	1	1	0
Tilley, John	....	Fr	1	1	0
Taylor, John	....	Rt	1	1	0

Wrangle—continued.

Name of Elector.	Residence, if out of the Parish.	Qual.	T.	W.	P.
Taylor, William	Boston	Fr			
Topham, James, Welford, Northamptonshire		Fr			
Underwood, Benjamin	....	Fr	0	0	1
Vessey, Henry John	Holton Holgate	Fr	1	1	0
Vessey, Samuel	Holton Holgate	Fr	1	0	0
Wright, Rev. Thomas Bailey	....	Fr	1	1	0
Wright, William	....	Fr	1	1	0
Waite, George	....	Fr			
Wright, George	....	Fr	1	1	0
Ward, Edward	....	Fr	1	0	1
Wainfer, John	....	Fr	1	1	0
Wright, Hotson	....	Fr	1	1	0
Wilson, John	Leake	Fr	1	0	1
Williams, Isaac	....	Fr	1	1	0
Wilcox, Simon William	Wainfleet All Saints	Fr	1	0	1
Wilks, Brown M., esq.	Chesterford, Saffron Walden, Essex	Fr			

Wyberton.

Name of Elector.	Residence, if out of the Parish.	Qual.	T.	W.	P.
Boardman, Joseph	....	Fr	1	1	0
Booth, Benjamin	Boston	Fr	0	0	1
Borman, Allen	Kirton	Rt	1	1	0
Cartwright, Thomas	Ragnall, Nottinghamshire	Fr	0	0	1
Crawford, Solomon	....	Rt	1	1	0
Creasy, George	....	Rt	1	1	0
Creasy, Bletcher	....	Rt	1	1	0
East, Jabez	....	Rt	0	0	1
Garfit, William, jun. Esq.	Boston	Fr	1	0	1
Garfit, Mark, Clerk	Maxey, Northamptonshire	Fr	1	0	1
Gibson, Henry	....	Fr	0	0	1
Goring, George	Boston	Fr	1	1	0
Keal, Richard	....	Fr	1	0	1
King, George, sen.	....	Rt	0	0	1
Kent, Samuel Harrison	Thimbleby	Fr			
Lister, Joseph	....	Rt	1	1	0
Minta, Thomas	....	Rt	0	0	1
Moore, Charles T. J., esq.	Frampton Hall	Fr			

Wyberton—continued.

Name of Elector.	Residence, if out of the Parish.	Qual.	T.	W.	P.
Mowbray, Marcham	....	Rt	1	0	1
Martin, Martin	....	Rt	1	1	0
Norton, John D.	Little Stanmore, Middlesex	Fr			
Parker, William	Thorton-le-Moor	Fr	1	1	0
Parkinson, Joseph	....	Fr	1	1	0
Popple, William	....	Fr	1	1	0
Roberts, John, jun.	....	Rt	0	0	1
Robinson, John Wright	....	Fr	1	1	0
Robinson, Christopher	....	Fr	1	1	0
Rogers, Thomas	....	Rt	1	1	0
Russell, William	West Ville	Fr	1	1	0
Sharp, John	Frampton	Fr			
Sheath, Rev. Martin	....	Fr	1	0	1
Short, John	....	Rt	1	0	1
Strattan, William	Little Birkhampstead	Fr			
Webster, William	....	Fr			
Wells, William	....	Rt	0	0	1
Watson, William	....	Fr	0	1	1
Worsley, Rev. Charles P.	Thurlby	Fr			
Watson, John	....	Fr	0	0	1

Whaplode.

Name of Elector.	Residence, if out of the Parish.	Qual.	T.	W.	P.
Nairn, Rev. Charles	Lincoln	Fr	1	1	0

No. 2.—POLLING DISTRICT ASSIGNED TO DONINGTON.

Bicker.

Name of Elector.	Residence, if out of the Parish.	Qual.	T.	W.	P.
Adkin, John	....	Fr	1	1	0
Bates, John	....	Fr	0	0	1
Best, Rev. Thomas	Kirkby on Bain	Fr	1	1	0
Bilsby, John	....	Fr	0	0	1
Boul, William	....	Fr	1	0	1
Burn, Edwin	....	Rt	0	0	1
Carrot, Peter Physick	....	Rt	0	0	1
Chester, Thomas	....	Fr	0	0	1
Collins, Richard	Kirk Burton, Yorkshire	Fr	*Clerk*		
Cooley, William Godbehere	....	Fr	0	0	1
Creasey, John	....	Fr			

Bicker—continued.

Name of Elector.	Residence, if out of the Parish.	Qual.	T.	W.	P.
Cooley, William	....	Rt	0	0	1
Cooley, Edward John	....	Rt	0	0	1
Dring, John	....	Rt	0	0	1
East, William	....	Fr	1	0	1
Fletcher, Henry Thomas *clerk, Vicar*		Fr	0	0	1
Godley, William	....	Fr	1	1	0
Godley, Joseph	....	Fr			
Gosling, John	....	Fr	1	1	0
Graham, George	....	Fr	0	0	1
Grice, Richard	....	Co	0	0	1
Godley, John Dawson	Skirbeck Quarter, Boston	Fr	0	0	1
Grewcock, George	Falkingham	Fr	0	1	1
Hall, William	....	Fr	0	0	1
Harley, David Bell	Frieston	Fr			
Holmes, John	....	Rt	0	0	1
Holland, John sen.	....	Fr	0	0	1
Hand, Richard	Spittlegate, near Grantham	Fr			
Hairby, James, esq. *m. x.*	Hundleby	Fr			
Houlden, Thomas	West Ashby	Fr	1	0	1
Higgs, Arthur	Kirton	Fr			
Jackson, John	Swineshead	Fr			
Jackson, William	....	Fr			
Jarvis, Thomas Razor	Boston	Fr			
Kirman, Joseph	....	Fr	0	0	1
Key, James	Bicker Cantlet	Rt	1	0	1
Lavesley, James	Sleaford	Fr			
Limbird, Richard	....	Co			
Morley, John William	....	Rt	1	1	0
Morley, William	Donington	Fr	1	1	0
Morley, Thomas	Donington	Fr	1	1	0
Mills, Charles	....	Rt	0	0	1
Norriss, George	Welbourne	Fr	0	0	1
Parker, Robert	....	Rt			
Payne, John	....	Fr	0	0	1
Pilkington, Rev. Charles	Stockton Rectory, near Southam, Warwickshire	Fr			
Peake, Henry *Soln*	New Sleaford	Fr			
Page, James	....	Fr	0	0	1

Bicker—continued.

Name of Elector.	Residence, if out of the Parish.	Qual.	T.	W.	P.
Ranby, Robert	....	Rt	0	1	1
Roworth, Joseph	....	Rt	0	0	1
Rowland, Benjamin	....	Rt	0	0	1
Sharp, Michael	Wigtoft	Fr			
Simpson, Hirst William	Falkingham *Clerk*	Fr			
Singleton, Jonathan	....	Fr	1	1	0
Smith, John	Frampton	Fr			
Smith, Samuel	Camberwell, Surrey	Fr			
Smith, Edward	....	Fr			
Stimson, Humphrey	....	Fr	0	0	1
Sharp, Joshua	....	Rt	0	0	1
Smith, Charles	....	Fr			
Sharpe, Joshua	....	Rt	1	0	1
Tawlks, John	....	Fr	0	0	1
Tawlks, Henry	....	Fr	0	0	1
Tomlinson, Thomas	....	Co	0	0	1
Trimnell, John George	....	Rt	1	1	0
West, Charles	....	Fr	1	1	0
White, Edward	....	Fr	1	0	1
Warnes, James Claxton	Saville-st., Leeds	Fr			
Wanewright, William	....	Fr	1	1	0
Winlow, John Bonner	....	Rt	0	0	1
Westmoreland, William	....	Rt	0	0	1

Donington.

Name of Elector.	Residence, if out of the Parish.	Qual.	T.	W.	P.
Artindale, William	....	Fr	0	0	1
Allen, Henry Clerk	Horsham, Sussex	Fr			
Bailey, Philip	....	Fr	1	1	0
Bemrose, Henry	....	Fr	0	1	1
Bedford, George	....	Fr	0	1	1
Bell, Thomas	....	Fr	0	1	1
Broughton, John	....	Fr	0	0	1
Bartram, Thomas	....	Fr	1	1	0
Barnsdale, George	....	Co	1	1	0
Bothamley, Samuel	....	Co	0	0	1
Brown, John	Hammersmith	Co			
Booth, George	....	Fr			
Baxter, Richard	....	Fr	0	1	1
Bacchus, Samuel	....	Fr	0	1	1
Cocks, Jonathan	....	Rt	1	1	0

Donington—continued.

Name of Elector.	Residence, if out of the Parish.	Qual	T.	W.	P
Clifton, John	....	Fr			
Clifton, David	....	Co			
Crampton, Joseph	....	Fr			
Cheavin, Squire	....	Fr	1	1	0
Cox, John	....	Fr	0	1	1
Carrington, William	....	Co	1	0	1
Carden, Thomas	....	Fr	0	0	1
Cragg, Edward	Threekingham	Fr			
Cocks, Thomas	....	Co	1	1	0
Cocks, Francis	....	Fr	0	1	0
Clifton, William	....	Co	1	0	1
Douglas, James Dee	Market Harborough	Fr			
Dods, Joseph	....	Fr	1	0	1
Dodd, Joseph	....	Co	1	1	0
Dolby, George	....	Fr			
Daubney, John Kent	Burton Coggles	Fr			
Day, Joseph	....	Rt	1	1	0
Dods, William	....	Fr	1	0	1
Dickinson, Joseph	....	Fr	1	1	0
Day, James	Sleaford	Co	1	1	0
Dawney, John William	Gosberton	Fr	1	1	0
Elston, Thomas	Swarby	Rt			
Elstone, John Harrison	....	Rt			
Elston, Robert	....	Rt			
Elston, Thomas, jun.	....	Rt	1	1	0
Edinborough, Thomas	....	Rt	1	1	0
Flowers, William	Surfleet	Fr			
Flowers, Henry	....	Fr	1	1	0
Fox, Samuel	....	Fr	0	0	1
Fowler, Benjamin	....	Rt	1	1	0
Flowers, Moses	....	Fr	1	1	0
Gleed, Joseph, esq.	....	Co	1	1	0
Graham, Joseph	....	Fr			
Green, William, jun.	....	Rt	1	1	0
Gunn, John	....	Fr			
Grenside, Rev. John D.	....	Fr	1	1	0
Gleed, Richard, esq.	....	Fr	1	1	0
Green, Bracebridge	....	Rt	1	1	0
Gadsby, Thomas	....	Rt	1	1	0
Hodson, Mark	....	Rt	0	0	1
Holland, Thomas	....	Fr	1	1	0

Donington—continued.

Name of Elector.	Residence, if out of the Parish.	Qual.	T.	W.	P.
Hickinbottom, John	. . . .	Rt	1	0	1
Holland, John	Liquorpond-street, Boston	Fr			
Holland, John Cragg	. . . .	Rt	1	1	0
Hinkley, Richard *Sol or* Lichfield		Fr			
Hoyes, Joseph	. . . .	Fr	0	1	1
Holmes, Richard	. . . .	Rt	0	0	1
Hickinbottom, Charles	. . . .	Co	1	0	1
Heffield, John	. . . .	Fr	0	1	0
Haw, William	. . . .	Co			
Haw, Thomas	. . . .	Fr	1	1	0
Jackson, Charles	. . . .	Fr	0	1	1
Johnson, George Dobson	. . . .	Fr	0	1	1
King, Charles	. . . .	Fr	1	1	0
Knowles, Richard	. . . .	Co	0	1	1
King, Thomas	. . . .	Fr	1	1	0
Kirk, Thomas	. . . .	Co	0	1	1
Lumby, John	. . . .	Fr			
Leatherland, Thomas	. . . .	Fr	1	0	1
Lawrence, John	. . . .	Co	1	0	1
Leach, Elijah	. . . .	Rt	1	1	0
Lake, Thomas	Revesby	Fr			
Millson, Enoch	. . . .	Co	0	1	1
Millson, William	. . . .	Fr	0	1	1
Mood, James	. . . .	Fr	0	0	1
Moore, John	. . . .	Fr	1	1	0
Milson, John Iron	. . . .	Fr			
Middlebrooke, Charles	. . . .	Co	0	1	0
Naylor, John	. . . .	Fr	1	1	0
Newton, Isaac	. . . .	Fr			
Parker, John	. . . .	Rt	0	1	1
Pearson, John	. . . .	Fr	1	1	1
Picker, William	. . . .	Fr	1	0	1
Porter, John	. . . .	Fr	1	0	1
Parry, Edward Humffreys	Surfleet *each*	Fr			
Page, Edward	. . . .	Rt	1	1	0
Pick, Charles	. . . .	Rt	0	1	1
Ridley, William	. . . .	Rt			
Rosling, William	. . . .	Rt	0	1	1
Raynor, John	. . . .	Fr	1	1	0

Donington—continued.

Name of Elector.	Residence, if out of the Parish.	Qual.	T.	W.	P.
Ranby, William	....	Rt	0	1	1
Rippon, Edwin	....	Fr	0	1	1
Roe, Abraham	....	Fr	0	1	1
Reek, John Boulding	....	Fr	1	1	0
Smith, Benjamin, *Sol*	Horbling	Fr			
Swift, Thomas	....	Rt	1	0	0
Stout, Thomas	....	Fr	0	0	1
Spendlow, John	Whittlesea	Fr			
Tenney, Thomas	....	Fr			
Torrington, Edward	Falkingham	Fr			
Thorlby, Joseph	....	Co	0	0	1
Thorold, Richard, *Esq*	Weelsby House, near Great Grimsby	Fr			
Thorold, Henry, *Esq*	Gloucester-square, Hyde Park	Fr			
Tebb, John	....	Co	0	1	1
Twigg, John	....	Fr	1	1	0
Wynn, Edward	....	Rt	1	1	0
Watson, Thomas	....	Fr	1	0	0
Willows, John	....	Rt	0	1	1
Woodhead, John	Quadring, Eaudyke	Fr	1	1	0
West, Simpson	....	Fr	1	1	0
Wells, Joseph Haw	....	Fr			
Worsdale, Dennis	....	Fr			
Worsdale, Joseph	....	Fr	1	1	0
Wilkinson, Edward	Horbling	Fr			
Watson, Joseph	....	Fr	0	1	1
Wilson, Richard	....	Rt	1	1	0
Weathers, James	....	Fr	0	1	1
Wigglesworth, Parkin, *Sol*	....	Rt			
White, George Chambers	....	Rt	1	1	0

Gosberton.

Name of Elector.	Residence, if out of the Parish.	Qual.	T.	W.	P.
Ashwell, Thomas	Gosberton-bank	Fr	0	0	1
Ashwell, Henry	Empingham, Rutland	Fr	0	0	1
Ashwell, William	....	Rt	0	1	1
Alcock, John	....	Fr	1	1	0
Andrew, John	....	Fr			
Atkinson, William	Gosberton Risegate	Rt	0	0	1
Bell, George	Moulton	Fr			
Brand, Richard	....	Rt	0	0	1

Gosberton—continued.

Name of Elector.	Residence, if out of the Parish.	Qual.	T.	W.	P.
Brown, George	Hammersmith, London	Fr			
Brand, Samuel	....	Fr	1	1	0
Butterfield, John	....	Fr			
Bicheno, William	....	Fr	1	0	1
Blackwell, John	....	Fr	1	1	0
Baxter, Samuel	....	Fr	0	0	1
Barnard, George Birkwood	....	Fr	1	1	0
Bray, William	Bourn	Fr			
Bull, George	....	Rt	1	1	0
Burrel, Charles	....	Rt	1	1	0
Berridge, John	....	Rt	0	0	1
Burrill, James	Gosberton Westhorpe	Rt	0	0	1
Brown, Edward	....	Rt	1	0	1
Bailey, John Thomas	....	Rt	1	0	1
Bicheno, Henry Smith	....	Fr	0	0	1
Browning, Edward	Broad-street, Stamford	Fr	1	1	0
Crosby, Benjamin	....	Rt	1	1	0
Coy, Thomas, jun.	....	Rt			
Coy, Thomas	....	Fr			
Cheavins, George	....	Fr	1	0	1
Cheavins, William	....	Fr	1	0	0
Chapman, Augustus	....	Fr			
Chambers, John Woodhead	....	Fr	1	1	0
Crow, Thomas	....	Rt			
Crosby, Benjamin	....	Fr			
Crosby, Richard Marriot	Gosberton, Risegate	Fr	0	0	1
Clifton, William	Donington	Fr			
Clark, John	....	Fr	0	0	1
Crosby, David	....	Rt	1	1	0
Crosby, William the Elder	....	Fr	1	1	0
Dickings, Robert	....	Fr	0	0	1
Draper, James	....	Fr	0	0	1
Dods, William, esq.	....	Fr	1	1	0
Dods, Henry, esq.	....	Fr	1	1	0
Dale, John	....	Fr	0	0	1
Dickings, William	....	Fr	0	0	1
Doubleday, John Millington	....	Fr	0	1	1
Dods, John Thomas	....	Rt	1	1	0
Dawson, Charles	Boston	Fr	1	0	1
Dale, John, jun.	....	Fr	1	1	0

Gosberton—continued.

Name of Elector.	Residence, if out of the Parish.	Qual.	T.	W.	P.
Dickinson, Kew	....	Co	1	1	0
Dickinson, William	....	Fr	0	0	1
Everard, Samuel, esq.	....	Fr	1	1	0
Epton, John	....	Fr			
Elson, George	Newark-upon-Trent, Nottinghamshire	Fr	1	1	0
Elsey, Abraham	....	Fr	0	0	1
Ellis, William	....	Rt	0	0	1
Foster, Thomas	....	Fr	1	0	1
Fox, Thomas Chesterfield	GosbertonRisegate	Fr			
Frazier, Thomas	....	Fr	1	1	0
Freir, William	....	Fr	1	0	1
Fedling, Henry	....	Co	0	0	1
Freemantle, Samuel	....	Fr	1	1	0
Freemantle, John	....	Fr	1	1	0
Fletcher, Thomas	Gosberton-fen	Rt	1	1	0
Faulkner, Cook	Tattershall	Rt	1	1	0
Faulkner, Matthew	....	Rt			
Freir, Samuel	....	Fr	1	1	0
Freir, William	Pinchbeck	Rt	1	1	0
Fountain, Moses	Surfleet	Fr	1	1	0
Green, Thomas	....	Fr	0	0	1
Gedney, James	....	Fr	0	0	1
Garner, Benjamin	....	Fr	1	1	0
Garner, William	....	Fr	1	0	1
Garner, William	Grantham	Fr			
Genn, Robert	Surfleet	Fr			
Gentle, James	....	Fr	1	0	1
Goodyear, Henry	Surfleet	Fr	0	1	1
Giddings, David	....	Rt	0	0	1
Garner, Henry	Gosberton Cheal	Fr	1	1	0
Gaunt, Kelham	....	Fr	0	0	1
Hardy, Thomas	....	Fr	0	0	1
Horn, Thomas Clerk	Mursley, Bucks.	Fr			
Horton, John	....	Rt	1	1	0
Hare, Robert Bellamy	....	Fr	0	0	1
Hare, Joseph	....	Fr	0	0	1
Hare, John	....	Fr	1	1	0
Harrison, Edward	....	Fr	0	0	1
Hopkinson, William	Stamford	Fr			
Hare, John	....	Rt	1	0	1

Gosberton—continued.

Name of Elector.	Residence, if out of the Parish.	Qual.	T.	W.	P.
Helliwell, James	....	Rt	0	0	1
Harrison, Francis Joseph	Tolethorpe	Fr			
Haresign, David	....	Rt	1	1	0
Haresign, George	....	Rt	1	1	0
Hickinbottom, John	....	Rt	1	1	0
Inkley, Joseph	....	Fr	1	1	0
Ingamells, William	....	Fr	0	0	1
Inkley, Barnes	....	Fr			
Johnson, John	....	Rt			
Johnson, Thomas	....	Fr	0	0	1
Knight, John	....	Fr	0	0	1
Kenning, John	....	Fr	1	1	0
Lilee, John	Quadring	Fr			
Leedell, William Patman	....	Fr	0	0	1
Long, John	....	Fr			
Ludlow, Squire	....	Fr	1	0	1
Lounds, Thomas, sen.	....	Rt	1	0	1
Morris, Henry	....	Fr	1	1	0
Mitchelson, George	....	Rt	1	1	0
Muxlow, Isaac	London	Fr			
Nutt, William Thomas	Edithweston, Rutland	Fr	1	0	1
North, William Horner	....	Fr	1	1	0
Nixon, Edward Augustus	....	Rt	0	0	1
Odam, Stephen	....	Fr	1	0	1
Oxman, John	....	Fr	1	0	1
Oliff, Jonathan Hanson	....	Fr			
Oldershaw, George, sen.	....	Fr			
Popple, John	....	Fr	0	0	1
Pridmore, Timothy	....	Fr			
Parsons, Henry	Upton St. Leonards, Gloucestershire	Fr			
Pennington, George	....	Fr	1	1	0
Panton, Robert	....	Rt			
Robinson, Henry	Spalding	Fr	1	1	0
Roper, John	....	Fr			
Rudkins, John Henry	Donington	Fr	0	0	1
Richardson, Benjamin	....	Fr	0	0	1
Riggall, Thomas	....	Rt	1	-1	0
Rowson, George	....	Fr	0	0	1
Smith, Benjamin	....	Rt	1	0	0

Gosberton—continued.

Name of Elector.	Residence, if out of the Parish.	Qual.	T.	W.	P.
Syson, Thomas, jun.	Empingham, Rutland	Fr	0	0	1
Smith, William Maples	....	Fr	1	1	0
Smith, Jacob	....	Rt			
Smith, Robert	....	Rt	1	1	0
Sandall, Thomas, sen.	Rippingale	Fr			
Sexton, William	Surfleet	Fr	0	0	1
Scott, William	....	Fr	0	1	1
Seymour, John	....	Fr	1	1	0
Sansom, Robert	....	Fr	1	1	0
Smith, William	Gosberton-fen	Fr			
Shaw, Joseph	....	Fr	1	0	1
Smith, Robinson	....	Rt	1	0	0
Smith, William	Spalding	Fr	0	0	1
Smith, Robert	Gosberton Belnie	Rt	1	0	1
Stevenson, William	....	Fr	0	1	1
Smith, John	....	Rt	1	1	0
Tomlinson, George	....	Rt	1	1	0
Tomblin, Joseph	High Lodge, Rutland	Fr			
Thorns, James	Boston	Fr	0	0	1
Thornby, David	Washingborough	Fr			
Twell, Abraham	....	Fr	0	0	1
Tunnard, Jacob	....	Fr	1	0	1
Twelves, William	....	Fr	1	0	1
Taylor, Isaac	Gosberton-fen	Fr	1	1	0
Torry, Parkinson	Skirbeck	Fr			
Thompson, John, sen.	....	Fr			
Topham, Rev. John	....	Fr	0	0	1
Todd, Samuel Campain	....	Rt	1	1	0
Wilson, Isaac	....	Fr	1	0	1
Wilkinson, John	Gosberton-fen	Fr	1	1	0
Wilson, Robert, sen.	....	Fr	0	0	1
Warde, William	....	Fr	0	0	1
Waite, John	....	Fr	1	1	0
Wilkinson, Thomas	....	Fr	0	0	1
Winters, George	....	Rt	1	1	0
Waite, William	Surfleet	Fr	1	0	1
Woodthorpe, James	....	Fr	1	0	1
Waite, Edmund Browne	Sibsey	Fr			
Warde, William	Huntingdon	Fr			

Gosberton—continued.

Name of Elector.	Residence, if out of the Parish.	Qual.	T.	W.	P.
Walpole, William	Grove-place, South Town, near Great Yarmouth	Fr			
Wilcock, Robert	....	Fr			
Wallis, John Thomas	....	Rt	1	1	0
Wilkinson, John	....	Fr			
Woodthorpe, James, jun.	Gosberton-fen	Fr	1	1	0
Wheat, James	....	Fr	0	0	1
Wakefield, William	....	Fr			
Watson, James	....	Rt	1	1	0
Young, Adam	Boston	Fr	1	0	1

Harts Grounds.

Name of Elector.	Residence, if out of the Parish.	Qual.	T.	W.	P.
Goose, Joseph	....	Rt	1	1	0
Mitchell, John	....	Rt	1	1	0
Pepper, William	....	Rt	0	0	1

Quadring.

Name of Elector.	Residence, if out of the Parish.	Qual.	T.	W.	P.
Allen, John	....	Fr	1	0	1
Abbott, Richard	....	Fr	1	1	0
Ashley, George	....	Co	1	1	0
Ackland, Thomas	....	Fr	0	0	1
Burrows, Howarth	Gosberton	Fr	0	0	1
Buddle, John	Swineshead	Fr			
Baldwick, Jacob	....	Rt	1	1	0
Betts, James	Wigtoft	Co	1	1	0
Bell, Ancill	North Kyme	Fr			
Bannister, Richard	....	Rt	1	0	1
Baldwick, Samuel	South Kyme	Fr			
Brooks, Austin	....	Fr	1	1	0
Bailey, James	Gosberton	Rt	1	1	0
Bramley, Richard	....	Co	1	1	0
Buzley, William	....	Fr			
Boyfield, Benjamin	....	Co	1	0	1
Casswell, Thomas Russell	....	Rt	1	1	0
Clarke, William	....	Fr	0	0	1
Crane, John	....	Fr	1	1	0
Clay, George	Donington	Co	0	0	1
Cropley, William	....	Fr	0	1	1
Cheavins, George	Gosberton	Fr			
Cartwright, John	....	Fr	0	1	1

Quadring—continued.

Name of Elector.	Residence, if out of the Parish.	Qual.	T.	W.	P.
Coy, William	Quadring Town	Fr	1	1	0
Creasy, John	High-fen	Rt	0	0	1
Duckett, Edward	....	Fr	1	1	0
Dobson, Benjamin	....	Fr	1	0	1
Dowse, John	....	Fr	0	0	1
Deeker, Robert, Rev.	Lyndon, Rutland	Fr	1	1	0
Ducket, Edward Thomas	Surfleet-fen	Rt	1	1	0
Farrow, Joseph	....	Fr			
Fowler, John	....	Fr	1	1	0
Fairbanks, James	....	Fr	1	1	0
Flatters, Thomas	Freiston	Fr	0	0	1
Freemantle, Samuel, jun.	Gosberton	Fr			
Gardner, William	....	Fr	1	0	0
Hurd, John	....	Fr	1	0	0
Harrison, Benjamin, sen.	....	Fr	1	1	0
Harrison, James	....	Fr	1	1	0
Harris, Thomas	....	Rt	1	0	1
Hotter, William	Old Bassford, Notts	Fr			
Jackson, John	....	Fr	1	1	0
Lewin, William Henry	Boston	Fr	1	0	1
Loughland, Thomas	....	Fr	1	1	0
Lilee, John Kitchen	....	Fr	1	1	0
Ludlow, Charles	....	Fr			
Maltby, John	....	Fr	1	0	1
Machin, William	....	Fr	1	1	0
Machin, Jonathan	....	Fr	1	1	0
Machin, Thomas	....	Fr	1	1	0
Machin, John	....	Fr	1	0	1
Mason, John	....	Fr	1	1	0
Machin, William	....	Fr	1	1	0
Marshall, James	Quadring-fen	Fr	1	1	0
M'Cann, Nicholas, esq.	50, Parliament-st., Westminster	Fr			
Mason, William	Quadring Eaudyke	Fr	1	1	0
Mason, Abraham	....	Fr	1	1	0
Naylor, Richard	Boston	Fr	1	0	1
Osborn, Thomas	....	Rt			
Osborn, Thomas, jun.	....	Rt	1	1	0
Ouzman, Charles	....	Rt	1	1	0
Pape, Benjamin	....	Fr	1	0	1

Quadring—continued.

Name of Elector.	Residence, if out of the Parish.	Qual.	T.	W.	P.
Perry, William	....	Rt	1	0	1
Peak, Thomas	....	Fr	1	1	0
Quilter, Rev. George	Canwick	Fr			
Rowe, James	....	Fr	0	0	1
Russell, Thomas	Gosberton	Fr			
Rowe, John Pinder	Quadring Eaudyke	Fr	1	0	0
Stevenson, Edward	....	Fr	0	0	1
Sinclair, George	Quadring Eaudyke	Fr	0	1	1
Sewards, William	....	Fr	1	0	1
Sandall, William	Rippingale	Fr			
Stimson, Joseph	....	Fr	1	1	0
Stevenson, Brookes J.	Burton Overy	Fr			
Sutton, Jonathan	....	Fr	1	1	0
Stanger, John	Swineshead	Co	1	0	0
Sewell, Joseph	Quadring Eaudyke	Rt	1	1	0
Thorogood, John	....	Rt	1	1	0
Tomlin, Rev. Charles	Langtoft	Fr			
Taylor, Robert	....	Fr	1	1	0
Todd, John	....	Fr	1	1	0
Wilson, Thomas	....	Fr	1	1	0
Woodhead, Richard	....	Co	1	1	0
Wallis, William	Fleet	Fr	1	1	0
Widall, John	Wigtoft	Fr	1	1	0
Whitfield, John	Nottingham	Fr			
Westerby, John, jun.	Peterborough	Fr			

Swineshead.

Name of Elector	Residence, if out of the Parish.	Qual.	T.	W.	P.
Adams, William *Clerk*	Throcking, Herts.	Fr			
Allen, William	....	Fr	0	1	1
Allen, James	....	Fr	1	0	1
Armstrong, Thomas	....	Fr	0	0	1
Aspland, Tunnard	....	Fr	0	0	1
Armstrong, William	....	Rt	1	1	0
Batterham, William	....	Rt	0	0	1
Blancher, William	....	Fr			
Bland, John George	Double-st., Spalding	Fr	1	1	0
Boyers, William	....	Fr	1	1	0
Brackenbury, Edward	....	Fr	0	0	1
Brewster, William	No. 65, New Bond-street, London	Fr			
Brown, John	....	Fr	0	1	1

Swineshead—continued.

Name of Elector.	Residence, if out of the Parish.	Qual.	T.	W.	P.
Burden, Joseph	....	Rt	1	1	0
Butheway, John	....	Fr	0	0	1
Brown, John, jun.	....	Rt			
Burden, Thomas	West Low Grounds	Rt	1	1	0
Black, Thomas	....	Fr	0	1	0
Casswell, Richard	Winter's-terrace,Skirbeck	Fr	1	1	0
Cawdron, Thomas	Bicker	Fr	1	1	0
Chambers,Benton William	....	Fr	0	1	1
Chamberlain, Joseph	Milk-st., London	Fr			
Cheetham, William	....	Fr	1	1	0
Clarke, William	....	Fr	1	1	0
Clarke, Henry	West Skirbeck	Fr	*dead*		
Cope, Edward	....	Fr	1	1	0
Cooper, Thomas L., Rev.	Empingham, Rutland	Fr	1	1	0
Cook, Robert	....	Fr	0	0	1
Cooper, John	....	Fr	1	1	0
Cole, George	....	Fr	1	1	0
Coates, Edward	....	Rt	0	0	1
Cook, William	....	Fr	1	1	0
Cox, William	Algarkirk	Fr	1	0	1
Cox, Joseph	Wisbeach	Fr			
Craven, Richard	....	Fr	1	0	1
Crown, Martin	....	Fr	1	0	1
Cook, Samuel	....	Fr	1	0	1
Dalton, John Neale	Greetham, Rutland	Fr			
Davison, Thomas	....	Fr	0	1	0
Dawson, Samuel	....	Fr	1	1	0
Dean, John	....	Fr	0	1	1
Edmunds, John	....	Fr	1	1	0
Ellwood, John	....	Fr	1	1	0
Fowler, John	....	Fr	1	1	0
Fox, William	....	Fr	1	1	0
Fox, Edward	....	Fr	0	0	1
Godbehere, William	....	Fr	0	0	1
Grimble, Ebenezer	....	Fr	1	1	0
Glassup, Sampson	....	Rt	0	0	1
Hallam, David	....	Le	1	1	0
Hall, Samuel	....	Fr	0	0	1
Harris, James	Exton, Rutland	Fr			

Swineshead—continued.

Name of Elector.	Residence, if out of the Parish.	Qual.	T.	W.	P.
Harrison, Richard	....	Fr	1	1	0
Harrison, William	....	Fr	0	1	0
Harrison, Joseph	Sibsey	Fr			
Harr, John	Willoughby	Fr			
Hart, Coxe	....	Rt	0	1	1
Hebblewhite, J. Thomas	Empingham,	Fr			
Hidés, Richard	....	Rt	0	0	1
Holmes, Thomas	....	Rt	1	1	0
Holmes, Joseph	....	Fr	1	1	0
Horner, Joseph	... .	Fr	1	1	0
Harwood, Henry *Sol*	High-street, Boston	Fr			
Hall, George	Reed-point, near Chapel-hill	Rt	0	1	1
Handley, Clement	North-end, Swineshead	Rt	1	1	0
Harris, William	....	Fr	1	1	0
Harrison, Jenken	....	Rt	1	1	0
Ingall, William Casswell	Gibbet-hills	Fr	1	1	0
Ingram, Herbert, esq.	Swineshead Abbey	Fr	1	0	1
Ingall, Richard	....	Rt	1	0	0
Idle, Henry	....	Rt	1	1	0
Jackson, John Burton	Greetham, Rutland	Fr			
Jackson, John	....	Fr	0	0	1
Jessop, Zebedee	....	Fr	0	0	1
Jessop, John	....	Fr	0	1	1
Johnson, John	....	Fr			
Jessop, John Brown	....	Co	0	0	1
Key, William	Great Brand-end	Fr			
Kynaston, William	Lad-lane, London	Fr			
Kinsley, Zachariah	near Chapel-hill	Rt	0	0	1
Lawson, Thomas	....	Fr	1	0	1
Lister, John	....	Fr			
Lister, William	... .	Fr	0	0	1
Lawson, Thomas	....	Fr			
Little, Charles Henry	....	Rt	0	0	1
Mayfield, Joseph	Swineshead Chapel-hill	Rt	0	1	1
Moody, Enos *Sol*	Wragby	Fr	0	0	1
Morris, William	....	Fr	1	0	1
Morris, Thomas	....	Fr			
Moore, Lemuel	....	Fr	0	1	1
Moss, John Robert	....	Rt	0	0	1

Swineshead—continued.

Name of Elector.	Residence, if out of the Parish.	Qual.	T.	W.	P.
Motley, Thomas	....	Fr	1	1	0
Nobles, Benjamin	....	Fr	1	1	0
Nundy, William	....	Fr	1	1	0
Nutsey, William	....	Fr	0	0	1
Pilgrim, William	....	Fr	0	0	1
Preston, James	....	Rt	0	1	1
Reddish, William Dolby	....	Fr	0	0	1
Reedman, Charles	....	Fr	1	0	1
Roberts, John	....	Fr	1	1	0
Robinson, John	....	Fr	1	0	1
Rilett, Joseph	LowGround,Swineshead	Rt	1	1	0
Sandall, John Stennett	....	Fr	1	1	0
Sewell, Francis	....	Fr	1	1	0
Sewell, John	....	Fr	0	0	1
Shaw, Robert	....	Rt	1	1	0
Shaw, John	....	Rt	1	0	1
Sharp, Joseph	....	Fr	1	1	0
Sharp, John	....	Fr	0	1	1
Sleight, John	....	Fr	1	0	1
Smith, George	Frampton Sandholme	Fr	1	0	1
Smith, Henry	....	Rt			
Smith, Robert	....	Fr	0	0	1
Smith, Thomas	Chapel-hill	Fr			
Sparrow, William	....	Rt	1	0	1
Stanley, Richard	Wigtoft	Fr	0	1	1
Stevenson, John	Pelham's-land	Fr	1	1	0
Stevenson, James	....	Fr	1	1	0
Stubley, Thomas	....	Fr	0	0	1
Stubley, Edward	....	Fr	0	1	1
Swainson, William	35,Cateaton-st.,London	Fr			
Stubley, Thomas, jun.	....	Fr	1	1	0
Snow, John	Doncaster,Yorkshire	Fr			
Stotherd, George	Chapel-hill	Fr	1	1	0
Smith, George	....	Fr	1	1	0
Smith, Robert	....	Fr			
Teesdale, Edward	....	Rt	1	1	0
Tennant, Joseph M., esq.	Littlewood-house, Leeds, Yorkshire	Fr	1	1	0
Tennant, William, esq.	Cowley-street, Westminster	Fr			

Swineshead—continued.

Name of Elector.	Residence, if out of the Parish.	Qual.	T.	W.	P.
Tennant, C. A., esq.	Dewsbury, Yorkshire	Fr	1	1	0
Thorpe, John	....	Fr	0	0	1
Thorpe, William	....	Fr	1	1	0
Tooley, James	Swineshead Chapel-hill	Fr			
Townhill, Joseph	Ditto	Fr			
Trickett, John, jun.	Deptford, Kent	Fr			
Tuffnell, John	....	Rt	1	1	0
Tyler, Francis	....	Fr			
Thorpe, David	....	Fr	0	0	1
Ulyatt, John	....	Fr	0	0	1
Vere, James, esq.	Suffolk-st., Pall Mall East, London	Fr			
Wanty, Samuel	....	Fr			
Wilkinson, William	Kirton Holme	Fr			
Woods, John	....	Fr	1	1	0
Woods, John, jun.	....	Fr	1	1	0
Woods, William	....	Fr	1	1	0
Woulds, William	....	Fr	1	1	0
Watts, John	....	Rt	0	0	1
Widall, Robert	....	Rt	1	0	1
Walton, William	....	Fr			
Woods, John	....	Rt	1	1	0
Woodcock, John	....	Fr	1	1	0
Young, Edward	....	Fr	0	0	1

Wigtoft.

Name of Elector.	Residence, if out of the Parish.	Qual.	T.	W.	P.
Ashwell, Jonathan	Horbling	Fr			
Bealby, James	....	Rt	1	0	1
Bell, John	....	Rt	1	1	0
Benington, William	....	Fr			
Blakey, John	Gainsborough	Fr	1	1	0
Brown, John	Swineshead	Fr	1	1	0
Brackenbury, William	....	Fr	1	1	0
Bates, Henry Edward	....	Rt	0	0	1
Boss, Thomas	....	Fr	0	0	1
Bonnett, Isaac	....	Fr	1	1	0
Blakey, John	Spalding	Fr			
Challans, Richard	....	Fr	0	1	1
Cartwright, Thomas	....	Fr	1	1	0
Chesman, David Newton	Kirton-fen	Fr	0	1	1

Wigtoft—continued.

Name of Elector.	Residence, if out of the Parish.	Qual.	T.	W.	
Craven, Brewster	....	Rt	1	0	1
Chatterton, Robert Grey	....	Rt	1	1	0
Chatterton, William	Tathwell	Rt	1	1	0
Chatterton, Richard	Hallington	Rt	1	1	0
Cole, John Charles	....	Fr			
Cole, James Edwin *Esq*	No. 2, Hare Court, Inner Temple, London	Fr			
Dowse, William	....	Fr			
Dowse, Richard	....	Rt	1	1	0
Day, William	....	Rt	1	1	0
Dickinson, Joseph	....	Fr	0	1	1
Daughty, John	....	Co	1	0	1
Dale, Whymont	....	Fr	1	0	1
Dowse, Richard John	....	Rt	0	0	1
Dowse, R. the Younger	....	Rt			
Fidler, James	....	Fr	1	1	0
Fox, Charles James	Newark	Fr	0	1	1
Gibson, John	....	Rt			
Gladding, Benjamin	....	Fr	1	1	0
Gladding, Bartholomew	....	Fr	1	1	0
Goodacre, John	....	Rt	1	1	0
Hart, Valentine	Doncaster	Fr			
Hartson, Thomas	....	Fr			
Hempshell, William	Swineshead	Fr	0	0	1
Holland, Charles George	Boston *Esq*	Fr	1	1	0
Johnson, Edward	....	Rt	0	1	1
Jackson, Richard	....	Rt	1	1	0
Johnson, John	....	Fr			
Langley, William	Wigtoft-fen	Rt	1	1	0
Langley, Henry	Wigtoft-fen	Rt	1	0	0
Leedale, Bates	....	Fr	1	1	0
Lupton, Robert	....	Fr	0	0	1
Maplethorpe, Hugh	....	Fr	1	1	0
Mansell, John	near Belvoir, Leicestershire	Fr	1	1	0
Millington, John Boyfield	Boston *Sol*	Fr			
Newton, Joseph	....	Fr	0	0	1
Newton, Michael	....	Fr			
Oliver, William	....	Rt	1	1	0

Wigtoft—continued.

Name of Elector.	Residence, if out of the Parish.	Qual.	T.	W.	P.
Parker, John	Swineshead	Rt	1	1	0
Pickwell, Wright	....	Fr	1	0	1
Preston, James	Wigtoft-fen	Rt	1	1	0
Powdrill, Richard	....	Rt	0	0	1
Roberts, Robert	Haverill, Suffolk	Fr			
Robinson, Randall W.	....	Fr			
Redshaw, James	....	Rt	0	1	0
Rayson, William	....	Fr	1	1	0
Sandall, Richard	....	Fr	1	0	1
Sharp, William	....	Fr	1	1	0
Soulby, Edward	....	Rt	1	0	1
Sharpe, J. the younger	....	Fr	0	0	1
Stephenson, Copping	....	Rt	1	1	0
Sharpe, Michael	Botolph Terrace, Lincoln	Fr	1	1	0
Towns, John	....	Fr	1	1	0
Vere, James, esq.	United University Club House, Suffolk-street, Pall Mall East, in the County of Middlesex	Fr			
West, John	....	Fr	1	1	0
Woods, George	Bicker	Fr	1	1	0
Woods, William	Swineshead	Fr			
Wilson, Rev. John	....	Fr	1	1	0

No. 3.—POLLING DISTRICT ASSIGNED TO SPALDING.

Cowbit.

Name of Elector.	Residence, if out of the Parish.	Qual.	T.	W.	P.
Atkin, Samuel	....	Fr	1	1	0
Atkin, Samuel, jun.	....	Fr	1	1	0
Allen, Jackson	....	Fr	1	0	0
Adkin, Benjamin	Ruskington, Lincolnshire	Fr			
Batterham, James	Deeping-fen-bank	Rt	1	1	0
Beeken, Thomas	Brotherhouse-bar	Fr	1	1	0
Burwell, Henry	....	Fr	0	0	1
Campain, Samuel	Deeping-fen	Rt			
Cape, Thomas	Cowbit North-fen	Fr	1	1	0

Cowbit—continued.

Name of Elector.	Residence, if out of the Parish.	Qual.	T.	W.	P.
Chesterfield, Henry	....	Fr	1	0	0
Chapman, Thomas	North Cowbit-fen	Fr			
Congreve, Daniel	Deeping-fen	Fr			
Calthrop, Everard	Deeping-fen	Rt	1	1	0
Cooling, Jonathan	....	Fr	1	1	0
Davis, James	....	Fr	1	1	0
Dyson, Jeremiah Francis	Spanish-place, London	Fr			
Dalton, Daniel	....	Fr	1	0	0
Decamps, William	....	Fr	0	0	1
Decamps, Edward	....	Rt	1	1	0
Dalton, Charles	....	Fr	1	0	0
Elves, Thomas	....	Fr	1	0	0
Everitt, Robert, jun.	Hunsdon Lodge, near Ware, Herts	Rt			
French, David	....	Fr	1	0	1
French, Charles	....	Fr	1	1	0
Gedney, John	....	Fr			
Gedney, Joseph	....	Fr	1	0	0
Giles, Thomas	....	Fr	1	1	0
Gibson, John, jun.	....	Fr	1	0	1
Guy, John	Spalding	Fr	0	0	1
Harwood, Henry	West-street, Boston	Fr			
Healey, John	Deeping-fen	Rt			
Hunt, William	Deeping-fen	Fr	1	1	0
Hall, Thomas	....	Fr			
Hall, Edward	....	Fr			
Hesson, William	....	Fr	1	1	0
Harrison, John	....	Fr			
Harrison, William	....	Fr	0	0	1
Henson, John	Thorney, Peterborough	Fr	0	0	1
Jackson, Joseph	....	Fr	1	0	0
Ledbetter, John	Cowbit, North-fen	Fr			
Morton, Richard	....	Rt	1	1	0
Madison, Charles	....	Fr	1	0	0
Newcomb, Robert N.	2, High-street, Stamford, Lincolnshire	Fr			
Pidduck, John	....	Fr	1	1	0
Pearson, Joseph	....	Fr	1	1	0
Pearson, Thomas	....	Fr	1	1	0

Cowbit—continued.

Name of Elector.	Residence, if out of the Parish.	Qual.	T.	W.	P.
Parker, John	....	Fr			
Riddlington, Thomas	....	Rt	1	1	0
Sewel, James	....	Fr	1	1	0
Smith, John	Deeping-bank	Rt			
Sutton, William	Cowbit North-fen	Fr	1	0	1
Steel, John	*incumbent.*	Fr			
Tye, Thomas	....	Fr			
Tabiner, Francis	....	Fr	0	0	1
Tabiner, Robert, jun.	....	Fr	0	0	1
Tyrrell, William	....	Fr	1	0	0
Tabiner, William	....	Fr	1	1	0
Winteringham, Joseph	....	Fr	0	0	1

Crowland.

Name of Elector.	Residence, if out of the Parish.	Qual.	T.	W.	P.
Atkin, George	....	Fr	1	1	0
Ayscough, William	....	Co	0	1	1
Aveling, Joseph	....	Fr	0	1	1
Ashby, William	Crowland Common	Rt	1	1	0
Alderman, James	Lodge Farm, Crowland	Co	1	0	0
Ager, Thomas	West-st., Crowland	Co			
Bates, Rev. John	....	Fr	1	1	0
Beeken, William	....	Co	0	0	1
Beeken, Thomas	....	Fr	1	1	0
Beasley, Thomas	....	Co	0	0	1
Bellaers, Henry	....	Co	1	1	0
Barron, James	Crowland Common	Rt			
Blood, William	....	Co	1	1	0
Blood, John	Sutton St. Edmund's	Co	1	1	0
Bee, Abraham	Deeping-bank	Rt	1	1	0
Bee, John	Ditto	Rt	1	1	0
Blood, Abraham	....	Co	1	1	0
Briggs, Joseph	....	Co	0	1	1
Bellamy, Thomas	King-street, Covent-garden, London	Fr			
Bains, Jonathan	....	Fr	1	0	1
Blood, William, jun.	....	Fr	1	1	0
Beal, Thomas, sen.	Peakhill	Fr	1	1	0
Beeken, William, jun.	....	Rt			
Byworth, Thomas	....	Rt	1	1	0
Bains, John	....	Co			

Crowland—continued.

Name of Elector.	Residence, if out of the Parish.	Qual.	T.	W.	P.
Boor, Jackson	....	Rt	1	1	0
Bains, Benjamin	....	Co			
Beeken, William, jun.	....	Co	0	0	1
Cherrington, George	....	Co			
Cooke, Robert Dalamore	....	Rt	1	1	0
Cooke, John	....	Fr	1	1	0
Casswell, Henry	....	Rt	1	1	0
Cooke, Robert	....	Rt			
Cherrington, William	....	Co	1	1	0
Cox, John	....	Rt	1	1	0
Cherrington, Richard J.	....	Rt	1	1	0
Cherrington, Stephen	....	Rt			
Cordley, William Bayes	....	Fr			
Dalton, Daniel	....	Co	1	1	0
Dixon, James	High-st., St. Martin's Stamford Baron, Northamptonshire	Co	1	1	0
Ealham, James	....	Fr	1	1	0
Ealham, Thomas	....	Fr	1	1	0
Ealham, John	....	Fr	1	1	0
Eakins, James	....	Fr	1	1	0
Edwards, William	....	Co	0	0	1
Eakins, James, jun.	....	Co	0	0	1
Empson, Charles	....	Rt	1	1	0
Eakins, William G.	....	Co	1	1	0
Frisby, Matthew	Deeping-bank	Fr	1	0	1
Fox, Henry	....	Fr	1	1	0
Fairchild, Joseph	Deeping-bank	Rt			
Fillingham, Thomas	....	Co			
Fillingham, Abraham	....	Fr	1	1	0
Fillingham, Thomas, jun.	....	Rt	1	1	0
Frisby, Henry	Deeping-bank	Fr	1	1	0
Fletcher, Thomas	....	Co	1	1	0
Fletcher, Joshua	....	Co	1	1	0
Fletcher, Thomas	Newborough, Northamptonshire	Rt	1	1	0
Fovargue, James, jun.	....	Co	1	1	0
Frisby, George	....	Fr	0	1	1
Goodwin, Felix	....	Rt	1	1	0
Harrison, Henry	....	Fr	1	1	0

Crowland—continued.

Name of Elector.	Residence, if out of the Parish.	Qual.	T.	W.	P.
Hobourne, James	....	Rt			
Hardy, Jacob Congreve	....	Rt	1	1	0
Hall, Joshua	....	Co	0	0	1
Hutchinson, Joseph	....	Co	0	0	1
Hickling, Thomas	....	Co	1	1	0
Hill, James	....	Fr	1	1	0
Hill, James	....	Fr	1	1	0
Hewson, William	Newborough, North-amptonshire	Fr	1	1	0
Hardy, Thomas	....	Rt	1	1	0
Hardy, Benjnmin	....	Rt	1	1	0
Hutchinson, William	....	Co	1	0	1
Hardy, John	....	Rt	1	1	0
Higgs, William	Burghley Park	Rt	1	1	0
Hack, Matthew	....	Rt			
Hastings, James Wirr	....	Fr	0	0	1
Hickling, William, jun.	....	Rt	1	1	0
Hickling, Charles	....	Rt	1	1	0
Ingram, William	....	Rt			
Jackson, Thomas	....	Fr	1	1	0
Jackson, John	....	Fr	1	1	0
Johnson, T. M. S., esq.	Spalding	Fr			
Kirby, John Barnes	Brighton, Sussex	Fr			
Leaton, Thomas	Deeping-bank	Rt	1	1	0
Leaton, Joseph	Ditto	Rt	0	0	1
Lucas, Gideon	Westgate, Peterborough	Fr			
Marfleet, Joseph	....	Co	1	1	0
Maxwell, Robert W.	Borough-fen	Rt			
Maxwell, Sutton G.	Ditto	Rt			
Miller, John	North-st., Peterborough	Fr	0	0	1
Nichols, Robert	....	Co	0	0	1
Pycraft, Francis	....	Fr	1	1	0
Pooler, Thomas	....	Co	1	1	0
Popple, Henry	....	Co			
Pitts, Isaac	....	Co	0	0	1
Pitts, William	....	Rt	1	1	0
Phillips, Philip	....	Rt	1	1	0
Riddlington, William	....	Co	1	1	0
Riddlington, Frederick	....	Co	1	1	0
Richardson, Martin	....	Rt	1	1	0

Crowland—continued.

Name of Elector.	Residence, if out of the Parish.	Qual.	T.	W.	P.
Sanderson, Benjamin	....	Co	0	0	1
Southwell, Christopher	....	Co	1	0	0
Sharpe, John	....	Fr	1	1	0
Smith, Sir Culling Eardley, Bart.	Bedwell Park, Hatfield, Herts.	Co			
Shelton, William	....	Co	1	1	0
Shelton, John	....	Co	1	1	0
Sanderson, William	....	Co	1	1	0
Stimpson, David	....	Fr	1	1	0
Tate, William	....	Co	0	0	1
Thompson, William	....	Co	1	1	0
Thompson, James	....	Fr			
Tookey, William	....	Co	1	1	0
Thompson, Thomas	....	Co	1	1	0
Tomlinson, William	Newark	Fr			
Trowell, John	....	Co	1	0	1
Tooley, George, sen.	....	Fr			
Tooley, George, jun.	....	Fr	0	0	1
Whitsed, John de Key	....	Rt	1	1	0
Whitsed, James	....	Rt	1	1	0
Whitsed, James	....	Fr			
Wyche, William	....	Rt	1	1	0
Whisker, Philip	....	Rt	1	1	0
Wright, John	....	Co			
Wright, Matthew	....	Co	1	1	0
Warwick, George M.	....	Rt	1	1	0
Wyche, Thomas	....	Fr	1	1	0
Wright, John	....	Rt	1	0	1
Wyche, Robert	....	Rt	1	1	0
Yardy, John	Gainsborough	Co			

Moulton.

Name of Elector.	Residence, if out of the Parish.	Qual.	T.	W.	P.
Atkinson, Thomas	Moulton Sea's-end	Fr	0	0	1
Atkinson, William	Moulton Sea's-end	Co	0	0	1
Booth, William Plowright	....	Rt	1	1	0
Betham, Edward	Lincoln	Fr	1	0	0
Blanchard, Daniel	Moulton Sea's-end	Rt			
Burngate, George	Moulton-fen-gate	Rt	1	1	0
Bird, Thomas	....	Fr	1	1	0
Burnham, Thomas	....	Fr	0	0	1

Moulton—continued.

Name of Elector.	Residence, if out of the Parish.	Qual.	T.	W.	P.
Bradford, Samuel	Chapel	Fr	1	0	1
Bacon, Jeremiah	Rippingale	Fr	1	0	1
Bailey, Thomas	....	Fr	0	0	1
Blanchard, Daniel	....	Rt	0	0	1
Brooks, Thomas	....	Fr	1	0	1
Chatterton, Robert Gray	Wigtoft	Fr			
Chatterton, William	Tathwell	Fr			
Cooley, William	....	Co			
Clark, Henry	Moulton Eaugate	Fr	1	0	1
Clark, Samuel Lee	Moulton Eaugate	Fr	1	0	1
Clay, Henry	....	Fr	1	1	0
Cowley, Becuda	....	Rt	1	0	0
Christie, Charles William	Lincoln's Inn, London	Fr			
Childers, John Walbanke	Cantley, Yorkshire	Le			
Chatterton, Richard	Hallington	Fr			
Clark, Matthew	....	Fr	1	0	1
Cock, John	....	Fr			
Crawley, John	Moulton Marsh	Rt	1	0	1
Cock, John	....	Fr			
Cowley, Becuda, jun.	....	Rt	1	0	1
Cooke, Benjamin	....	Rt			
Chesterfield, John	....	Rt	1	1	0
Dowding, Rev. Charles	Steeple Langford, Heytesbury, Wilts	Co	1	1	0
Dyball, Robert	Loosegate	Fr	0	0	1
Dodson, John Harrop	....	Fr	1	1	0
Dalton, Charles	Moulton Chapel	Fr			
Day, Charles	....	Fr	0	0	1
Earl, Robert	Moulton Sea's-end	Rt	1	1	0
Elsdale, Robinson	....	Fr	0	0	1
Francis, Daniel	Moulton Sea's-end	Rt	0	0	1
Fydell, William	Moulton Chapel	Fr	1	1	0
Foster, Thomas	....	Rt	1	0	0
Foster, William	Moulton Chapel	Fr			
Footit, John	Eaugate	Rt	1	0	1
Foster, Henry	Moulton Common	Co	0	0	1
Free, Isaac	....	Fr	1	0	1
Guy, William	Moulton Salt Marsh	Rt			
Gainsley, Benjamin B.	....	Fr	1	0	1

Moulton—continued.

Name of Elector.	Residence, if out of the Parish.	Qual.	T.	W.	P.
Huntsman, Edmund	Chapel-gate	Fr	1	1	0
Harpham, Benjamin	Sea's-end	Rt	0	0	1
Hodson, Edward	Moulton Eaugate	Fr	1	0	1
Hannah, Abraham	Moulton Marsh	Rt	1	0	1
Holbrook, James	Monmouth	Fr			
Hill, Wynn	Easton, near Stamford	Fr	1	1	0
Horton, David	....	Rt	1	0	1
Holmes, Matthew	....	Fr	0	0	1
Holland, Thomas	....	Rt	1	1	0
Inkley, James	Moulton Eaugate	Fr	1	0	0
Jarvis, John	....	Fr	1	0	1
Johnson, Benjamin	....	Rt	1	0	1
Jones, Thomas Alley	No. 1, Clifford's Inn, London	Fr			
King, Robert	....	Fr	1	0	1
King, James Measure	....	Rt	0	0	1
Kisby, William	Chapel-gate	Fr	0	0	1
Lawson, James	....	Rt			
Lee, Joseph	....	Fr	1	1	0
Leaver, William	....	Co	1	1	0
Maugham, George R.	....	Fr	1	1	0
Mawson, Samuel	....	Fr	1	1	0
Maples, Thomas	Moulton Marsh	Rt	0	1	1
Markham, Thomas	Moulton Marsh	Rt	1	1	0
Moore, Rev. Charles	....	Fr			
Moore, George A., esq.	the Vicarage, Moulton	Rt	1	1	0
Meadows, Samuel	....	Fr	0	0	1
Morfoot, William	Hogsgate	Fr	0	0	1
Markham, William	....	Fr	0	0	1
Morfoot, William, jun.	....	Fr	0	1	1
Morfoot, John	....	Fr	0	0	1
Newton, Thomas	....	Fr	1	0	0
Osborne, James	....	Co	0	1	1
Pattison, John	Moulton Marsh	Fr	0	0	1
Pick, William	Holbeach	Fr			
Pocklington, Robert	Moulton Austendike	Rt	1	0	1
Ranby, Low	Moulton West-fen	Rt	1	0	1
Robinson, George	Pinchbeck Marsh	Fr	1	1	0
Routhan, John	....	Rt	0	0	1

Moulton—continued.

Name of Elector.	Residence, if out of the Parish.	Qual.	T.	W.	P.
Rower, Thomas	Moulton Loosegate	Fr	0	0	1
Rosling, Clement	Moulton Eaugate	Rt	1	0	1
Robinson, Thomas	Moulton Chapel	Rt	1	0	0
Robinson, William	Moulton Eaugate	Fr	1	1	0
Reed, John	Moulton Common	Rt	0	0	1
Robinson, Adonijah	Moulton Chapel	Rt	1	1	0
Robinson, Richard	....	Rt	1	1	0
Robinson, Samuel	....	Fr	1	0	1
Reed, George	....	Rt	0	0	1
Ranby, Low, jun.	....	Fr	0	1	1
Smith, William	Town	Fr	1	0	1
Smith, Sergeant	Moulton Chapel	Fr	1	1	0
Smith, William	....	Fr	0	0	1
Savage, William	....	Fr	0	0	1
Savage, John Pearson	....	Co	0	0	1
Skeath, Benjamin	....	Co	1	0	1
Smith, William	Moulton Turnpike	Fr	1	0	1
Turnbull, John	Moulton Chapel	Fr			
Turnbull, William	Moulton Chapel	Rt	1	1	0
Turnbull, Richard	Moulton Eaugate	Rt	0	0	1
Thorpe, Francis	....	Rt	1	0	1
Teesdale, John	....	Fr			
Tatam, John	Moulton Austendike	Co			
Tawn, Abraham	Moulton Marsh	Fr			
Thorpe, Robert	....	Fr	1	0	1
Taylor, John	Moulton Eaugate	Rt	0	1	0
Taylor, William	Grantham	Fr			
Turnbull, John	Moulton Eaugate	Rt	1	0	0
Thimbleby, Daniel	Lutton	Fr	1	1	0
Tatam, Henry Hardy	Moulton Sea's-end	Rt	0	0	1
Tooley, George	Crowland	Co			
Twell, Henry	Moulton Common	Fr	0	0	1
Twell, Zachariah	Moulton Washway	Rt	1	0	1
Thorpe, William	....	Rt			
Turnbull, Job	....	Rt	1	0	1
Turnbull, Robert	....	Rt	1	0	1
Vickers, John	Moulton Sea's-end	Fr	0	0	1
Vickers, William	Moulton Chapel	Co	1	0	1
Wrout, Frederick	Moulton Common	Rt	0	0	1
Watts, Thomas	....	Fr	0	0	1

Moulton—continued.

Name of Elector.	Residence, if out of the Parish.	Qual.	T.	W.	P.
Wiseman, William	Moulton East-fen	Fr	1	0	0
Watson, Thomas	Woodgate, near Moulton Chapel	Rt			
Whitehead, Henry	Easton, Northamptonshire	Fr	0	0	1
Webster, Joseph	....	Rt	1	1	0
Wiseman, John	....	Rt	0	0	1
Williamson, Samuel	....	Co	1	0	1

Pinchbeck.

Name of Elector.	Residence, if out of the Parish.	Qual.	T.	W.	P.
Arnsby, John	....	Fr	1	1	0
Allen, Charles, jun.	....	Rt	1	1	0
Allen, Robert	....	Fr	0	1	1
Allen, Robert, jun.	....	Rt	1	1	0
Allen, Charles	....	Fr	1	1	0
Allen, George	....	Fr	1	1	0
Ashby, Charles	....	Rt			
Ashby, Charles	Saxilby	Fr	0	0	1
Atkinson, James	....	Fr	0	0	1
Atty, James, esq.	Penley Hall	Fr	1	1	0
Ayscough, William	....	Rt	0	0	1
Andrew, John	Long Sutton	Rt			
Aitken, Thomas	....	Rt			
Aitken, Martin Irving	....	Fr	0	0	1
Aitken, Andrew	....	Co	0	0	1
Allen, Henry	....	Rt	1	0	0
Allen, William	....	Fr	1	0	0
Atty, James, esq.	Rugby, Warwickshire	Fr			
Anderson, Benjamin	....	Fr	1	1	0
Blake, Richard	Spalding	Fr	0	0	1
Braderwick, James	....	Fr	1	0	0
Branton, William	....	Fr	0	0	1
Booth, William	....	Rt	1	1	0
Burdall, Thomas	....	Rt	1	1	0
Bennett, William	....	Fr	1	1	0
Benner, Emanuel	....	Rt	1	1	0
Beach, Samuel	Spalding	Fr			
Bowcock, John	....	Co	1	0	1
Bell, Edward	....	Fr	1	0	1
Burden, John	London	Fr			

Pinchbeck—continued.

Name of Elector.	Residence, if out of the Parish.	Qual.	T.	W.	P.
Bradford, Samuel	Edenham	Fr	0	0	1
Bonner, Charles *Sol*	Spalding	Fr	*dead*		
Brown, Matthew	....	Fr	1	1	0
Buckle, Samuel	5, Beauchamp-square, Leamington	Fr	1	1	0
Buckworth, T. R., esq.	Cockley Cley, Norfolk	Fr	1	1	0
Buckworth, Rev. C. P.	Ditto	Fr			
Beaston, Auby	Canterbury	Fr	1	1	0
Buckle, Samuel	Saint John's-street,				
Bevan, John	....	Fr	0	0	1
Banks, Thomas Young	Spalding	Rt	1	1	0
Barnet, James	....	Rt	1	1	0
Benner, Charles	....	Fr	1	1	0
Black, William	....	Fr			
Bonner, John George	Clapham Common, Surrey	Fr	1	1	0
Boothby, Thomas S.	....	Rt	1	1	0
Booth, William	....	Fr			
Brittain, Benjamin	....	Rt	1	1	0
Burdall, Jonathan	....	Fr	1	1	0
Bullard, John	....	Rt	1	1	0
Capes, John	....	Fr	1	0	1
Cock, Stephen	....	Rt	1	1	0
Colvin, William	....	Fr	0	0	1
Cowham, John	....	Fr	1	0	1
Cheaven, George	....	Fr			
Carter, John	....	Fr	1	1	0
Chatterton, Bollon	....	Fr			
Caulton, William	....	Rt	1	1	0
Cock, William S.	....	Rt	1	1	0
Chatterton, Joseph	....	Fr	1	1	0
Clarke, Henry James	Burley	Fr	1	1	0
Cooling, Robert	....	Rt	1	1	0
Chamberlain, William	....	Rt	1	1	0
Chatterton, Thomas	....	Fr	1	0	1
Dowse, Robert	....	Fr	1	1	0
Durance, Thomas	....	Fr	1	0	1
Darley, Robert	....	Rt	1	0	0
Elsdale, Robinson	Moulton	Fr			
Elderkin, William	....	Fr	1	0	1

Pinchbeck—continued.

Name of Elector.	Residence, if out of the Parish.	Qual.	T.	W.	P.
Everitt, Robert	Ware	Fr	1	1	0
Frost, William	....	Fr			
Freeman, William	....	Fr	1	0	1
Fisher, Dale	Deeping-fen	Rt	1	0	1
Freir, Samuel	Gosberton-fen	Fr			
Freir, William	....	Rt			
Fisher, Thomas	Weston	Fr	1	1	0
Green, Martin J.	Lincoln College, Oxford	Fr			
Green, Christopher	....	Fr	1	1	0
Goodale, Wallet	Peterborough	Rt			
Gilson, John	Regent's Terrace, King's-road, Chelsea	Fr	1	1	0
Grassam, Adam N.	....	Fr	1	0	1
Gates, John	Peterborough	Fr	1	0	0
Gilson, John	Gloucester Terrace, Park-wall, Chelsea	Fr			
Gedney, William	....	Fr	1	1	0
Garratt, John	....	Fr	1	0	1
Garratt, Upton Henry	New York, U S.	Fr			
Garwell, Thomas	....	Fr	0	1	1
Green, John	....	Fr	1	1	0
Grummitt, John	....	Fr	0	0	1
Guy, Richard	....	Fr	1	0	0
Harrison, Thomas D.	Loughborough	Fr			
Houldon, George M.	....	Fr	0	0	1
Hewerdine, Thomas	Stamford	Fr			
Hewitt, John	Hall-street, Spalding	Fr			
Haddon, William	....	Fr	1	1	0
Hardy, William	....	Rt			
Heffield, John	Donington	Fr			
Hughes, William	Cowbit	Fr			
Hartley, John	....	Fr	1	0	0
Hill, William	....	Fr	1	1	0
Hicks, Robert	....	Fr			
Harrod, Thomas	....	Fr			
Hewerson, Matthew	....	Fr	1	1	0
Harrison, William	....	Rt	1	1	0
Huddlestone, Moses	....	Fr	0	0	1
Harwood, John	....	Fr	1	1	0
Hensman, John	....	Fr	1	1	0

Pinchbeck—continued.

Name of Elector.	Residence, if out of the Parish.	Qual	T.	W.	P.
Hardy, Henry	....	Fr	1	1	0
Hicks, Robert	Sutton Bar, near Retford	Fr	1	1	0
Islip, William	....	Rt	1	1	0
Ingram, Robert	....	Fr	1	1	0
Judd, Robert	Spalding	Fr			
Johnson, Richard	....	Fr	1	1	0
Jackson, Richard	....	Rt			
Jackson, Richard	....	Rt	1	1	0
King, Samuel	Spalding	Fr	0	0	1
Kelley, Thomas	....	Fr	0	0	1
Kendall, Thomas	Gosberton	Fr	0	0	1
Kerlew, William	....	Co	1	1	0
Kingston, Robert	....	Fr	1	0	0
Love, Thomas	....	Fr	1	0	0
Lacey, Timothy	....	Fr	0	1	1
Laxton, Thomas	....	Fr	1	1	0
Langton, William	....	Fr	0	0	1
Lindsey, John, jun.	....	Rt	0	0	1
Lacey, John	Oakham	Fr	0	0	1
Lenton, John	....	Fr	1	1	0
Ladd, Thomas	....	Fr	0	0	1
Lane, Isaac	....	Fr			
Leadbetter, John	Cowbit North-fen	Fr			
Lindsey, John	Spalding Marsh	Fr	1	1	0
Laxton, Clement	Cowbit Allotment, Pinchbeck West	Rt	1	1	0
Lewis, Robert	....	Fr	1	1	0
Loveley, John	....	Fr	1	0	0
Marshall, Isaiah	....	Fr	1	1	0
Measure, John	London	Fr			
Maples, George	Clifton House, Wavertree, Liverpool	Fr	1	1	0
Marvin, Edward	....	Fr	1	1	0
Muskett, John	....	Fr	1	1	0
Miller, Thomas	Redway	Fr			
Musson, Samuel	....	Fr	1	1	0
Merriman, John	....	Rt	0	0	1
Moore, George Augustus	Moulton Esq	Fr			
Mitchell, Charles	....	Fr	1	0	0

Pinchbeck—continued.

Name of Elector.	Residence, if out of the Parish.	Qual.	T.	W.	P.
Mann, Charles	....	Fr	0	0	1
Molcher, Henry	....	Rt	1	1	0
Nelson, Hector	West Pinchbeck	Fr			
North, Richard	....	Rt	1	1	0
Otter, James	....	Fr	1	0	1
Parker, William Barton	Stamford	Fr			
Plowright, Thomas	....	Fr	1	1	0
Plowright, James	....	Fr	1	1	0
Phillips, George	North-fen	Rt			
Platt, Samuel	....	Rt			
Plowright, Thomas	....	Fr	1	0	0
Porter, George	Easton	Fr			
Porter, Daniel	Easton	Fr	1	1	0
Porter, James	Spalding	Fr			
Plowright, William	Spalding	Fr	1	1	0
Parker, Thomas King	Saint Mary's-street, Stamford	Fr	1	0	1
Palmer, John	....	Rt	1	1	0
Portors, William	....	Fr	1	0	0
Pearson, Joseph	....	Fr	0	0	1
Patchett, John	....	Fr	1	0	0
Robinson, Edward	....	Rt	1	1	0
Robinson, George	....	Fr			
Robinson, John W.	East Keal	Fr	1	1	0
Robinson, William, jun.	....	Rt	1	0	1
Risely, John	....	Fr			
Redmile, John	....	Fr			
Reynolds, Joseph	....	Fr	1	1	0
Ramm, John	....	Fr			
Robinson, Samuel	....	Rt	0	0	1
Robinson, John, sen.	....	Rt	1	0	1
Robinson, Stephen	....	Rt	1	0	1
Robinson, John, jun.	....	Rt	1	0	1
Sharp, Joel	Spalding	Fr			
Sharp, Edward	....	Fr	1	1	0
Simpson, George	....	Fr	1	1	0
Squier, Frederick	Knight-street	Fr	0	0	1
Spreckley, Zachariah	....	Rt			
Squire, William	....	Fr	0	0	1
Styles, Thomas	....	Fr	1	0	1

Pinchbeck—continued.

Name of Elector.	Residence, if out of the Parish.	Qual.	T.	W.	P.
Stableforth, Charles	....	Fr			
Sharp, William	....	Fr	1	1	0
Sellers, Joseph	....	Fr	1	0	1
Swingler, Robert Lenton	Ketton, Rutland-shire	Fr	0	0	1
Stubley, William	....	Rt	1	1	0
Storey, William	....	Fr	0	0	1
Sewell, Edward	....	Rt	1	1	0
Sharman, Thomas	Bourn-road, Spalding	Fr			
Simpson, William	....	Rt	0	0	1
Swift, Robert	....	Rt	1	1	0
Shepperson, Joseph	Deeping St. Nicholas	Fr			
Saxton, Francis	....	Fr	1	0	1
Speechly, James	Spalding	Fr	1	1	0
Sutton, John	....	Fr	0	0	1
Swinton, Jacob	....	Fr	1	1	0
Swinton, John	....	Fr			
Tateson, John	Market Rasen	Fr			
Tomlin, John	....	Fr			
Tomlinson, John	....	Rt	1	1	0
Upton, Henry	....	Fr	0	0	1
Wayet, Rev. West	....	Fr	1	1	0
Wait, William	....	Fr	1	1	0
Walling, Francis	....	Fr	1	0	0
Wood, William	....	Fr			
Wright, Francis	Deeping-fen	Rt	0	0	1
Wells, William	....	Fr	0	0	1
Webster, James	....	Rt	1	1	0
Woods, William	....	Fr	1	0	0
Woods, John	....	Fr	1	0	0
Woodward, Isaac	....	Fr	1	0	1
Woodward, Isaac, jun.	....	Rt	0	0	1
Webb, William	....	Co	1	1	0
Wilson, John	....	Fr	1	0	1
White, John	Surfleet	Fr			
Wardall, Thomas Green	....	Co	1	1	0
Whitfield, John Sisson	Long Sutton	Fr			
Western, John	....	Rt	1	1	0
Yarrard, Michael	....	Fr	1	1	0

Spalding.

Name of Elector.	Residence, if out of the Parish.	Qual.	T.	W.	P.
Albin, Thomas	Plymouth	Fr			
Allen, Joseph	....	Fr	0	0	1
Amos, Thomas	Spalding Common	Rt	0	0	1
Andrew, James	....	Fr	0	1	1
Armstrong, Charles	Fulney	Fr	1	1	0
Armstrong, George	....	Fr	1	0	1
Armstrong, William	....	Fr	1	0	1
Atkin, Samuel	....	Fr	0	0	1
Ayre, John	12, Church-row, Hampstead, Middlesex	Fr			
Adeane, R. J., esq.	Babraham, Cambridgeshire	Fr			
Asling, Brelsford	....	Rt	1	0	1
Bales, Benjamin	......	Fr	1	0	1
Banks, Thomas	Gedney	Fr	1	1	0
Barnes, Joseph	....	Fr	1	0	1
Barnes, William	Deeping-fen	Rt			
Barns, Henry	St. Martin's, Stamford	Fr	1	1	0
Barrell, William	....	Fr	1	0	0
Bellairs, Rev. Henry	Bedworth, Warwickshire	Fr			
Bemrose, Thomas	....	Fr	1	1	0
Bemrose, Thomas	....	Rt			
Boardman, Joseph	Spalding-fen	Rt	1	0	1
Bonner, Charles Foster	....	Fr	1	1	0
Booth, George	....	Fr	0	0	1
Booth, John	....	Fr	1	1	0
Brainsby, William	....	Fr			
Brighton, George	....	Fr	1	0	1
Brice, John	....	Fr	0	0	1
Brown, William	....	Co	1	0	1
Buckle, S. C. W.	Church-st., Peterborough	Fr			
Buckworth, Theophilus Russell, esq.	Cockley Cley Hall, Norfolk	Fr			
Bugg, Henry	....	Rt	1	0	0
Ball, Ancell	....	Fr	1	0	1
Brand, Richard	....	Fr	0	0	1
Bothamley, Richard	....	Fr			
Brett, Charles	....	Fr	0	0	1
Barnes, Joseph, jun.	....	Co	0	0	1
Barnwell, Edward	Deeping St. Nicholas	Fr	1	1	0

Spalding—continued.

Name of Elector.	Residence, if out of the Parish.	Qual.	T.	W.	P.
Briggs, Jonathan T.	....	Fr	1	1	0
Barnes, James	....	Fr	1	0	1
Bowles, Benjamin	....	Rt	1	0	1
Bridges, Joseph	....	Rt	1	1	0
Betts, George William	....	Rt	1	1	0
Bingham, William	....	Rt	1	0	1
Bates, Henry	....	Rt	1	1	0
Calthrop, James T.	Deeping-fen	Rt	1	1	0
Cammack, Thomas *m. a.*	....	Fr	1	0	1
Campain, Joseph, jun.	Deeping-fen	Rt	1	0	1
Campain, Samuel	Ditto	Rt			
Cape, Charles	....	Fr	0	0	1
Capps, Joseph	Wisbeach	Fr			
Carter, John	....	Rt	*dead*		
Carter, John R., esq. *Sol*	....	Fr	1	1	0
Cartwright, John	....	Fr	1	1	0
Casswell, George	....	Fr	0	0	1
Caulton, John	North-fen	Fr	1	1	0
Caulton, William	....	Fr	1	1	0
Cave, John	Fulney	Fr	0	0	1
Cherrington, Stephen	....	Rt			
Childers, John W., esq.	Cantley, York	Co	0	0	1
Clark, John	....	Fr	1	0	1
Clark, John, jun.	....	Fr	0	0	1
Congreve, Daniel	Deeping-fen	Rt	1	1	0
Congreve, David	....	Fr			
Congreve, Abraham	....	Fr	0	0	1
Congreve, Thomas, jun.	Deeping-fen	Rt	1	0	0
Cooke, William	....	Rt	1	1	0
Cooper, Richard Marshall	....	Fr	1	1	0
Cope, William	....	Fr			
Copping, Charles	....	Rt	0	0	1
Cotton, Joseph	....	Fr	1	1	0
Cotton, Thomas	....	Fr	1	1	0
Cotton, William Lusby	....	Fr	1	1	0
Coulson, Daniel	....	Fr	0	1	0
Craps, John *minister*	Lincoln	Fr	0	0	1
Croskill, William	Beverley, Yorkshire	Fr			
Crust, John	....	Fr	1	0	1
Crust, Richard	....	Rt	1	0	1

Spalding—continued.

Name of Elector.	Residence, if out of the Parish.	Qual.	T.	W.	P.
Culy, Benjamin	....	Co	1	1	0
Culpin, Richard, sen.	....	Fr	0	0	1
Clark, William Simpson	Holbeach *Esq*	Fr	1	1	0
Cunnington, Thomas	....	Fr	0	0	1
Cunnington, John	....	Fr	0	0	1
Capps, John	....	Fr	1	0	1
Clark, William	....	Fr	0	0	1
Carter, Rev. George	Coningsby, Lincolnshire	Fr	1	1	0
Cave, John, jun.	....	Rt	1	1	0
Capps, William Thomas	....	Fr	1	0	1
Cave, Joseph	....	Fr			
Caulton, Henry	....	Fr	1	1	0
Case, John, jun.	....	Rt			
Caister, George	....	Fr	1	1	0
Cartwright, Augustus F.	*Solicitor*	Fr	0	0	1
Dallicoat, George	....	Fr	0	0	1
Dieppe, Thomas	Hull	Fr			
Dixon, Richard	....	Fr	0	0	1
Dolman, Samuel	....	Fr	1	0	1
Doria, Alexander *Esq*	Clipsham Hall, Rutland	Fr			
Draper, Thomas	....	Fr	1	0	1
Dolby, Charles	Manor House	Rt	1	1	0
Dawson, Stephen	....	Fr	1	1	0
Dolman, Edmund	....	Fr	1	0	1
Duffin, Stephen	....	Fr	0	0	1
Dalton, James	....	Fr	0	0	1
Dawson, Stephen	....	Fr			
Dixon, Moses	....	Fr	1	0	1
Eayrs, William	Pickworth, Rutland	Fr			
Eaton, Rev. Charles O. *Esq*	Tixover, Rutland	Fr	1	1	0
Eaton, John R., esq.	Tixover Hall, Rutland	Fr	1	1	0
Edwards, William	....	Fr	1	0	1
Everard, Henry, esq.	Fulney, Spalding	Fr	1	1	0
Everard, Robert, esq.	Ditto	Fr	1	1	0
Everitt, Robert	Saffron Walden, Essex	Fr	1	1	0
Exton, Thomas	Empingham, Rutland	Fr			
Elsom, Isaac	....	Fr	1	0	1
Edwards, Samuel	....	Fr	0	0	1
Facon, John	....	Fr			
Fletcher, John Ballett	Golden-sq., London	Fr			

Spalding—continued.

Name of Elector.	Residence, if out of the Parish.	Qual.	T.	W.	P.
Foster, Edward	....	Fr	1	0	1
Foster, Thomas	Moulton	Fr			
Fisher, Edward	....	Co	1	0	1
Fox William Henry, Beeston, Notting-hamshire		Fr	1	1	0
Fox, Charles Wright, Jesus College, Cam-bridge		Fr			
France, James	....	Fr	1	1	0
Geeson, Francis	Bottesford, Leicester-shire	Fr			
Godley, John	....	Fr	0	0	1
Gooch, George	....	Fr	1	0	1
Goodale, John	Market Deeping	Rt			
Goodwin, William	....	Fr	1	0	1
Grantham, Charles,	Ketton Lodge	Fr			
Green, John	....	Fr	0	0	1
Green, William	....	Fr			
Grist, Henry	....	Fr	0	0	1
Gulson, John	Spalding Common	Fr	1	0	0
Glen, William, jun.	....	Fr	0	0	1
Goodale, Wallet	Deeping High-bank	Fr	1	0	1
Green, James	....	Rt			
Gilbert, Edward	....	Rt	1	1	0
Gilbert, Francis Cutto	Leeds	Fr			
Garner, William	....	Rt	0	0	1
Hall, Cornelius	Commercial Road	Fr	1	1	0
Hall, William	Bourn Road	Fr			
Hames, Francis	Pinchbeck Road	Co	0	0	1
Hames, William	New Road	Fr	0	0	1
Hames, Charles	....	Fr			
Hanslip, Charles	London	Fr	1	1	0
Harrison, Thomas	Spalding Common	Fr			
Harvey, Charles	Gashouse-street	Fr	0	0	1
Hawkes, Henry, esq.	Brighton	Fr			
Healey, John	Deeping-fen	Rt			
Hewitt, Richard	Hall-street	Fr	0	0	1
Hewitt, John	Pinchbeck-road	Fr	0	0	1
Hiley, Thomas	Hall-street	Fr	1	0	1
Hobson, William	London Road	Fr			
Hockerston, Francis	London Road	Fr	0	0	1

Spalding—continued.

Name of Elector.	Residence, if out of the Parish.	Qual.	T.	W.	P.
Holdich, William H.	Sleaford	Fr			
Hopkins, Samuel	Boston	Fr			
Horn, William	Winsover	Fr			
Howard, William J.	Race-ground	Fr	0	0	1
Hudson, Ephraim	....	Fr	0	0	1
Hunt, Thomas	Spalding-fen-ends	Fr	0	0	1
Hewitt, Hilary	St. Martin's Stamford	Fr	1	1	0
Hall, Asa	....	Fr	1	0	1
Hill, Sleight	Cowbit Road	Rt	1	1	0
Hockerston, John	Pode Hole, Pinchbeck	Fr	0	0	1
Harrison, John	....	Fr	0	0	1
Hurry, William Charles	....	Fr	1	1	0
James, William	Holbeach Road	Co	1	0	1
James, Thomas	....	Fr	0	0	1
Jennings, Charles D.	Bridge-street	Rt	1	1	0
Jepson, John	Winsover	Fr	0	0	1
Jepson, William	Winsover	Rt	0	0	1
Johnson, John	Winsover	Fr			
Johnson, Maurice, esq.	~~Hotham Hall, Yorks~~.	Fr	1	1	0
Johnson, Tyrer	London Road	Co	1	0	1
Judd, Robert	Sessions House	Fr	1	1	0
Jinks, John	....	Fr	1	1	0
Jones, John Chatwin	....	Fr	1	0	1
Johnson, Maurice, esq.	Redgrave Hall, Botesdale, Suffolk	Fr	*voted*		
Johnson, T. M. S. esq.	....	Fr	1	1	0
Kelk, Jacob	near Chain-bridge	Fr	0	0	1
Kemp, Francis	High-street, Spalding	Fr	0	0	1
Kerr, James	Bourn Road	Fr	0	0	1
King, George	near Chain-bridge	Co	1	1	0
King, Thomas	Crackpool-lane	Fr			
Kirk, Frederick A.	Bourn Road	Fr	0	0	1
Kingston, Samuel, jun.	5, Welland Terrace	Fr	1	0	1
Laming, Samuel	Low Fields	Fr	1	1	0
Langcaster, Joseph	Bourn Road	Fr	0	0	1
Lansdale, Hamerton	Spalding, Double-street	Fr	0	0	1
Law, Thomas	Deeping Bank	Fr			
Lawson, John	Whittlesea	Fr	0	0	1
Lewis, John	London Road	Co	0	0	1
Lindsey, Philip	Deeping-fen	Rt	1	1	0

Spalding—continued.

Name of Elector.	Residence, if out of the Parish.	Qual.	T.	W.	P.
Longbottom, James	Holbeach Marsh, Lincolnshire	Fr			
Longbottom, Jonathan	Holbeach Marsh, Lincolnshire	Fr			
Lowden, George	Spalding Marsh	Fr	1	1	0
Lowe, William	New-road, Spalding	Fr	1	1	0
Lyon, John	Winsover, Spalding	Fr	1	0	1
Louth, Thomas	....	Fr	0	1	0
Lagnel, Jaques F. U.	....	Fr	0	0	1
Leach, Henry	....	Fr	1	1	0
Luck, Thomas	....	Fr	1	1	0
Mallet, Parmer	Walpole St. Peter's, Norfolk	Fr			
Maples, Ashley *Sol*	High-street	Rt	1	1	0
Maples, Edward Palmer	High-street	Fr	0	0	1
Maples, Coates	Deeping Saint Nicholas	Rt	1	1	0
Maples, Henry	Cowbit Road	Fr	1	1	0
Martell, Moses	London Road	Fr	0	1	1
Mawby, Robert, jun.	Spalding Marsh	Rt	0	0	1
Maxwell, William	New Hall, Ware	Fr			
Measures, Richard	....	Rt	1	1	0
Metherell, Richard	....	Fr	0	0	1
Middleton, John	....	Fr	1	0	1
Middleton, Adlard	Deeping-fen	Rt	1	1	0
Millns, Francis	London Road	Fr	1	1	0
Moore, William, D.D.	Church-street	Fr	1	1	0
Mounteny, Bartholomew	Market-place	Fr	0	0	1
Mousley, Richard	MoultonTurnpike-road to Holbeach	Fr			
Musson, William	Winsover, Spalding	Fr	0	0	1
Moore, John	....	Fr	0	0	1
Maxwell, William	Guyhurn, Wisbeach Saint Mary's	Fr	1	1	0
Moyer, Samuel	Bridge-street	Fr	1	0	1
Molson, William *als*	Hogsthorpe, near Alford	Fr	1	1	0
Maccann, Hillham	....	Fr	0	0	1
Measures, Joseph R.	....	Rt	0	0	1
Man, William	....	Fr	0	0	1
Mason, Robert Johnson	....	Fr	1	0	1
Neal, Benjamin	Monks' House	Rt	0	0	1

Spalding—continued.

Name of Elector.	Residence, if out of the Parish.	Qual	T.	W.	P.
Neave, James	Market-place	Fr	0	0	1
Nichols, William	near Chain-bridge	Fr	1	1	0
Newton, Robert	....	Rt	1	0	1
Osborn, James Dent, jun.	Crescent	Fr	0	0	1
Oliver, Robert	Deeping-fen	Fr	1	1	0
Osborn, James Dent	Crescent	Fr	0	0	1
Osbourn, James	Whaplode	Fr			
Owen, Joshua	Deeping-fen	Rt	0	0	1
Osborn, George Corney	....	Fr	1	0	1
Parkinson, John	Frog Hall	Fr	1	1	0
Parkinson, Thomas	....	Fr	0	0	1
Parr, John	St. Paul's-street, in the Parish of St. George, Stamford, Lincolnshire	Fr			
Pear, Thomas	Bedford Cottage, Spalding	Fr			
Pears, Joseph	Double-street	Fr	1	0	1
Pearson, Joseph	Pinchbeck-road	Fr			
Pepper, Thomas	Bourn-road	Fr	0	0	1
Peppercorn, William	Eaton Solken, Beds.	Fr			
Perry, John	Deeping-fen	Rt	1	0	1
Phillips, George	Spalding-fen	Rt	0	0	1
Pickering, John P.	Abbey-yard	Fr	1	[illegible]	1
Pickering, Thomas	Fen-ends	Fr	0	0	1
Pickworth, William	Hall-street	Fr	0	0	1
Pitcher, Christopher	Little London	Fr	1	1	0
Platt, Samuel	Spalding Marsh	Rt	0	0	1
Ponton, James	Clipsham	Fr	1	1	0
Pratt, Robert Parr	Deeping-fen	Rt	0	0	1
Preston, Richard	at the Park, Nottingham, in the County of Nottingham	Fr	0	0	1
Proctor, William	....	Co	0	0	1
Proctor, Edward	Wykeham	Rt	1	1	0
Platten, William, jun.	....	Fr			
Parr, Robert	Tinwell, Rutland	Fr	1	1	0
Pike, William	....	Fr	1	0	1
Plowright, John Hurrey	Manea, Cambridgeshire	Rt	1	1	0

Spalding—continued.

Name of Elector.	Residence, if out of the Parish.	Qual.	T.	W.	P.
Parke, Samuel, esq.	....	Rt	1	1	0
Percival, William	....	Rt			
Reedmon, John	Spalding-fen	Fr	1	1	0
Rogers, Newcombe	Little Gonerby, near Grantham	Fr			
Rose, William	Commercial-road	Fr	0	0	1
Reek, Thomas	....	Fr	0	0	1
Rainey, Charles	....	Fr			
Rainey, Edward	Spilsby	Co			
Roberts, Thomas	Ram Skin Inn	Fr			
Sanderson, Francis	Hedgehill, Warwick	Fr			
Saul, Stephen	Market-place	Fr	1	0	1
Scott, Thomas Basely	Empingham, near Stamford	Co	0	0	1
Seward, Samuel	Commercial-road	Fr	1	0	1
Seawell, Thomas Samuel	Mareylands, near Farnham, Surrey	Fr	*dead*		
Seymour, James	Bourn-road	Fr	0	0	1
Shadford, Major	Market-place	Fr	0	0	1
Sharman, Thomas	....	Fr	0	1	1
Shaw, George	Billericay, Essex	Fr			
Sherrad, George	King's Ripton, Hunts	Fr			
Sindall, Zachariah	Weston Marsh	Fr			
Sindall, John	Spalding-fen-ends	Fr	1	0	1
Skeath, Edward	Cradge-bank, Spalding	Fr	0	0	1
Skeath, William	Cradge-bank, Spalding	Fr	0	0	1
Smith, James	....	Fr	0	0	1
Smith, John	Abbey-yard	Fr	1	0	1
Smith, John	Deeping-fen-bank	Rt	0	0	1
Smith, Joseph	....	Fr			
Smith, David	Fulney-lane, Spalding	Rt	1	1	0
Smith, Thomas	....	Co	1	1	0
Sneath, James	Kentish Town, near London	Fr			
Spooner, Henry	Hall-street	Fr	1	1	0
Stableforth, John	High-street, Spalding	Fr	0	0	1
Stennett, Michael	Spalding Marsh	Rt	0	0	1
Storr, Edward	Winsover-road	Fr	1	0	1
Strong, Thomas Linwood	Sedgefield Rectory, County of Durham	Fr	*cch*		

Spalding—continued.

Name of Elector.	Residence, if out of the Parish.	Qual.	T.	W.	P.
Sharp, Joel	Albion-street	Fr	1	1	0
Soulby, Charles	....	Rt	1	1	0
Stubbs, William	Market-place	Fr			
Southwell, Thomas Gue	Hall-street	Fr	0	0	1
Stevenson, John	....	Fr	0	0	1
Sutton, George	Chapel-lane	Fr	1	1	0
Sharman, William	....	Fr	1	0	1
Sharman, William, jun.	....	Fr	1	0	1
Storey, May	....	Rt	1	0	0
Smith, Robert	....	Rt			
Smith, Samuel	....	Fr	0	0	1
Soulby, Henry	Toynton All Saints, Spilsby	Fr	1	1	0
Taylor, Dennis	Huntingdon	Fr			
Taylor, Thomas	....	Fr	0	0	1
Teesdale, Isaac	Wykeham	Rt	1	1	0
Thompson, George	Spalding Marsh	Fr			
Thompson, William	Weston	Fr			
Thorpe, Matthew	....	Fr	0	0	1
Thorpe, Richard Francis	....	Fr	0	0	1
Thornton, James	Pig Market	Fr	0	0	1
Thory, John	Winsover	Fr	0	0	1
Tidwell, Joseph	Little London	Fr	1	0	1
Tidswell, James W. H.	....	Fr	1	1	0
Tointon, James	Bourn-road	Fr	1	0	1
Tricket, John	Pinchbeck	Fr			
Turner, Isaac	Deeping Bank	Fr	1	1	0
Tye, Joseph	....	Fr	1	1	0
Thompson, Edward	....	Fr	0	0	1
Todd, William	Bourn	Rt			
Todd, Samuel Campain	Spalding-fen	Rt			
Tingey, William	....	Rt	1	0	1
Tory, George	....	Fr			
Turner, William	....	Fr	1	0	1
Vere, James Esq	United University Club, Suffolk-st., Pall Mall, East Middlesex	Fr			
Vise, Charles	....	Fr	1	1	0
Vergette, Thomas	Boro'-fen	Rt	1	1	0

Spalding—continued.

Name of Elector.	Residence, if out of the Parish.	Qual.	T.	W.	P.
Wadeson, Thomas	Forty-foot-bank	Rt	0	1	0
Walden, Mark	London-road, Spalding	Fr	1	1	0
Wallis, Robert	Pinchbeck-street	Fr	1	1	0
Waltham, Joseph	Deeping-fen	Rt	0	0	1
Waltham, Robert	....	Fr	1	0	0
Watson, Edward	....	Fr	0	0	1
Watson, James	Crackpool-lane, Spalding	Fr	0	0	1
Webster, James	Spalding North-fen	Rt			
Wellband, Edward	London-road	Fr			
Wells, William, jun.	Spalding-fen	Rt	1	0	0
White, Thomas	Bourn-road	Fr	0	0	1
White, William	Sheep Market	Fr	0	0	1
White, William	Commercial-road	Co	1	1	0
Wilson, John	....	Fr			
Willmot, John	Market-place	Fr	1	1	0
Willson, James	York	Fr			
Wilson, William	Commercial-road	Fr	1	1	0
Wisher, John	Albert-street	Fr	1	1	0
Withers, Thomas	Bourn-road	Fr	0	0	1
Whitwell, Walter	Holbeach-road, Spalding	Fr	1	1	0
Wooley, Robert	Bourn-road	Fr	1	0	1
Wright, Thomas	Weston Hills	Fr			
Ward, William	....	Rt	0	0	1
Wright, Samuel	7, Grantham-place, Lincoln	Fr	0	0	1
Wright, William	Stamford	Fr			
Wooley, Morton	....	Fr	1	0	1
Welborn, Edward	....	Fr	1	1	0
Watson, John	....	Fr	0	1	1
Webster, George	....	Fr	1	0	1
Willson, John	....	Rt	1	1	0
Whitwell, Walter	....	Fr			
Willson, John	Crescent	Fr	1	1	0
Watkinson, Henry	....	Rt	1	0	1
Youlden, Abraham	Henley-upon-Thames	Fr			

Surfleet.

Name of Elector.	Residence, if out of the Parish.	Qual.	T.	W.	P.
Allen, Valentine Ingram	....	Rt	1	1	0
Ash, John	....	Fr	0	0	1

Surfleet—continued.

Name of Elector.	Residence, if out of the Parish.	Qual.	T.	W.	P.
Beasley, William *Esqr*	Osborn Villa, Folk-stone, Kent	Fr			
Barton, Thomas	....	Fr	1	1	0
Baxter, Joseph	....	Fr	1	0	1
Belsham Abraham	Pinchbeck	Fr	1	1	0
Boothby, Edward	....	Fr	0	0	1
Boothby, Edward J.	....	Rt	0	0	1
Barsley, John	....	Fr	1	0	1
Beasley, William Cole	Middlesex	Fr			
Burrell, George	....	Rt	1	1	0
Brown, William	Cressey Hall, Surfleet	Rt	1	1	0
Boothby, Thomas S.	....	Fr	0	0	1
Barton, Frederick	....	Rt	1	1	0
Brittain, Richard	....	Rt	1	1	0
Cooper, John	....	Fr	1	0	1
Coxell, James	....	Fr	1	1	0
Clay, Henry	....	Fr	0	0	1
Crow, Thomas	....	Rt	1	0	0
Ducket, Clark Armston	....	Fr			
Drewery, William	....	Fr	1	1	0
Ellsey, Edward	....	Fr	0	0	1
Flowers, William	....	Fr	1	1	0
Fox, Thomas C.	Gosberton	Fr	1	1	0
Garritt, William	....	Fr	0	0	1
Godwin, Robert	....	Fr			
Goulding, Thomas	....	Fr	1	1	0
Genn, Robert	Peterborough	Fr	0	0	1
Grant, James	Fishtoft	Fr			
Ingram, James	....	Fr	1	1	0
Ingram, Robert	Pinchbeck	Fr			
Inkley, Robert	....	Fr	0	0	1
Knight, Samuel	....	Rt	1	1	0
Law, Joseph	....	Rt	0	1	0
Lane, Edmund	....	Rt	1	1	0
Long, John	Gosberton	Fr	0	0	1
Melson, Samuel	....	Rt	1	0	1
Melson, Charles	....	Fr	0	0	1
Muckslow, William	Gosberton	Fr	1	1	0
Melson, John	7, Arlington-st., New North Rd., London	Fr			

Surfleet—continued.

Name of Elector.	Residence, if out of the Parish.	Qual.	T.	W.	P.
Musson, John	....	Fr	1	0	0
Needham, John	....	Fr	1	1	0
North, William Horner	Gosberton	Fr			
Northon, Edward	....	Fr	0	0	1
Nale, William	....	Fr	1	0	0
Pickworth, Francis	....	Rt	1	1	0
Parry, Humphries E. *Incumbent*		Fr	0	1	1
Reynolds, John Skinner	....	Fr	1	1	0
Robinson, Henry	....	Fr			
Roe, Nicholas	....	Fr	1	0	1
Robinson, John	....	Rt	1	1	0
Smith, Robert	....	Fr	1	1	0
Speed, Henry	....	Fr	0	0	1
Smith, William	....	Rt	1	0	1
Suthrell, John	Gosberton	Fr			
Skerritt, John	Pinchbeck	Fr	1	1	0
Taylor, James	....	Fr	0	1	1
Taylor, Isaac	....	Fr			
Twelves, Robert	....	Fr	0	0	1
Taylor, Richard	No. 4, Queen's Row, Stockwell, Surrey	Fr			
Tenant, Ottiwell	*El*Holme, Huntingdonshire	Fr			
Tupholme, Joseph	....	Rt	1	1	0
Wade, David	....	Fr	0	1	1
Wade, John	....	Fr	1	1	0
Winkley, John	....	Fr	1	1	0
Watson, Thomas	....	Fr			
White, John	....	Fr	1	1	0
Whaley, Samuel	....	Rt			
Wilson, Charles	....	Rt	1	1	0

Weston.

Name of Elector.	Residence, if out of the Parish.	Qual.	T.	W.	P.
Allen, Walpole	Spalding	Rt	0	0	1
Armstrong, Thomas	....	Co	1	1	0
Bellamy, James	Bourn	Fr	1	1	0
Bycraft, John	Moulton	Co	0	0	1
Black, Edward	....	Fr	1	0	0
Beeston, Peter Petelion	....	Fr	1	1	0
Benner, William	....	Fr	1	0	1
Bell, Joseph	Bourn	Fr			

Weston—continued.

Name of Elector.	Residence, if out of the Parish.	Qual.	T.	W.	P.
Bell, Joseph	Bourn	Fr	1	1	0
Blackburn, Charles	....	Fr	1	1	0
Blackburn, Robinson	....	Fr	1	1	0
Bradford, John	....	Fr	1	1	0
Benner, Robert	....	Fr	1	0	0
Cordley, William, sen.	....	Fr	1	0	1
Copping, Henry	....	Fr	1	0	0
Cock, John	Moulton	Rt	0	0	1
Crook, Amos	....	Fr	1	0	1
Chambers, William	....	Rt	1	1	0
Campain, Joseph, sen.	Deeping-fen	Fr	1	1	0
Clayton, John	....	Co	1	1	0
Clayton, William	....	Fr	1	0	1
Clayton, David	....	Fr	1	0	1
Clark, Thomas John	....	Rt	1	1	0
Clark, Charles	....	Fr	1	1	0
Durance, Charles	Bourn Bedehouse	Rt			
Desborough, John	....	Fr	1	0	0
Ellis, William	Bourn	Fr			
French, Isaac	....	Co			
Francis, John	Bourn Bedehouse	Rt			
Flint, William	....	Fr	1	0	0
Gedney, John	Cowbit	Fr			
Grummitt, William, sen.	....	Fr	1	0	1
Gibson, John	....	Fr	1	1	0
Green, William	....	Co	1	1	0
Gedney, John	Cowbit	Fr	1	1	0
Grummitt, William, jun.	....	Fr	0	0	1
Gedney, William	....	Fr	1	1	0
Grummitt, Joseph	....	Fr	1	0	1
Howard, John	....	Rt	1	1	0
Hazelgreave, John	Bourn	Fr	1	1	0
Hutchinson, John	....	Fr	1	0	1
Hawley, Nathaniel	....	Fr	1	1	0
Johnson, Charles F.	Northfield	Fr			
Mousley, John	....	Fr	1	1	0
Moore, Rev. Edward	Master's Lodge, Church-lane, Spalding	Rt	1	1	0
Ogden, John	....	Rt	1	1	0
Ogden, William	Weston Hills	Rt	1	0	1

Weston—continued.

Name of Elector.	Residence, if out of the Parish.	Qual.	T.	W.	P.
Pick, Abraham	....	Fr	1	0	1
Perkins, James	Weston Hills	Rt	1	1	0
Payling, George	Ditto	Fr	1	1	0
Raines, William	....	Rt	1	0	0
Sindall, Zachariah	....	Rt	0	1	1
Spence, Rev. John	East Keal	Fr			
Snell, Robert Holmes	Weston Hills	Fr	1	1	0
Skeels, William	....	Fr	1	0	0
Sharp, William	Deeping Bank	Rt	1	0	0
Smith, Charles Handley	....	Rt	0	0	1
Sindall, Thomas William	....	Fr	1	0	0
Smith, James	....	Fr	1	1	0
Tidswell, James	....	Fr	1	1	0
Thompson, William	....	Fr	1	1	0
Walker, John	....	Fr	1	0	1
Wilson, Aqquilla	....	Rt	1	0	1
Waite, William	....	Rt	1	0	1
Welbourn, John	....	Co	1	1	0
Wright, Thomas	....	Fr	1	1	0
Wilson, William	....	Fr	1	1	0
Webster, Thomas	....	Co	1	0	1
Wiseman, William	....	Fr	1	1	0

No. 4.—POLLING DISTRICT ASSIGNED TO HOLBEACH.

Fleet.

Name of Elector.	Residence, if out of the Parish.	Qual.	T.	W.	P.
Ashton, James	....	Rt	0	0	1
Aucock, Robert	Fleet-bank	Fr	0	0	1
Bailey, William	....	Fr	0	0	1
Bedford, Thomas	....	Fr	1	0	1
Buckworth, Joseph	Glinton, Northamptonshire	Fr			
Bothamley, John	....	Fr	0	0	1
Bothamley, James	Gedney	Fr	0	0	1
Bayston, Joseph	....	Co	0	0	1
Bailey, Richard C.	Thorney Abbey	Fr	0	0	1
Brown, John	Pear Tree Hills, Elm, Cambridge	Fr	1	0	1

Fleet—continued.

Name of Elector.	Residence, if out of the Parish.	Qual.	T.	W.	P.
Barker, Thomas, jun.	Gedney-dyke	Co			
Butters, John	Fleet-bank	Fr	0	1	1
Britain, Robert	....	Rt	1	1	0
Crosby, William	....	Fr			
Clifton, George	Peterborough, Northamptonshire	Fr			
Crane, Wright	Thorney, Cambridgeshire	Fr			
Collins, John William	....	Fr			
Creek, Joseph	Fleet-fen	Fr	0	0	1
Chamberlain, Farmer	....	Fr	0	0	1
Creek, Thomas	Fleet-fen	Fr	0	0	1
Clarke, James	Fleet-fen	Rt	0	0	1
Duckering, Samuel	....	Fr	0	0	1
Duncombe, Philip Duncombe Pauncefort, esq.	Great Brick-hill Manor, Bucks.	Fr			
Ellis, Robert	....	Fr	0	0	1
Ellis, Matthew	....	Fr	1	0	1
Edwards, David Owen	15, Cheyney-walk, Chelsea, Middlesex	Fr			
Ellis, Anthony	....	Fr	0	0	1
Franks, Lawrence	....	Rt	1	0	1
Fish, John, Cordwainer	....	Fr	0	0	1
Graves, Thomas	....	Fr			
Garner, Thomas	....	Fr	0	0	1
Griffin, Philip	Powder Blue, Parish of Eye, in the County of Northampton	Rt	1	0	1
Hunter, Francis	....	Rt			
Hallifax, William	....	Fr			
Haines, Jonathan	....	Fr	0	0	1
Hakeman, Joseph	Fleet-fen-ends	Rt	0	0	1
Hilliam, Robert	....	Rt	0	0	1
Herris, George Headen	Fleet Hargate	Fr	0	0	1
Kemp, Edwin Richard	....	Fr	0	0	1
Larrington, Joseph	....	Fr	0	0	1
Loughton, William	....	Fr			
Maddock, Samuel, Clerk	Ropley, Hampshire	Fr			
Musson, William	Knipton	Fr			

Fleet—continued.

Name of Elector.	Residence, if out of the Parish.	Qual.	T.	W.	P.
Maskill, Christopher	....	Fr	0	0	1
Massey, John	....	Fr			
Markham, Thomas	....	Fr			
Marriott, Edward	....	Fr	0	0	1
Manton, William	....	Fr	0	0	1
Morris, Richard	....	Rt	1	1	0
Millington, John Boyfield	Boston	Fr			
Metcalf, Charles, jun.	Wisbeach, Cambridgeshire	Fr			
Norwood, Edward	....	Fr	0	0	1
Oliver, David	....	Rt	1	1	0
Parke, Samuel, esq.	Ayscough Fee-hall, Spalding	Fr			
Proctor, James	....	Fr	0	0	1
Rhodes, Charles	Fleet-fen	Fr	0	0	1
Ratcliffe, John, jun.	Boston	Fr			
Ridlington, William	No. 1, Rockingham-row West, New Kent-road, London	Fr	1	1	0
Slator, Barnett	....	Fr	0	0	1
Stokes, Samuel	Parish of Saint Sepulchre, Northamptonshire	Fr			
Smith, Samuel	....	Rt	0	0	1
Sturton, Jacob	....	Fr			
Seawell, Thomas A.	Marelands, in the Parish of Bentley, in the County of Southampton	Fr	0	0	1
Townsend, Nathan	Long Sutton	Fr	0	0	1
Walker, John	Spalding	Fr			
Wanty, Edwin	Fleet-fen	Fr	0	0	1
Wilkinson, Matthew	Holbeach-drove	Fr			
Wadeson, James	....	Le	0	0	1
Wilkins, Thomas	Ringstead House, Northamptonshire	Fr			
Winkley, John	Fleet-fen	Fr	1	0	0
White, John	Spalding	Fr			
Walker, Henry James	Spalding	Fr	0	0	1
Waterman, John	....	Rt	1	1	0

Gedney.

Name of Elector.	Residence, if out of the Parish.	Qual.	T.	W.	P.
Aubin, John	. . . .	Fr	0	0	1
Atkin, James	. . . .	Rt	1	0	0
Barwell, Thomas	Gedney-fen	Rt	0	1	1
Bass, Edward	. . . .	Fr	1	1	0
Bertie, Edward	. . . .	Fr			
Boucher, Charles	South Brink, Wisbeach St. Peter's	Fr			
Boynton, Robert	Gedney-fen	Rt	0	0	1
Bird, Leonard	Farcet, Huntingdonshire	Rt	0	0	1
Bird, Robert	Farcet-fen, Huntingdonshire	Rt	0	0	1
Bellamy, John	Stevenage, Herts.	Fr			
Bothamley, Thomas	Gedney-fen	Rt	0	0	1
Barnes, William	. . . .	Rt	1	1	0
Buffham, William	Gedney Marsh	Rt	1	0	1
Bailey, William	Holbeach Marsh	Fr	0	0	1
Butters, David	. . . .	Co	1	1	0
Bristow, Samuel	Gedney-drove-end	Fr	0	1	1
Barker, Francis	. . . .	Co	0	0	1
Clarke, Algernon John	Long Sutton	Rt			
Clarke, James	. . . .	Rt	1	0	1
Collins, John William	Fleet	Fr	1	1	0
Clifton, John	. . . .	Fr	0	0	1
Chantry, Joseph	. . . .	Rt	0	0	1
Cooper, John	Tydd St. Giles, Cambridgeshire	Fr			
Clifton, Joseph	. . . .	Fr	0	0	1
Clifton, Robert	. . . .	Fr			
Chapman, Mowbray	Gedney Broad-gate	Rt	0	0	1
Cropper, James	Sutton St. Mary	Fr	0	0	1
Coats, Charles	Gedney-drove-end	Fr	1	1	0
Cooper, Thomas	Ditto	Fr	1	1	0
Cunnington, William, jun.	Lutton	Fr	1	1	0
Cocks, Thomas Somers	Harley-st., Middlesex	Rt			
Cocks, T. S., jun, esq.	Hereford-st., Middlesex	Fr	1	1	0
Cardwell, Charles	28, Chester Terrace, Regent's Park, London	Fr			
Cardwell, Edward	Whitehall Gardens, Westminster	Fr			
Cooper, John	. . . .	Co	0	0	1
Derry, Charles, esq.	. . . .	Co	1	1	0

Gedney—continued.

Name of Elector.	Residence, if out of the Parish.	Qual.	T.	W.	P.
Dring, Thomas Boyes	Claxby, near Spilsby	Rt	0	1	0
Escot, Rev. Thomas S.	*Kirton ... dead*	Fr			
Fardell, Charles Esq.	Holbeck, near Horncastle	Fr			
Freeman, Richard	....	Fr			
Faulkner, Isaac	....	Fr	1	1	0
Franks, Samuel	Gedney-fen-ends	Co	0	0	1
Goodale, Mark	Sutton St. Mary	Fr	1	1	0
Goose, John	....	Rt	1	1	0
Gibbons, Robert	6 Percy-place, Clapham-rd., Surrey	Fr			
Gott, George	....	Fr			
Goulton, Benjamin	Gedney Marsh	Rt	1	0	1
Harrison, Thomas	Gedney-dyke	Rt	1	1	0
Haines, James	....	Co	0	1	1
Hill, Luke	....	Fr			
Holbourn, Edward	....	Rt	0	0	1
Holbourn, Matthew	....	Rt	0	0	1
Howard, Thomas	14, Buckingham-st., Strand, London, & Upper Court Lodge, Wolhingham	Fr			
Hutchinson, Proctor	....	Fr	0	0	1
Hicks, William	Gedney Marsh	Rt	1	0	1
Hutchinson, Jonathan	Selby, Yorkshire	Fr			
Halifax, William	....	Fr	0	0	1
Holbourn, George	Gedney Marsh	Rt	1	1	0
Holt, Charles	....	Co	0	0	1
Hurling, John	Sutton St. Mary	Fr	0	0	1
Hutchinson, John	Selby, Yorkshire	Fr			
Hutchinson, William	Gedney-drove-end	Fr	1	1	0
Hart, Henry	....	Rt	0	0	1
Haynes, William	Gedney Dyke	Co	0	0	1
Jerrad, Robert	....	Co	0	0	1
Kent, Robert T., esq.	8, Trinity-sq., Southwark, Surrey	Fr			
Kent, Thomas J., esq.	9, Trinity-sq., Southwark, Surrey	Fr			
Kent, Anthony, esq.	Somerby, near Grantham	Fr			
Kirkby, James	Moulton Marsh	Co			
Kitchen, Richard	....	Co	0	0	1

Gedney—continued.

Name of Elector.	Residence, if out of the Parish.	Qual.	T.	W.	P.
Lavender, Edmund	....	Co	0	0	1
Long, John Hume	....	Fr	1	1	0
Long, William	....	Rt	1	1	0
Long, Edward	....	Rt	1	1	0
Larrington, Thomas	....	Co	0	0	1
Lawrence, William	Peterborough, North-amptonshire	Fr			
Landing, William	....	Fr			
Laws, Samuel	....	Fr	0	0	1
Loughton, William	....	Fr			
Loughton, Henry	....	Fr			
Manton, John	....	Fr	1	1	0
Mason, Robert	....	Co	0	0	1
Maston, Frederick	....	Rt	1	0	1
Moore, Rev. Edward	Church-st., Spalding	Fr			
Morris, Hosea	....	Le	1	1	0
Millington, Edward	Fleet Lodge	Co			
Morris, Solomon	Sutton St. James	Co			
Mitchell, William	....	Fr	1	1	0
Munson, William	....	Rt	0	1	1
Oldershaw, Burrell	Gedney Broadgate	Rt	0	0	1
Parr, Richard	....	Fr	0	0	1
Peele, Thomas	Sutton St. Mary	Fr			
Piggins, George	....	Fr	1	1	0
Patchett, William Gibson	Gedney Marsh	Fr	1	1	0
Peck, William	....	Co	0	1	1
Perkins, George	....	Rt	1	1	0
Pettors, Samuel	....	Fr	0	0	1
Rubbins, Isaac	Stamford	Fr	1	1	0
Reed, Howard	Gedney Marsh	Rt			
Reynolds, Charles	London-road, Spalding	Fr	1	1	0
Smith, William Watson	Pimlico, London, but no certain residence	Co			
Smith, Isaac	Fleet	Fr	0	0	1
Slator, Luke	Gedney Drove-end	Fr	0	0	1
Sharpe, John	....	Co	0	0	1
Taylor, James Wickham	....	Co			
Thistlewood, Thomas	Gedney Broadgate	Co	0	0	1
Vincent, John	....	Co			

Gedney—continued.

Name of Elector.	Residence, if out of the Parish.	Qual.	T.	W.	P.
Ward, Joseph	Walpole, Norfolk	Fr			
Wing, Rev. John	Thornaugh, Northamptonshire	Co			
Welbourn, Edward	Long Sutton	Co	0	1	1
Waterfield, Joseph	....	Fr	0	0	1
Wilkinson, Samuel	....	Rt	0	0	1
Wilkinson, Joseph S.	Great Marlow, Bucks.	Fr			
Walker, John	....	Co	0	0	1
Wilkinson, Frederick	....	Rt	0	1	0
Young, Thomas	Gedney Dyke	Rt	1	1	0

Gedney Hill.

Name of Elector.	Residence, if out of the Parish.	Qual.	T.	W.	P.
Allen, Thomas	....	Co	0	0	1
Barrens, Joseph	....	Co	0	0	1
Barton, George	....	Rt			
Brown, Joseph	....	Rt	0	0	1
Cook, Edwin	....	Co	1	0	1
Cooke, John	....	Rt			
Cooper, Richard	....	Co	1	1	0
Edens, John	....	Rt	0	0	1
Flint, John	....	Co			
Foreman, Samuel	....	Rt			
Foyster, Joseph Ansil	....	Fr	0	0	1
Harrison, Charles	....	Rt	1	1	0
Heys, James	....	Co	0	0	1
Hurn, James	....	Fr	1	0	0
Jackson, James	....	Fr	1	1	0
Jones, John	....	Co			
Larnett, William	....	Fr			
Lenton, William	Whaplode Drove	Fr	0	0	1
Lound, William	Cowgate, Peterborough	Fr	0	0	1
Maxwell, John	Thorney, Cambridgeshire	Rt	0	0	1
Mears, Isaac	....	Fr	0	0	1
Mears, Seth	....	Co	0	0	1
Robinson, Zachariah	....	Co	1	1	0
Richardson, James Scribo	....	Co	1	1	0
Seaton, Thomas	....	Co	0	0	1
Wyles, William	....	Fr	0	0	1

Holbeach.

Name of Elector.	Residence, if out of the Parish.	Qual.	T.	W.	P.
Aldgate, Stephen	....	Fr	0	0	1
Allen, John	Sutton St. Edmunds	Fr	1	1	0
Archer, John	Mansfield-road, Not- tingham	Fr			
Ash, William	Dyke, near Bourn	Fr			
Atkinson, Henry	Fleet .	Fr	0	1	1
Aldgate, James	Market-place, Peter- borough	Fr	0	0	1
Beeston, Frederick W.	....	Co	0	0	1
Banks, Charles	Holbeach Marsh	Rt	0	0	1
Belgrave, Rev. W.,	Preston, in the County of Rutland	Fr	1	1	0
Belgrave, William, jun.	Preston, Rutland	Fr	1	1	0
Beeston, Brittain	....	Fr	1	0	0
Birkbeck, Henry *Esq*	Keswick, Norfolk	Fr			
Bimrose, William W.	....	Fr	0	0	1
Boardman, John	Holbeach-fen-ends	Rt	0	0	1
Booth, Richard	Wainfleet	Fr	1	1	0
Byron, John	Horncastle	Fr	1	1	0
Brown, George	Holbeach Marsh	Rt	0	0	1
Buffham, Charles	Spalding	Fr	0	0	1
Barker, Joseph C. esq.	....	Fr	1	1	0
Burchnall, William	Holbeach Drove	Fr	0	0	1
Boston, William	Holbeach Marsh	Fr	0	0	1
Burgess, William	Holbeach-fen	Rt	0	0	1
Beagles, William	Holbeach Drove	Fr	0	0	1
Bailey, John	Holbeach Wash-way	Fr	1	0	1
Burton, Edward	Whaplode	Fr	0	0	1
Banks, Thomas	Holbeach Hurn	Rt	0	0	1
Banks, Christopher	Holbeach Hurn	Rt	0	0	1
Bailey, Joseph	Holbeach Hurn	Rt	0	0	1
Black, James	....	Fr			
Boon, William	....	Fr	1	0	1
Brister, Edward	....	Fr	0	0	1
Caparn, Richard *Sol*	....	Fr	1	1	0
Congreve, Samuel	....	Fr	0	0	1
Connington, James	Holbeach-fen	Fr	1	0	1
Curtis, Thomas West	....	Fr	1	0	1
Chamberlain, Palmer	Fleet	Fr			
Cain, John	....	Fr	1	0	1

Holbeach—continued.

Name of Elector.	Residence, if out of the Parish.	Qual.	T.	W.	P.
Capp, James	Fleet	Fr	0	0	1
Carbutt, William	Holbeach Marsh	Rt			
Claxton, William	Holbeach-bank	Fr			
Carter, John	....	Rt	0	0	1
Clifton, Henry	Ruddington, Nottinghamshire	Fr			
Clifton, John	Bottesford, Leicestershire	Fr			
Clarke, William	....	Fr	0	0	1
Clement, George	....	Fr			
Cope, Thomas	....	Fr	1	0	1
Cooke, George	Kirton	Fr			
Cook, Jarvis	....	Fr	0	0	1
Cooke, Isaac	Clenchwarton, Norfolk	Fr	1	1	0
Cross, David	Holbeach-fen	Rt	0	0	1
Cheshire, Thomas	Cowgate, in the City of Peterborough	Fr			
Cox, George	Holbeach-fen-ends	Rt	0	0	1
Craven, Joseph	....	Rt	1	1	0
Cross, John	Holbeach Common	Fr			
Cross, David	Whaplode-drove	Fr	1	0	1
Coxon, Hugh C.	Holbeach Battlefields	Fr	0	0	1
Clarke, Samuel	....	Fr	0	0	1
Crofts, John	....	Fr	0	0	1
Cartwright, George	....	Rt	1	1	0
Capp, James Robert	....	Fr	0	0	1
Codling, John	Whaplode	Rt			
Crawley, William	Holbeach Marsh	Rt	0	0	1
Cordeaux, John	Hoyland Parsonage, near Barnsley, Yorkshire	Fr			
Carbutt, William	Holbeach Marsh	Fr			
Dobson, Isaac	Gedney-drove-end	Fr	0	0	1
Darley, John	....	Fr	1	0	1
Digby, James	Spalding	Fr			
Dickins, John	....	Rt	0	0	1
Downham, William	Holbeach-bank, near the Hurn	Fr			
Dolby, Thomas	Wignall's-gate	Rt	0	0	1
Dodds, Joseph	....	Rt	1	0	1

Holbeach—continued.

Name of Elector.	Residence, if out of the Parish.	Qual.	T.	W.	P.
Daubney, W. H., esq. *Sol*	Great Grimsby	Fr	1	1	0
Eldred, John	....	Fr	0	0	1
Ellis, Thomas	....	Fr	0	0	1
Ellis, Henry	....	Fr	0	0	1
Eldred, John Bass	Albert-street, Holbeach	Fr	0	0	1
Eason, William K.	Holbeach Drove	Rt	0	0	1
Eliff, Joseph	....	Rt	0	0	1
Fawn, James	Holbeach-fen	Fr	1	0	1
Farmer, Thomas	Holbeach Marsh	Fr	1	1	0
Franks, John	Holbeach Drove	Fr	0	0	1
Friskney, John	Fleet	Fr	0	0	1
Franks, Samuel	....	Fr	0	0	1
Field, Jonathan, esq.	Laceby	Fr	1	1	0
Garner, Henry	Holbeach-fen	Rt	0	0	1
Goulding, Robert	....	Rt	1	1	0
Grundy, Stephen	....	Fr	0	0	1
Gott, Matthew	....	Fr	0	0	⸌1
Griffin, John	Borough-fen, Northamptonshire	Rt			
Gunthorpe, William H.	....	Fr	1	1	0
Harrison, Richard	Holbeach-fen	Fr	0	0	1
Harrisson, Alfred	Barrington-gate, Holbeach	Fr	1	0	0
Harrison, Seth Thomas	....	Rt	0	0	1
Hawley, Sir Joseph H.	Leybourne Grange, Kent	Fr			
Hunt, Amos	....	Fr	0	0	1
Harris, William	Holbeach Drove	Fr	0	0	1
Harrison, Joseph	....	Fr			
Higdon, Francis	....	Rt	1	1	0
Harrison, John	....	Fr	0	0	1
Harris, Richard	Cowfield, Gold	Rt	0	1	1
Hickson, Richard	....	Rt	1	0	0
Head, Henry	Wash-way-road	Fr			
Hunter, Charles Vicars	Kilbourne, in the County of Derby	Fr			
Hardell, John	Sutton St. James	Fr	1	0	1
Hilliam, Robert	Fleet	Rt			
Haythorp, Zachariah	Holbeach-bank	Fr	0	1	1

Holbeach—continued.

Name of Elector.	Residence, if out of the Parish.	Qual.	T.	W.	P.
Holah, Joseph	....	Rt	0	0	1
James, John *J. J.*	Peterborough	Fr			
Jeffreys, John	....	Rt	1	1	0
Johnson, Edmund	....	Fr	0	0	1
Johnson, Sturton	Great Stanmore, Middlesex	Fr			
Johnson, Edward Davey	No. 7, Gray's Inn Square, Middlesex	Fr	1	1	0
Kirkbride, John	3, St. Martin's Court, Ludgate-hill, London	Fr			
Kirkby, William	....	Rt	0	0	1
Kirton, William	....	Fr	0	0	1
Keal, Robert	Penny-hill, Holbeach	Rt	0	0	1
Kirkbride, Robert	47, Market-place, Kingston-upon-Hull	Fr			
Laws, William	....	Fr	0	0	1
Lawrence, Atkinson	....	Fr	0	0	1
Longbottom, Jonathan	Holbeach Marsh	Rt	1	0	1
Lawson, William	Whaplode-drove	Fr	0	0	1
Latham, Robert Gordon	29, Upper Southwark-st., London	Le	0	0	1
Lundy, Robert	....	Rt	0	0	1
Leatherland, James	Holbeach-drove	Fr	0	0	1
Long, James John	....	Fr			
Longbottom, James	....	Rt	0	0	1
Meatheringham, W. B.	Holbeach Marsh	Rt	0	0	1
Mendham, Robert	Holbeach-drove	Fr	1	1	0
Mackman, Joseph	Holbeach-drove	Fr	0	0	1
Moulds, William	Holbeach Marsh	Fr			
Morton, James	....	Fr	1	0	1
Mayson, James	....	Fr	1	0	1
Mossop, Benjamin A.	Spalding	Fr	1	0	0
Merryman, Charles	....	Fr	0	0	1
Milns, Robert	....	Fr	1	0	1
Morton, John	Egleton	Fr	1	1	0
Naylor, John	63, Blackfriar's-road, London	Fr			
Newton, Robert	Chatteriss	Fr	1	1	0
Newton, William	East Retford	Fr			

Holbeach—continued.

Name of Elector.	Residence, if out of the Parish.	Qual.	T.	W.	P.
Nichols, Robert	....	Fr	1	0	1
Nichols, James	Holbeach-bank	Fr	0	0	1
Nussey, Joshua *clk*	Vicarage, Oundle, Northamptonshire	Fr			
Naylor, John	No. 114, Whitechapel-road, London, Middlesex	Fr			
Ogden, John	Holbeach-drove	Fr	0	0	1
Oliver, James	....	Fr	1	0	1
Parsons, John Mowbray	....	Fr	0	0	1
Paxton, Viney	....	Fr	1	0	1
Pennington, John	Holbeach-wash-way	Rt	0	0	1
Pennington, Thomas	....	Fr	0	0	1
Perkins, Benjamin	Holbeach Marsh	Rt	1	1	0
Parr, John	Deeping-fen	Fr			
Peet, Major Flintham	....	Fr	0	0	1
Perkins, Joseph	Holbeach-fen-ends	Fr			
Phœnix, James	....	Fr	0	0	1
Peckover, William	Wisbeach St. Peter's Cambridgeshire	Fr	0	0	1
Pine, Thomas	....	Fr	0	0	1
Porter, Charles	St. Martin's, Stamford Baron, Northamptonshire	Fr			
Pridgeon, Thomas	....	Fr			
Phœnix, John	Holbeach-drove	Fr	0	0	1
Pope, James	Holbeach-drove	Fr	0	0	1
Priestley, George	Holbeach-fen	Fr	1	0	1
Pearson, William	Little London, Spalding	Fr			
Pick, William	Hall Hill, Holbeach	Fr	0	0	1
Ransom, John	Dog-drove, Holbeach	Fr	1	0	1
Rose, Frederick	Holbeach-fen	Rt	0	0	1
Robinson, John	Pinchbeck	Fr			
Reed, Thomas Depear	Whaplode	Fr	1	0	1
Regester, Thomas	....	Fr	0	0	1
Rhodes, John	Spilsby	Fr			
Robinson, William	....	Fr	0	1	1
Robbs, John, jun.	....	Fr	1	0	1
Reynolds, William	Holbeach-fen	Fr	0	0	1
Ravensdale, Thomas	Holbeach-drove	Fr			

Holbeach—continued.

Name of Elector.	Residence, if out of the Parish.	Qual.	T.	W.	P.
Ravel, Richard	....	Fr	0	1	1
Rouse, Thomas	Holbeach-drove	Fr			
Rickerby, William	Terrington, St. Clements, in the County of Norfolk	Fr	1	0	1
Richards, Thomas Wallis	....	Fr	1	1	0
Richardson, John Alpress	Sutton St. Mary	Fr			
Rogers, George	Holbeach-fen	Rt	1	1	0
Sheppard, Robert	Boston	Fr			
Speck, William	....	Fr	1	0	0
Savage, Seth	Fleet	Rt	0	0	1
Smith, Fryer	Holbeach Hurn	Fr	0	0	1
Slator, Henry	....	Fr	0	0	1
Stevenson, David	Swineshead	Fr			
Stevenson, William	....		0	0	1
Snaith, Frederick *m. 2.*	Boston	Fr	0	0	1
Smith, Edward	....	Rt			
Savage, Thomas Edward	....	Fr	0	0	1
Savage, Seth Holliday	Holbeach Marsh	Fr	0	0	1
Sturton, John	Peterborough	Fr			
Tatam, Charles Hardy	....	Fr	0	0	1
Taylor, John	....	Rt	0	0	1
Taylor, Edward	....	Fr	1	1	0
Thornton, John	....	Fr			
Townsend, Richard	Moulton Marsh	Fr			
Tryer, Jonathan	....	Fr			
Tinsley, William	....	Fr	0	0	1
Tinsley, Henry	Holbeach Drove	Fr	1	1	0
Tingle, William	Gedney	Fr	0	0	1
Tupholme, Thomas	Holbeach-fen	Fr			
Tryer, Samuel C.	Holbeach Wash-way	Fr	1	0	1
Tinsley, George	Ditto	Rt	0	0	1
Thomas, William	Leadenhall, Holbeach Marsh	Rt			
Thompson, Edward	....	Fr	0	0	1
Tomline, George *Cy*	Riby-grove, near Brigg	Fr			
Tuxford, Joseph	....	Fr	0	0	1
Teesdale, John	Holbeach Marsh	Rt	1	1	0
Thompson, Edward, jun.	....	Fr	0	0	1
Thornton, John	....	Fr			

Holbeach—continued.

Name of Elector.	Residence, if out of the Parish.	Qual.	T.	W.	P.
Vise, Edward Blythe	....	Fr			
Vorley, John	Holbeach Hurn	Fr	0	0	1
Walker, William	......	Rt	0	0	1
Wayne, William Henry	Morville, in the Parish of Cavers-wall, Stafford	Fr			
Wood, James Suttell *clk*	Woodhall Beadle, Yorkshire	Fr			
Wilkinson, John	Holbeach-bank	Fr	0	0	1
Woods, Samuel	Washway-road	Fr	0	1	1
Walker, John	....	Fr	1	0	1
Woolley, William	Manthorpe	Rt			
Wingfield, C. W., esq.	Woolwich, Kent	Fr	1	1	0
Wingfield, Rev. E. O.	Market Overton, Rutlandshire	Fr			
Wingfield, George, esq.	Glanton, Hunting-donshire	Fr			
Wingfield, T. H., esq.	Head Quarters of H. M. 32nd Regt.	Fr			
Worth, Thomas	....	Fr	1	1	0
Welsh, William, jun.	Holbeach Washway	Rt	1	1	0
Wraithby, Thomas, jun.	Holbeach-fen-ends	Rt	1	0	1
Wray, Thomas	....	Fr	0	0	1
Woolley, John	Holbeach Hurn	Rt	0	0	1
White, Robert	Whaplode	Fr	0	0	1
Wing, Elkana	Fleet-fen	Fr	0	0	1
Woodhouse, George C.	Wellingore	Fr			
Wilson, James	Scawby, Lincolnshire	Fr	0	0	1
Ward, Richard	Holbeach Marsh	Rt	1	0	1
Ward, Isaac	Guyhirn	Fr	1	1	0
Watson, Thomas	....	Fr			
Woolley, John Austin	Holbeach Marsh	Rt	1	1	0

Lutton.

Name of Elector.	Residence, if out of the Parish.	Qual.	T.	W.	P.
Adcock, Samuel	Long Sutton	Fr	0	0	1
Amory, Isaac Bingley	Sutton Saint Mary	Fr	1	1	0
Allcock, Ephraim	....	Co	0	0	1
Anderson, Henry	Long Sutton	Rt			
Andrew, John	Lutton Marsh	Rt	1	1	0
Baxter, Matthew John	Ditto	Rt	1	1	0
Bertie, Charles H., esq.	....	Fr			

Lutton—continued.

Name of Elector.	Residence, if out of the Parish.	Qual.	T.	W.	P.
Bettinson, George	Lutton Marsh	Rt	1	0	1
Briggs, William	....	Fr			
Black, Edward	....	Fr			
Black, Richard	Gedney	Fr	1	1	0
Brown, George Henry	....	Fr	1	0	1
Bland, George Banks	Sutton St. Nicholas otherwise Lutton	Rt	1	1	0
Cave, John	....	Co			
Cunnington, Robert	....	Fr	1	0	1
Cunnington, William	....	Fr	1	1	0
Cutter, Matthias Kirkby	....	Co	0	0	1
Clifton, Robert	....	Fr	0	0	1
Cooper, John	Chapel-bridge	Fr	0	0	1
Crosby, William	....	Fr	1	0	1
Cunnington, John	....	Fr	1	1	0
Dilehoy, Isaac	....	Fr	1	0	0
Fields, Peter	....	Fr	0	0	1
Gibbons, John Williams	Sutton	Fr			
Harrison, William	....	Fr	1	1	0
Howard, Daniel	Lutton Marsh	Rt	1	1	0
Hudson, John	....	Fr	1	1	0
Kirkham, Richard	Lutton Garnsgate	Rt	0	0	1
Knight, Richard	Sutton St. Mary	Fr	1	0	1
Mason, Henry Bence	White House, Wareham, Norfolk	Fr			
Mayer, Jeremiah	Gedney	Fr			
Montagu, James	Normanton, near Stamford	Fr	1	1	0
Mason, Henry Baxter B.	Wareham, Norfolk	Fr	1	1	0
Millns, Robert William	....	Co			
Moyer, Stephen	Roman-bank, Lutton	Rt	0	0	1
Parke, Samuel, esq.	Leatherhead, Surrey	Fr			
Pinch, Thomas	....	Fr	1	0	0
Smith, Edward	....	Fr			
Smith, Robert	....	Fr	1	1	0
Staveley, Michael	....	Fr	1	1	0
Searson, Henry	....	Fr			
Smalley, William	Gedney	Fr			
Taylor, Charles B., esq.	....	Fr	1	1	0
Thompson, Samuel	Long Sutton	Rt			

Lutton—continued.

Name of Elector.	Residence, if out of the Parish.	Qual.	T.	W.	P.
Thompson, John Wilson	Lutton Marsh	Rt	1	1	0
Wroot, William	....	Fr			
Whitfield, William	....	Fr	1	0	1
Wilkinson, George	Long Sutton	Fr			

Sutton Saint Edmund.

Name of Elector.	Residence, if out of the Parish.	Qual.	T.	W.	P.
Allatt, William	Glinton, Northamptonshire	Rt	1	0	1
Bailey, Henry Cole	....	Rt	0	0	1
Bell, Thomas	Leverington, Cambridgeshire	Fr	1	1	0
Barker, Charles	Gedney	Co			
Bellamy, William	....	Rt	1	1	0
Butcher, Richard	....	Fr	0	0	1
Berridge, William	....	Rt	1	1	0
Bailey, Richard Flour	Wood-st., London	Fr			
Cattle, Christopher	Inkerson-fen	Fr	1	1	0
Castle, John	....	Co	1	1	0
Clipham, James	....	Co	0	0	1
Cole, Thomas	....	Co	1	1	0
Cole, John	....	Rt	1	1	0
Castle, George	....	Co			
Gee, Thomas, jun.	Thorney Abbey, Cambridgeshire	Co	0	0	1
Handley, John	....	Fr			
Household, John	No. 10, Crescent, Peterborough	Fr			
Hopkinson, William	Sutton, Northamptonshire	Fr	1	1	0
Howard, Adderley, esq.	Long Sutton	Fr	1	0	1
Hanbury, James	Newborough, near Peterborough	Fr			
Hunt, William	Deeping-fen	Fr			
Haines, James	....	Fr	1	1	0
Hilton, William	....	Rt	1	1	0
Jealous, Michael	Parson Drove, Isle of Ely	Fr			
Jones, Joseph	Gedney Hill	Co	0	0	1
Johnson, George W.	Midgate, Peterboro	Fr	0	1	1
Kingston, Clement Usill	....	Co	1	1	0

Sutton St. Edmund's—continued.

Name of Elector.	Residence, if out of the Parish.	Qual.	T.	W.	P.
Moore, William	Elm, Cambridgeshire	Co	1	1	0
Morris, George	Peterborough	Fr			
Morris, Bryan William	Thorney	'Rt	1	1	0
Ollard, Henry	Walsoken, Norfolk	Fr			
Provost, Samuel	Thorney, Cambridgeshire	Fr			
Phillips, Edward	Wisbeach, South Brink	Co			
Pawlett, John Thomas	Rippingale	Fr			
Rowlett, Thomas	....	Rt	1	1	0
Redhead, John	....	Rt	1	1	0
Reeve, William	Sibson, near Stibbington	Fr			
Scott, John	....	Fr	0	0	1
Smith, John Thomas	Thornby, Northamptonshire	Fr	1	0	0
Sheepshanks, Thomas	Bishop-st., Trinity, Coventry	Co			
Speechly, Benjamin	....	Fr	,0	0	1
Speechly, Zachariah	....	Co	1	1	0
Strickling, William	Parson Drove, Cambridgeshire	Fr			
Starbuck, Mark	....	Fr			
Storey, Henry Spendlove	Hull, Yorkshire	Co			
Taylor, John	North Terrace, Wisbeach	Fr			
Taylor, Samuel	....	Fr	1	0	0
Thompson, Thomas	....	Co			
Tigardine, Jacob	....	Rt	1	1	0
Taylor, Francis	....	Rt	1	0	0
Taylor, Benjamin	....	Rt	1	0	0
Taylor, Francis	....	Rt			
Whitsed, Isaac, esq.	....	Fr	1	1	0
Webster, James	Peakirk	Rt	1	0	1
Willoughby, Francis, jun.	Hunstanton	Fr			
Webster, Daniel	Maxey, Northamptonshire	Fr	1	0	1
Whitehead, Stephen	....	Rt	1	0	1
Whitsed, Abraham	....	Rt	1	1	0
Walker, John	....	Rt	1	0	1

Sutton Saint James.

Name of Elector.	Residence, if out of the Parish.	Qual.	T.	W.	P.
Allenby, Henry H.	Louth	Fr			
Armstrong, John	....	Fr	1	0	1

Sutton St. James—continued.

Name of Elector.	Residence, if out of the Parish.	Qual.	T.	W.	P.
Barton, James	. . . .	Fr			
Bellamy, John	Lynn-road, Wisbeach Saint Peters	Co	1	1	0
Berkeley, C. P., esq.	Oundle, Northamptonshire	Fr	1	1	0
Belton, Joseph	. . . .	Fr			
Belton, Benjamin	. . . .	Fr	0	0	1
Bass, Thomas	Tydd Saint Mary	Fr	0	0	1
Baker, John	. . . .	Fr	0	0	1
Boardman, Abraham	. . . .	Fr	1	1	0
Boardman, Matthew	. . . .	Fr	0	0	1
Booth, Thomas Marshall	. . . .	Fr	1	1	0
Brown, Henry	. . . .	Fr	1	1	0
Craven, Thomas	. . . .	Fr	0	0	1
Cartwright, William	. . . .	Co	0	0	1
Cartwright, John	. . . .	Fr	1	1	0
Chantry, Joseph	Gedney	Fr			
Chamberlain, Palmer	Fleet	Fr			
Clifton, Joseph	Lutton	Fr			
Coulson, William Brett	. . . .	Fr	1	1	0
Colton, William	Holbeach	Fr	0	0	1
Dawes, Rev. Septimus	. . . .	Fr	0	0	1
Diggle, Thomas	. . . .	Fr	1	0	0
Eate, John	. . . .	Fr			
Edgley, William	. . . .	Rt	0	1	1
Heanes, Robert	. . . .	Fr	0	0	1
Heanes, Jonathan	. . . .	Fr			
Heanes, William	. . . .	Fr	0	0	1
Hardell, John	. . . .	Rt			
Hardy, Joseph	. . . .	Rt			
Hardy, John	Old Market, Wisbeach Saint Peters	Fr			
Howes, Robert	. . . .	Fr	1	0	1
Harris, Edward	. . . .	Co	1	1	0
Horn, William	. . . .	Rt	1	1	0
Horn, Isaac	. . . .	Rt	1	1	0
Hall, Henry, Clerk	Fishpond-st., Abbey Parish St. Albans,	Fr			
Jackson, W. G., esq.	North Brink, Wisbeach Saint Peters	Fr	1	1	0

Sutton St. James—continued.

Name of Elector.	Residence, if out of the Parish.	Qual.	T.	W.	P.
Johnson, James	....	Co	0	0	1
Keach, John	....	Fr	0	0	1
Maxey, Richard	....	Co	1	1	0
Morris, Solomon	....	Fr	0	0	1
Morrel, Robert	....	Fr	1	1	0
Nichols, John	....	Fr	0	0	1
Pate, Robert Francis *2y*	North Brink, Wisbeach Saint Peters	Fr	*dead*		
Pridmore, Thomas	....	Fr	1	1	0
Parke, Samuel, esq.	Ayscough Feehall, Spalding	Fr			
Putterill, Francis	....	Fr	0	0	1
Sleight, William	....	Co			
Scotney, Edward	....	Fr	0	0	1
Scrimshaw, Joseph	....	Fr	0	0	1
Stubley, John	....	Rt	0	0	1
Thistlewood, John	....	Rt	1	1	0
Webb, Thomas	....	Co	0	0	1
Wright, John Spikins	....	Fr	0	0	1
Wollas, William	....	Fr	0	0	1

Sutton Saint Mary.

Name of Elector.	Residence, if out of the Parish.	Qual.	T.	W.	P.
Allen, John *cele*	Long Sutton	Co	1	1	0
Anderson, Henry	Long Sutton	Fr	0	0	1
Allenby, Hynman R. *2y*	Kenwick House, near Louth	Fr	0	0	1
Adams, Edward	Long Sutton	Fr			
Amory, Isaac Bingley	....	Fr			
Atkinson, William	Long Sutton	Fr	0	0	1
Atkinson, John Ashby	Tydd Saint Mary	Fr	0	0	1
Andrews, William	Sutton Bridge	Fr	1	1	0
Bennett, Rev. E. L.	Long Sutton	Fr	1	1	0
Bailey, John	Ditto	Fr			
Burrell, John	Ditto	Fr	0	0	1
Bennett, George Bright	Primrose-hill Place, Coventry	Fr	1	1	0
Bennett, George Carter	Market-place, Long Sutton	Fr	1	1	0
Buckle, Francis	Long Sutton	Fr			
Baxter, Baker Matthews	Holbeach-bank	Fr	0	1	1

Sutton Saint Mary—continued.

Name of Elector.	Residence, if out of the Parish.	Qual.	T.	W.	P.
Baxter, James	Lutton	Fr	0	1	1
Brett, Robert	Mill-hill	Fr	0	0	1
Bellamy, John	Wisbeach, County of Cambridge	Fr			
Bowstock, John	Long Sutton	Co	0	0	1
Bracking, John	Ditto	Fr			
Bush, John	Ditto	Fr	0	0	1
Blower, Joseph	Long Terrace, Long Sutton	Fr	1	1	0
Buzacott, Aaron, B.A.	Long Sutton	Fr	0	0	1
Cartwright, John	Sutton Saint James	Fr	1	1	0
Copeman, Philip	Long Sutton	Fr	0	0	1
Copeman, Rev. P. W.	Minster Lovel Oxford	Fr			
Clarke, John	Sutton Marsh	Rt	1	0	1
Clarke, Thomas William	Sutton-bridge	Rt	1	1	0
Copeman, Thomas	6, Sackville-street, Saint James, Westminster	Fr			
Carbut, David	Holbeach	Co	0	0	1
Cartwright, Thomas	Long Sutton	Fr			
Cheney, Thomas	Wisbeach Saint Peters, Isle of Ely	Fr			
Chaplin, Thomas	Wisbeach Saint Peters,	Fr			
Cook, Thomas	Union-place, Higham, Norwich	Fr			
Cole, Edward F.	Long Sutton	Fr	0	0	1
Cole, John	Market-street, Long Sutton	Fr	0	0	1
Dawes, Rev. Septimus	Long Sutton	Co			
Dring, John Maddison	....	Rt	1	1	0
Emberson, John	....	Fr	0	0	1
Ewen, Henry	Long Sutton	Co	0	0	1
Eno, Joseph	Sutton Crossas	Rt	0	0	1
Ellis, George	Long Sutton	Fr	0	0	1
Fletcher, William	Ditto	Fr	0	0	1
Franks, Henry	Ditto	Fr	0	0	1
Fawley, Henry Baxter	Lutton	Fr	0	0	1
Fryer, John Richardson	Denvor, Norfolk	Fr	1	1	0
Goodacre, John	Long Sutton	Co	0	0	1
Gibbs, Edward	Long Sutton Marsh	Rt	0	0	1

Sutton Saint Mary—continued.

Name of Elector.	Residence, if out of the Parish.	Qual.	T.	W.	P.
Giddens, William	Walsoken, Norfolk	Fr	0	0	1
Grant, Francis	Long Sutton	Co	0	0	1
Gray, John	Ditto	Fr	0	0	1
Garner, Thomas	Sutton Marsh	Rt	1	1	0
Green, Edward H.	Hinxon Hall, County of Cambridge	Fr			
Garthwaite, William	....	Fr	0	0	1
Hardy, John	Wisbeach Saint Peters, Isle of Ely	Fr			
Hayes, Henry	Sutton-bridge	Fr	1	1	0
Howard, John Sands	Long Sutton	Rt	1	0	1
Hobson, John George	Sutton Saint Mary's Marsh	Rt	1	1	0
Howard, John	....	Fr	1	0	1
Howard, Thomas	14, Buckingham-st., Strand, London	Fr			
Hobson, John Overton	....	Rt	1	0	1
Hainsworth, John T.	....	Fr	0	1	1
Hickman, James	Little London, near Long Sutton	Fr	0	0	1
Image, Henry	Sutton-bridge	Fr	1	1	0
Jerram, Rev. James	Fleet	Co	1	1	0
James, Joseph	Market-place, Long Sutton	Fr	0	0	1
King, Thomas	Long Sutton	Fr	0	0	1
Little, William	Ditto	Co	0	0	1
Longland, Joseph	Sutton-bridge	Rt	1	0	0
Mumby, John	Sutton Marsh	Rt	1	1	0
Mossop, Robert	Long Sutton	Fr	0	0	1
Medd, Edward	Ditto	Fr	1	0	1
Newman, James	Ditto	Fr	0	0	1
Naylor, Thomas	Fold-house, Long Sutton	Rt			
Oldfield, Matthew	Sutton-bridge	Fr	0	0	1
Peele, John	Sutton Town	Rt	1	0	1
Peele, Thomas	Long Sutton	Fr	1	0	1
Piggins, William	....	Fr	1	1	0
Porter, James	Long Sutton	Fr	1	1	0
Prest, George	Sutton-bridge	Fr	1	0	1
Peacock, John	Long Sutton	Rt	1	0	0

Sutton Saint Mary—continued.

Name of Elector.	Residence, if out of the Parish.	Qual.	T.	W.	P.
Peck, James	Roman-bank, Long Sutton	Fr	0	0	1
Patrick, Robert Crosby	Long Sutton	Co	0	0	1
Payne, John	Ditto	Rt	1	1	0
Peek, Jonathan	....	Fr	0	0	1
Peek, Thomas	Long Sutton	Co	0	0	1
Read, James	Duddington, North-amptonshire	Fr			
Richardson, John	....	Fr	0	0	1
Roberts, Robert	Long Sutton	Fr	0	0	1
Ream, William	North Kirkgate, Long Sutton	Fr			
Roberts, John	Long Sutton	Co			
Roper, Watts	Ditto	Fr	0	1	1
Richardson, John A.	....	Fr	0	0	1
Roper, John	Tydd Saint Mary	Fr	1	1	0
Sanby, Kemp	Nottingham	Fr	0	0	1
Scott, William	Downham, Norfolk	Fr	0	0	1
Skelton, William, esq.	Sutton-bridge	Co	1	1	0
Skelton, Spencer, esq.	Ditto	Rt	1	1	0
Shearcroft, William	Long Sutton	Fr	0	1	1
Spendla, William	Ditto	Fr	0	0	1
Sainty, Barnard	Ditto	Fr	0	1	1
Swain, John	Ditto	Co			
Skelton, Edward D.	Sutton-bridge	Rt	1	1	0
Skelton, John Thomas	Sutton Marsh	Rt	1	1	0
Stutevant, John	Sutton St. Matthew	Fr	1	0	0
Shearcroft, George	Long Sutton	Fr	0	0	1
Stephenson, John Fred.	Ditto	Fr	0	0	1
Sutterby, Jonathan Nixon	Ditto	Rt	0	0	1
Triffitt, Charles	Ditto	Fr	0	0	1
Tagg, William	Ditto	Rt	0	0	1
Threadgill, John	Ditto	Rt	0	1	0
Taylor, John	Sutton-bridge	Fr	1	1	0
Townsend, Christopher	Long Sutton	Co	1	0	0
Thompson, Samuel	Ditto	Fr	0	1	1
Usill, Harley Matthew Esq.	Wisbeach St. Peter	Fr			
Wrought, Charles	Long Sutton	Co	0	0	1
Ward, William Henry Esq.	Wisbeach	Fr	1	1	0
Wroot, Henry W.	Everton, near Liverpool	Fr			
Wing, Thomas	Long Sutton	Rt			

Sutton Saint Mary—continued.

Name of Elector.	Residence, if out of the Parish.	Qual.	T.	W.	P.
Wright, William	Long Sutton	Rt	1	1	0
Wilkinson, George	Ditto	Fr	0	0	1
Winter, Francis Andrew	Ditto	Fr	1	0	1
Wykes, James	Lutton	Fr			
Wade, Henry	Sutton-bridge	Rt	1	1	0
Walpole, Richard Henry Vade, *Esqr*	38, Upper Brook-st., Grosvenor-square, London	Fr			
Young, Thomas Drake *clerk*	Sutton-bridge	Fr	1	1	0

Tydd Saint Mary.

Name of Elector.	Residence, if out of the Parish.	Qual.	T.	W.	P.
Bailey, John Bennett	....	Rt	0	0	1
Burrell, Thomas	....	Fr			
Brown, Rev. Thomas	Somersham, Hunts.	Fr			
Brewin, Charles	Tydd Gote	Fr	0	0	1
Bass, Thomas	....	Rt			
Boor, Robert	Newton, Isle of Ely	Fr	1	1	0
Burrell, Edward	Mornington-road, Regent's Park, Middlesex	Fr			
Bills, William	Star Inn, Tydd Saint Mary	Rt	1	0	1
Cole, Michael	Wisbeach	Fr			
Clark, Rev. Thomas	Gedney Hill	Fr	1	1	0
Clarke, Thomas	....	Fr	0	1	1
Cox, Joseph *2y*	Wisbeach	Fr	0	0	1
Cross, Thomas	....	Fr	0	0	1
Dowse, Thomas	....	Fr	1	0	1
Dack, Joseph	....	Rt			
Day, Thomas	Walpole Saint Andrew's	Fr	0	0	1
England, George	Wisbeach Saint Peter's	Fr	1	1	0
Edens, Benjamin	....	Fr	0	0	1
Edwards, John	Tydd Saint Mary-fen	Fr	1	1	0
Edwards, Charles	Stow Bardolph, Norfolk	Fr			
Foster, William	....	Fr			
Gilbert, James	....	Fr	0	0	1
Gostelow, Thomas	Tydd Gote	Fr	1	1	0
Greeves, Emanuel	....	Rt	1	1	0
Greeves, Thomas, sen.	Tydd Saint Giles	Rt	1	1	0
Gutteridge, John	Tydd Saint Mary-fen	Fr			

Tydd Saint Mary—continued.

Name of Elector.	Residence, if out of the Parish.	Qual.	T.	W.	P.
Heanes, John	Sutton Saint James	Fr	0	0	1
Hopkinson, William	Tydd Saint Mary-fen	Fr	0	0	1
Henson, William	....	Fr	1	1	0
Hannath, Joseph	Tydd Saint Giles	Fr			
Harris, John	....	Rt	1	1	0
Kilham, Richard	....	Fr	1	0	1
Kilham, William	Tydd Saint Giles	Fr	1	0	1
Lowe, John Edward	Foul Anchor	Fr	1	1	0
Long, Samuel, Colonel	Bromley-hill, Kent	Fr	1	1	0
Larmet, Joseph	Wisbeach	Fr	1	1	0
Marshall, Joseph	Elm, County of Cambridge	Fr			
Marshall, Thomas	Tydd Gote	Fr	1	1	0
Marshall, John Thomas	Tydd Gote	Fr			
Mallett, John	....	Fr	1	1	0
Mackenzie, Rev. Henry	Rectory House, Tydd Saint Mary	Fr	1	1	0
Nichols, Henry James	Camden-street, Birkenhead, County of Chester	Fr			
Palmer, John	....	Fr	1	0	1
Pollard, Robert	....	Fr	1	0	1
Peck, John, jun.	Parson-drove	Fr	1	1	0
Robinson, William	in the Village	Fr			
Robinson, John	Tydd Gote	Fr	1	1	0
Roper, Benjamin	....	Fr	0	1	1
Richardson, John Alpress	Sutton Saint Mary	Fr			
Roberts, John	....	Fr	1	1	0
Scattergood, Robert	....	Fr	0	0	1
Sparkhall, Robert	King's Lynn, Norfolk	Fr			
Snushall, William	....	Rt	1	0	1
Snushall, John	Sutton Saint Edmunds	Rt	1	0	1
Smith, John	March, Cambridgeshire	Fr			
Scrimshaw, William W.	Parson Drove	Fr	1	0	1
Stubley, John	Tydd Gote	Fr	1	1	0
Sikes, Rev. Joseph	Chantry House, Newark	Fr			
Spikins, John, jun.	Walpole Saint Peters, Norfolk	Rt	1	1	0
Spikins, William	Tydd Marsh	Rt	1	1	0
Tenant, Henry H.	Castle Bytham	Fr	1	1	0

Tydd Saint Mary—continued.

Name of Elector.	Residence, if out of the Parish.	Qual.	T.	W.	P.
Tilbrook, John	. . . .	Fr			
Thorpe, John	. . . .	Fr	0	1	1
Tindall, Richard Joseph	Tretton House	Rt	1	0	1
Threadgill, Phineas B.	. . . .	Rt	1	1	0
Tennant, Edmund	Hanley, Staffordshire	Fr			
Warren, Samuel	. . . .	Rt	0	0	1
Wilkinson, John Capps	. . . .	Fr	0	0	1
Wade, Henry	Tydd Gote	Fr	1	1	0
Wiles, Stephen	Tydd Gote	Fr			
Whaler, James	Trafford House, Tydd Saint Mary	Rt	1	1	0
Young, Richard	Wisbeach	Fr	1	0	1

Whaplode.

Name of Elector.	Residence, if out of the Parish.	Qual.	T.	W.	P.
Ashby, Charles	. . . .	Rt	1	0	1
Abbot, John	. . . .	Fr	1	0	0
Allen, Thomas	. . . .	Rt	1	0	0
Armstrong, Michael	. . . .	Rt			
Ashby, Thomas	. . . .	Fr	1	1	0
Almond, Henry	. . . .	Fr	0	0	1
Aveling, Joseph	Dowsdale, Whaplode-drove	Fr	1	1	0
Ash, John	Whaplode-drove	Fr	1	1	0
Anniss, Robert	. . . .	Fr	1	0	1
Barchard, Francis	Ashcombe, Saint Anne, Lewis	Fr			
Boardman, James	. . . .	Rt	1	1	0
Burton, William Fitz-william	Burton Hall, County of Carlow, Ireland	Fr			
Brown, George	. . . .	Fr			
Benner, William	. . . .	Fr	1	0	0
Black, Edward	. . . .	Rt	1	0	1
Beagles, Robert	Whaplode-drove	Fr	1	1	0
Barker, Francis	. . . .	Rt	1	1	0
Campain, Samuel	Spalding	Fr			
Cram, Robert	. . . .	Fr	0	1	1
Collins, Robert	Lincoln	Fr	1	1	0
Collins, William	. . . .	Fr	0	1	0
Chapman, Edward	Postland	Fr	1	1	0
Cook, Arthur	. . . .	Rt	1	0	1

Whaplode—continued.

Name of Elector.	Residence, if out of the Parish.	Qual.	T.	W.	P.
Congreve, Abraham	Peterborough	Fr			
Congreve, Nelson	Holbeach	Fr	0	0	1
Custance, William	Saint Giles, Cambridgeshire	Fr			
Cook, Robert	Postland, in Crowland	Fr			
Crampton, James	....	Fr	1	0	1
Culy, Robert	....	Fr	0	0	1
Culy, Benjamin	....	Fr	1	1	0
Culy, Joseph	....	Fr	0	0	1
Codling, John	....	Fr	1	1	0
Cooke, Isaac	Clenchwarton, Norfolk	Fr			
Clayton, William, jun.	Whaplode-drove	Fr			
Cooper, Robert	Whaplode-drove	Co	0	1	1
Cooke, Benjamin, jun.	Moulton Chapel	Rt	1	1	0
Croft, Matthew Edward	Market Deeping	Co			
Coddington, Edward	....	Rt	1	0	1
Copping, Wright	....	Fr	1	1	0
Dennis, John	....	Fr	1	0	1
Depear, John	....	Rt	1	0	0
Depear, Matthew	....	Rt			
Dickenson, Joseph	....	Fr	0	0	1
Dieppe, William	Whaplode-drove	Fr	1	1	0
Donington, George	Whaplode-drove, Lawson's Lane	Rt	0	0	1
Donington, John	Whaplode-drove	Rt	0	0	1
Dodes, Thomas	Dowsdale, Whaplode-drove	Fr	1	0	0
Duncombe, Philip Duncombe Pauncefort	Great Brick Hill Manor, Bucks.	Fr			
Darlow, James	Bull Inn, Newborough, Northamptonshire	Fr	0	0	1
Edings, John	....	Fr			
Earl, John	Hagbeach-drove, Whaplode-drove	Rt			
Essam, John	Whaplode-bank	Rt			
England, Cue William	Whaplode Common-bank	Fr	0	0	1
Eason, James Huckbody	Whaplode-drove	Co	0	0	1
Earl, John	Whaplode-drove	Fr	0	1	0
Fletcher, Robert	....	Fr	1	0	1

Whaplode—continued.

Name of Elector.	Residence, if out of the Parish.	Qual.	T.	W.	P.
Freeman, Thomas	....	Fr			
Faulkner, Thomas	Whaplode Common-bank	Fr	1	1	0
Farrow, Joseph	Dowsdale, Whaplode-drove	Fr	1	1	0
Farrow, Thomas	Dowsdale	Fr	1	0	0
Farrow, William	Dowsdale, Whaplode-drove	Fr			
Fields, William Freeman	Holbeach	Fr			
Fletcher, Joshua	Postland	Fr	1	1	0
Faulkner, John	Tydd Saint Giles	Fr			
Green, Charles *Sol*	Spalding	Fr	*absent*		
Gostelow, William	....	Fr	1	0	1
Green, Thomas	....	Rt	0	0	1
Graham, William	....	Fr	0	0	1
Goodger, William	Elm	Fr	1	1	0
Gee, Thomas	Ship Eau Stow, Whaplode-drove	Fr	1	0	0
Goodger, Samuel	Ufford	Fr			
Hanson, Richard	....	Rt	1	0	1
Harrison, Thomas	....	Rt	1	1	0
Harrison, Thomas	....	Fr	0	0	1
Hawley, Robert	Oakham	Fr	0	0	1
Hunter, Benjamin	....	Fr	1	1	0
Harward, Rev. John	....	Fr	1	1	0
Hardy, Thomas	Spalding	Co	0	0	1
Healey, Joseph	Whaplode Marsh	Rt			
Healey, William	Ditto	Rt	0	0	1
Hill, Mark	Moulton Chapel	Rt	0	0	1
Jackson, William	....	Rt	0	0	1
Kearby, William	Moulton	Fr	0	0	1
Kenney, William	Morton	Fr			
Kingston, Charles, jun.	Little Postland	Rt			
Kingerley, Richard	Whaplode-fen	Rt	0	0	1
Lawson, John	....	Fr	1	1	0
Lawson, William	Whaplode-drove	Fr	0	1	1
Lowery, Robert	Ditto	Fr			
Lilley, Rev. Charles	Ware, Herts.	Fr			
Lavender, Richard Brand	Bridge-st., Spalding	Fr	1	0	1
Long, James John	Holbeach	Fr			

Whaplode—continued.

Name of Elector.	Residence, if out of the Parish.	Qual	T.	W.	P.
Mimmick, John	....	Fr			
Molesworth, Thomas C.	Easton, near Stamford	Fr	1	1	0
Molesworth, John	....	Fr	0	0	1
Molesworth, Thomas	....	Fr	1	1	0
Mews, William	Ship Eau Bank	Fr	0	0	1
Money, William Wilcock	Chapel-drove	Fr	0	1	1
Mawford, William	Whaplode-drove	Fr	0	0	1
Musket, Joseph	Ditto	Fr	0	0	1
Moore, Rev. Edward	Church-st., Spalding	Fr			
Mackinder, Joseph	Whaplode-drove	Rt	0	0	1
Mackinder, Edward	Ditto	Rt	0	0	1
Millington, John Boyfield	Boston	Fr			
Nunnerley, John	....	Fr	1	1	0
Naylor, James	....	Rt	1	1	0
Nutt, Henry	....	Fr	0	0	1
Nairne, Rev. Charles	Lincoln	Fr			
Newton, Thomas	....	Fr			
Nichols, Thomas	....	Rt	1	0	1
Osborn, James	Moulton	Fr			
Osborn, James, jun.	....	Fr			
Palmer, Charles Everson	....	Fr			
Palmer, Jacob David	....	Fr	1	0	0
Parker, Thomas	....	Rt	1	0	1
Pearce, John, jun.	Craig's-court, Middlesex	Fr			
Pawley, Thomas	Dowsdale	Fr	1	1	0
Pridgeon, William Blake	Whaplode-drove	Rt	1	1	0
Peet, Zachariah	Ditto	Fr	0	1	1
Porter, Matthew	....	Rt	1	1	0
Robinson, John, jun.	Pinchbeck North-fen	Fr			
Robinson, Jonathan	....	Fr	0	0	1
Robinson, Joseph	....	Rt	1	0	1
Robinson, William	....	Fr			
Rouse, John	....	Fr	0	0	1
Robinson, William	Chapel-drove	Fr	1	1	0
Read, William	Whaplode-drove	Co	0	0	1
Rose, John	....	Fr	0	0	1
Rogerson, William	....	Rt			
Shepherd, John Dixon	....	Fr	1	0	1
Slator, John	....	Fr	0	0	1

Whaplode—continued.

Name of Elector.	Residence, if out of the Parish.	Qual.	T.	W.	P.
Smith, James	....	Fr	1	1	0
Shackle, James	Wansford	Fr			
Stennett, Michael	....	Rt	0	0	1
Smith, John	....	Fr	1	0	0
Smith, Robert	....	Fr	ʁ	0	1
Scupham, John	Moulton	Fr	1	1	0
Sisson, Rev. Michael	Spalding	Fr	1	1	0
Smith, Isaac	Whaplode-drove	Rt	1	1	0
Smith, Thomas	Ditto	Rt	1	1	0
Smith, William	Ditto	Co	1	1	0
Stokes, John	Ditto	Fr	1	0	0
Sergeant, John, sen.	Ditto	Fr	1	1	0
Sergeant, Henry	Ditto	Fr	1	1	0
Smith, John	Holbeach	Rt	0	0	1
Smith, Robert	Ditto	Rt	0	0	1
Sturton, John Phipps *Sol*	Ditto	Fr	1	1	0
Stainsby, George	Whaplode-drove	Fr	1	0	0
Smith, Theophilus	....	Rt	1	0	1
Thistlewood, Henry	Gedney	Fr			
Tupholme, William	Whaplode-fen	Fr	0	0	1
Thurlby, Joseph	....	Rt	1	1	0
Taylor, Thomas	Gosberton	Rt			
Taylor, Francis	North-st., Stamford	Fr	1	1	0
Thistlewood, Thomas	Gedney Broadgate	Fr			
Thornton, John	Holbeach	Fr			
Ullett, James	....	Rt	1	0	1
Vise, Jacob Davey, esq.	Holbeach	Rt	1	1	0
Watson, John	....	Fr	1	0	0
Watson, James	....	Fr	1	0	0
Wing, Rev. William	Stibbington, Huntingdonshire	Fr			
Ward, Middleton Seth	Upper Stamford-st., Surrey	Rt			
Wiseman, Henry	Whaplode-fen-ends	Rt	1	0	1
Wright, Henry	Wyberton	Fr			
Watson, William	....	Fr	0	0	1
Waltham, William	....	Fr	0	0	1
Watson, Thomas	Holbeach	Fr	1	0	1
Wilkerson, Robert	Fleet-fen	Fr			
Wright, Joseph	Whaplode-drove	Fr	1	1	0

Whaplode—continued.

Name of Elector.	Residence, if out of the Parish.	Qual.	T.	W.	P.
Walker, Captain Isaac	Hendregadno, Yny- scynheiarn, Car- narvon, Wales	Fr			
Wing, John, jun.	Whaplode-drove	Fr			
Wright, Luke	Ditto	Fr	1	1	0
Winkley, James	Ditto	Fr	1	1	0
Wright, Richard	....	Fr	1	0	1

INDEX.

WILLIAM FAWCETT,

Printer, Bookseller, Stationer, Binder,

DEALER IN PAPER HANGINGS,

MUSICAL INSTRUMENTS,

PATENT MEDICINES, ETC.,

MARKET PLACE, SLEAFORD.

Parcels from London Daily.

THE TIMES & OTHER DAILY NEWSPAPERS SUPPLIED.

Agent to the Lincolnshire Chronicle, Stamford Mercury, and all London and Country Newspapers.

A LARGE STOCK OF SECOND-HAND BOOKS ALWAYS ON SALE.